Paul Obiechefu Nwandu

Religious Education in the Diocese of Ahiara (Nigeria) and in the Archdiocese of Munich and Freising (Germany): A Comparative Study

I0876889

eligious Education in the Dio PB
119499
9783830676355

THEOLOGISCHE REIHE, BAND 097

Paul Obiechefu Nwandu

Religious Education in the Diocese of Ahiara (Nigeria) and in the Archdiocese of Munich and Freising (Germany): A Comparative Study

eos

1. Auflage 2013

Deutsche Erstausgabe
Zugleich auch Dissertation zur Erlangung des Akademischen Grades
eines Doktors der Theologie an der Theologischen Fakultät
der Ludwig-Maximilians-Universität München,
angenommen im Jahre 2013.

Copyright © 2013 by EOS Verlag Sankt Ottilien
mail@eos-verlag.de
www.eos-verlag.de

ISBN 978-3-8306-7635-5

Bibliografische Information der Deutschen Bibliothek
Die Deutsche Bibliothek verzeichnet diese Publikation
in der Deutschen Nationalbibliografie;
detaillierte bibliografische Angaben
sind im Internet unter http://dnb.ddb.de abrufbar.

Alle Rechte vorbehalten.
Kein Teil des Werkes darf in irgendeiner Form
(durch Fotografie, Mikrofilm oder ein anderes Verfahren)
ohne schriftliche Genehmigung des Verlags
reproduziert oder unter Verwendung elektronischer Systeme
verarbeitet, vervielfältigt und verbreitet werden.

Gedruckt auf säurefreiem, chlorfrei gebleichtem Papier.
Printed in Germany

Acknowledgement

The rapid growth of anti-religiosity especially in the European Christian world is a great concern not only for religious education but also for the moral and pastoral aspects of theology. Just as the trees lose their leaves in autumn Christianity appears to have lost most of its members with post-modernity. Efforts are now being made to bring about a possible new springtime in Christendom so that its members can find a convincing reason to return to their faith. The Catholic Church raised the awareness of the signs of the time during the Second Vatican Council. Under this dispensation, the Church calls for the necessity to introduce new means of evangelization which can address the interest of the different age demographies of the present time. Young people are brought into the focal point of religious education under this category. This is because they constitute the humanly possible hope for the continued transmission of Christianity. The majority of them have also drifted from the practice of the faith. This situation gives the Church the great task of devising new means of keeping young people in the Christian faith. Under the pastoral care of the youth, the Catholic Church has drawn up captivating programmes which can encourage the commitment of young people in the practice and spread of the Christian teachings. The need for this has been stated by the African bishops in their expression that young people need witnesses and teachers who can walk with them, teaching them to love the Gospel and share it, especially with their peers, and thus to become authentic and credible messengers.[1] To achieve this, they need to be loved, esteemed and respected because youth is a time when genuine and irrepressible questions arise about the meaning of life and the direction our lives should take.[2] This explains the choice of the title of this work.

As a comparative study using the diocese of Ahiara (Nigeria) and the archdiocese of Munich and Freising (Germany) as its basis, this work aims at finding out the role of religious education in the unification of cultures and national development in both Nigeria and Germany. Although the method of teaching religion in these two places is different, this study strives to establish the impact of religious education in the practice of religion among young people in both areas of investigation. Under this dispensation, a line is drawn between religious knowledge and religious practice. This is because one can be very well educated in religious studies without necessarily adhering to any religious practice. Hence, to foster both the study of Christian religion and its practice in

1 Cf. Africae Munus, (AM), 2011, 60.

2 Cf. Ibid.

the two areas of investigation, attention is focused on how these two resource areas can benefit from each other. Thus, what can the diocese of Ahiara borrow from the arch-diocese of Munich and Freising in the teaching of religion and vice versa? This work also attempts to draw attention to some aspects of religious education and religious practices in these two dioceses which require certain levels of improvement. A separate and neutral introduction is given in the body of the work. This introduction gives both the state of the research and the structure of the entire work.

This work is meant to give rise to further research on the youth and religious education. Therefore, constructive and helpful criticisms on the work will be very much appreciated, with the hope that the work and the motivated criticisms will lead to an on-going research on the topic.

In recognition of many peoples' assistance both in my journey to the priesthood and my educational pursuits, I am grateful to my late local ordinary and spiritual father, Most Rev. Dr. Victor Adibe Chikwe, whose inspiring support motivated the need to engage in this study. I am greatly indebted to my academic mentor, Prof. Dr. Stephan Leimgruber, the professor and head of the department of religious education and didactic of religious studies at the Ludwig Maximilian University Munich, for his academic guidance in the course of this doctoral research. He is not just a supervisor, but also serves as a co-researcher, in the academic welfare of his students. I also thank his assistants and my post-graduate seminar group members, Dr. Angelika Sirch, Bernhard Flassak (MA), Annette Wermuth and Silvia Warnke for their friendliness and team work. The same thanks go to the secretary of the religious education and didactic of religious studies department Monika Podlesak, for her readiness to help. My unalloyed gratitude goes to Prof. Dr. Markus Vogt, who accepted the request to evaluate this work despite the shortness of notice. I also appreciate the roles of Prof. Dr. Bertram Stubenrauch and Prof. Dr. Knut Backhaus in conducting the defence of this work.

I wish to express my heartfelt gratitude to the Catholic Archdiocese of Munich and Freising for her financial support throughout the period of my studies in Germany. On a special note, I recognise the scholarship granted me by St. Korbinians Verein e.V (St. Corbinian's Society) of the Archdiocese of Munich and Freising which also included assistance in the publication of this work. I am as well grateful to the parishioners and workers of Maria Trost and St. Raphael in Untermenzing for their spirit of accommodation during the period of my stay with them. Similarly I appreciate the love and care of the parishioners of my present habitat, St. Michael in Perlach, St. Georg in Unterbieberg and Verklärung Christi in Ramersdorf. My thanks also go my parish priest in Maria Trost and St. Raphael, Leslaw Magdziarek and his pastoral team, for their fraternity. I am also appreciative of the love and care of my present parish priest, the other priests, deacons and the lay members of the pastoral team, Christian Penzkofer, Dr. Wolfgang Rothe, Prof. Dr. Thomas Bohrmann, Dr. Karl Schimmel, Bast Udo and Martin Holzner. The same thanks go to the parish workers: Gabriele Brose, Christa Axnick and Astrid Penzior for their assistance. I remain grateful to the Kirchenverwaltung (Church Finance Council) of St. Michael's Parish, Perlach for her financial solicitude.

In a special way, I express my deep thanks to Shelia Sullivan and Rev. Dr. Chrysogonus Nwele for their painstaking efforts to proof-read and make corrections in the entire work.

I very much appreciate the suggestions and pieces of advice of my fellow Nigerian priests studying or working in various parts of Germany especially Dr. Justine Anaele, Dr. Cyprain Anyanwu, Dr. Pius Adiele, Dr. Gerald Njoku, Dr. Moses Nnajiofor, Dr. Alex Uzor and Michael Ukpong. I also acknowledge the encouraging support of my relatives, friends and benefactors especially Dr. Nich. Uwazie and family, Rose Anne Borg, Bernadette Rothes, Renate and Max Steierer and family, Rev. Fr. Bernhard Bielasik, Rev. Fr. Felix Schnetgöke, Rev. Fr. Rudi Spatschek, Lydia and Bernhard Schröer, Elisabeth Holmann, Gabriele Wich, Christel Müter, Agathe and Karl Streicher and family, Hildergard and Heinrich Telaak and family, Christa and Franz Hübl and family, Christa and Bernhard Herbst and family, Kemi and George Oni and family, Rev. Dr. Martin Elekwachi, Rev. Dr. Emmanuel Nwaoru, Rev. Dr. Joseph Egbule, Rev. Fr. Gabriel Ahiarakwem, Msgr. Vincent Uwazie, Rev. Dr. Benedict Nwachukwudaku, Rev. Fr. Donatus Uwaeme, Rev. Fr. Francis Njoku, Rev. Fr. Christian Echewodo, Rev. Dr. Celestine Uzondu, Dr. Buchi Eze, Sr. Keyna Onyekwelеariri, Sr. Perpetua Nwaigwe, Sr. Anne Anoruo, Sr. Noel Marie Agba, Sr. Emmanuela Umunna, Sr. Bernadine Ohuakanwa, Ernest Ezeani and Ogechukwu Nwaenyi.

Finally, I wish to express my filial thanks to my family. I acknowledge the loving care of my late father, Athanasius Nwandu, who longed to see the fulfilment of this dream. May God grant him eternal rest! I appreciate the loving wishes and support of my mother, Josephine Nwandu, my brothers and sisters and numerous relatives. May God reward you all!

Paul Obiechefu Nwandu

This work is dedicated
to my late father
Mr. Athanasius Ndiukwuegbulem Nwandu
and all lovers of education

Table of Contents

Abbreviations

AG	Action Group
AM	Africae Munus
ATR	African Traditional Religion
CBCN	Catholic Bishops' Conference of Nigeria
CCC	Catechism of the Catholic Church
Cf.	Confer
CRK	Christian Religious Knowledge
CRS	Christian Religious Studies
CT	Catechesi Tradendae
CYON	Catholic Youth Organization of Nigeria
Ed.	Editor
Eds.	Editors
EFA	Education for all
EN	Evangelii Nuntiandi
GE	Gravissimum Educationis
Gen. Ed.	General Editor
GS	Gaudium et Spes
Hg.	Herausgeber (Editor)
Ibid.	Ibidem (same place cited)
IRK	Islamic Religious Knowledge
IS	Islamic Studies
JAMB	Joint Admissions and Matriculation Board
JSS	Junior Secondary School
LexRP	Lexikon der Religionspädagogik
LG.	Lumen Gentium
MDGs	Millennium Development Goals
MOD	Man of Order and Discipline
NCE	National Council on Education
NCNC	National Council of Nigeria and the Cameroons
NEEDS	National Economic Empowerment and Development Strategies
NEPU	Northern Elements of Progressive Union
NERDC	Nigerian Educational research and Development Council
NFCS	Nigeria Federation of Catholic Students
NNDP	Nigerian National Democratic Party
NPC	Northern Peoples Congress
NPE	National policy on Education

NYM	Nigerian Youth Movement
NYSC	National Youth Service Corps
QS	Quam Singulari
SSS	Senior Secondary School
Trans.	Translator
UBE	Universal Basic Education
UNFPA	United Nations Population Fund
UNESCO	United Nations Educational, Scientific and Cultural Organisation
UPE	Universal Primary Education
Vol.	Volume
YCS	Young Catholic Students of Nigeria
YMCA	Young Men Christian Association of Nigeria
YOUCAT	Youth Catechism of the Catholic Church

0. Preliminaries

Religious education as an inter-disciplinary subject deals with the understanding of the relationship between human beings and the supernatural. It is a practical branch of theology, which is concerned with the transmission of religious beliefs as a means of contributing to sustainable human development and the eradication of ignorance in the society. It plays a key role in the achievement of moral policies and the maintenance of social norms. It encourages social interaction among human beings, so that as believing communities, they can team up in the global fight against poverty and contribute towards environmental protection.[1] This means that religious education is not only concerned with the religious formation of an individual, but also with his or her social well-being and ethical disposition. It is in collaboration with other theological and scientific disciplines such as Biblical exegesis, Church history, systematic theology, psychology and the social sciences.[2] The aim of the preliminary section of this work is to state its background and research methodology. It begins with a general introduction in which the scope of the work will be stated.

0.1 General Introduction

The study of religion is a sensitive area of human searching. This is because religion deals with one of the most non-phenomenological aspects of inquiry knowable through myths, mystery, faith, reason and the senses. Religion touches the entire fabric of the human person both within and without. It dwells alongside individuals irrespective of their level of consciousness of its influences in their lives. This is why religion exacts an unprecedented influence in the life of people. According to Idowu:

> *Religion is very much and always with us. It is with us at every moment of life – in our innermost beings and with regard to the great or minor events of life; it is discussed daily in the newspapers, through the*

1 Cf. Vogt M., Zur Rolle der Ethik im Programm "Bildung für nachhaltige Entwicklung", in: Münk H. J. (Hg.), Wann ist Bildung gerecht? Ethische und theologische Beiträge im interdisziplinären Kontext, Bielefeld, 2008, 270.

2 Cf. Kalloch C., Leimgruber S., Schwab U., Lehrbuch der Religionsdidaktik, Für Studium und Praxis in ökumenischer Perspektive, Freiburg, 2009, 21.

radio and television, and in our conversations. It is with all of us inevitably; whatever may be our individual, avowed attitudes to it.[3]

Religion in this sense (as understood from an African perspective) cannot be separated from the life of human beings and indeed from the society in which they live. This is because the human person by nature is religious. This means that most people believe in some form of force that controls the entire universe, even when this force is not identified as God, the Supreme Being.[4] Idowu expresses this religiosity of the human person as he says:

... everybody is interested in 'religion', be he a believer to whom his faith is a matter of ultimate concern, or a person who thinks that he does not believe and cannot believe in the divine rulership of the universe.[5]

Religion has always served the purpose of shaping the lives of individuals. This means that religion is an inevitable phenomenon in the life of every individual person. This inevitability according to Idowu "is deep down in the nature of every person; there is an inherent urge in man which makes religion a matter of ultimate concern".[6] Religion, therefore, is understood from different perspectives depending upon the frame of mind and dispositions of those involved in it. This understanding of religion runs across the barrier of age, race, gender or colour.

The youth as human beings are in the African view also religious. Their knowledge of religion, however, is not intuitive. They have to be taught and it has to be learnt (cf. Rom. 10:17). Hence religious education is important. The essence of religious education is to make religion educational and make education a religious thing. Thus religious education exposes a person to the idea of God and the truth concerning the supernatural, and how he or she is related to it. The need for religious education in the life of human beings especially from the formative stages of their lives is revealed in the biblical injunction: "Train up a child in the way he should go, and even when he grows old he will not depart from it" (Prov. 22:6).[7]

---

3 Idowu E. B., African Traditional Religion, A Definition, London, 1973, 1.

4 There is a great contrast between African and Western understanding of religion. In the Western world, religion is not primarily identified with the individual. It is acquired through learning and exposure. The Africans see it as a "primum datum", so that each individual recognises his or her allegiance to a deity as a natural phenomenon.

5 Idowu E. B., African Traditional Religion, A Definition, London, 1973, 1.

6 Ibid., 3.

7 Biblical quotations in this work are taken from the New Revised Standard Version, Catholic Edition of the Holy Bible.

In this work, attention will be focused on exploring the meaning of religion and its relationship with education. The research will be based on questions such as: can religion be studied, especially in our post-modern age? The influence of culture, the media, the experience and needs of the present-day human person will also be studied as they relate to religion. Human life situations and their readiness to assimilate religious teachings will form the basis of assessing the meaningfulness of religious education. Hence, there is a need to find out the mode and atmosphere in which these teachings should be carried out.

Other questions to be considered include: where can this religious education take place? This involves the context and contents of religious educational curricula, the politics behind the designing of these curricula, the role of the environment and the subjects of religious education. How is it to be carried out? Who takes up its responsibility? These important questions will play a basic role in the development of this work.

0.2 Background of the Work

This work is drawn from the background of two separate worlds: the developed world and developing world, using Germany and Nigeria as a case study. At the beginning of Western civilisation, Christianity is said to have made its way throughout ancient Europe. The Europeans accepted Christianity as a religion which bears a certainty of faith which would ensure the salvation of its adherents. From this perspective, religious education in Germany has passed through the ages and has developed alongside the technological advancement of the country. In Nigeria, Christianity came in conjunction with the colonialism in the 19th century. Religious education in this country, therefore, is still at its developmental stage along with the economic, political, cultural, religious and technological level of the country.

These two countries will be used to assess the impact of religious education on the life of an individual, irrespective of his/her level of environmental and mental development. It is meant to ascertain whether the contemporary conception of religion depends upon the standard of living of the individual, his/her cultural background or his/her nature purely as a human person. Such assessment will truly help to understand the role which religious education plays in imparting religious knowledge and encouraging its practices in the life of our present day youth.

0.3 Statement of the Problem

The study of religion in the present day situation takes place only within a remote part of the entire institutionalised and authoritative aspects of human learning. In the multi-pluralistic and social world of the post-modern era, the human person is constantly in search of absolute freedom and desires to live independent of organised religion. This is the observation of Kunstmann when he remarked that, many post-modern people regard the teachings on faith and religion only as alternative means of acquiring knowledge in the midst of many other fields of learning.[8] According to him, the assertions of the entire religious teachings, their validity and profession no longer seem to meet up with the life situation of many post-modern people.[9] Thus under the condition of incomprehensibility, religious teachings have been termed unproductive and obsolete by many post-modern individuals. They are no longer seen to be relevant to the constant changes that have characterised the life of the post-modern person.

Religious education has always had the goal of educating young people especially in the faith and its practice. Religious education, therefore, influences them in their choice of faith and adherence to religious principles. This type of education, according to the Second Vatican Council:

> *...not only develops the maturity of the human person ..., but is especially directed towards ensuring that those who have been baptised, ... are gradually introduced to a knowledge of the mystery of salvation, become daily more appreciative of the gift of faith which they have received.*[10]

The use of the word "faith" here is meant to indicate that religion is not meant to be dormant. It has to be practiced within a faith, which in this work is understood to be Christian.

To what extent then has religious education led young people to the practice of the Christian faith? What are the contents and perspectives of the religious education they receive in their families, schools and Christian communities? Are they given a qualitative religious teaching that is capable of introducing and holding them in the practice of their faith or has this teaching not permeated into the main stream of their lives? Do religious education teachers teach them with the proper religious language? At what age should a child begin to receive religious teachings? A visit to any Christian Church ses-

8 Cf. Kunstmann J., Religionspädagogik, Eine Einführung, Tübingen, 2004,1.

9 Cf. Ibid.

10 Dillon M. (Trans.), Gravissimum Educationis (GE), 2, in: Flannery A., (Gen. Ed.), Vatican Council II, The Conciliar and Post-Conciliar Documents, Mumbai, 2007, 644.

sion in Germany for instance will instantly provoke the question of the future of Christianity. This is because young people are not numerically well represented in the Churches. Church attendance is increasingly left for the old and a handful of middle aged people. This development indicates that religion is losing its relevance and grip in the lives of many contemporary youth. Some of them claim that they no longer find full expression of themselves within organised religions. Organised religion, such as Christianity, according to them limits their freedom and worldview. Such youth claim that religious activities are dull and do not conform to the contemporary norms of life. That is why these young people prefer commercialism and materialism to contemplation and asceticism. A life of religion is for this group boring and unacceptable. The problem, therefore, consists in the fact that some young people of the present age are very neutral concerning Church activities and religious practices. This situation calls for urgent action because it is an indication that the Church may cease to exist in the near future.

To identify properly the problem of religious practices in the life of the contemporary youth, certain further questions need to be asked: How has religion lost its flare among the youth? Where does the problem of this non-conformity to religious matters lie? What has replaced the position of religion in their lives? Does the problem identify itself with lack of religious education or the manner in which the given religious education is carried out? What has actually gone wrong? Is it that the society no longer needs religion? Is religion to be thrown away as out-modish? Has the problem something to do with the anthropological development of human beings or their social environment? The answers to these and other similar questions will help in stating the actual problem that exists as well as finding a possible solution to it.

0.4 Motivation of the Work

The decision to enquire into the impact of religious education in the lives of the youth is motivated by a number of factors. Firstly, young adults' lack of interest in religious activities and practices creates doubts as to the usefulness of religion in the contemporary human society. According to a study by Ziebertz, Kalbheim and Riegel on the religiosity of the youth in Germany in 2003, only about 16.7% are engaged in Church activities, about 20.6% are only functionally religious, about 20% are Christians but belong to no particular Church, about 27.4% are doubtful of the Church and religion while about 15.3% are completely non-believers.[11] Although these figures may have changed in the

11 Cf. Ziebertz H. G., Kalbheim B., Riegel U., Religiöse Signaturen heute, Ein religionspädagogischer Beitrag zur empirischen Jugendforschung, Gütersloh, 2003, 394.

course of time, they reveal a frightening reality. This is because young people are the hope and future of the Church and as such the subsequent bearers of her faith, moral, social and religious norms.[12] Their involvement in the life of the Church therefore is an important area of educational scrutiny. Their unchecked absence and lack of interest in the life of the Church will not be to the favour of the Church.

Although the Nigerian situation is not at the same level with that of Germany, one cannot totally rule out the fact of religious laxity in these two countries. In this instance, the involvement of the youth in the activities of the Church is comparatively better in Nigeria in the sense that the youth form more than 50% of the membership of both the Church and Nigerian population.[13] They play leadership roles in various aspects of the Church's life especially in the teaching of catechism and organising youth associations. However it is noticeable that the situation has undergone some negative changes in the past 20 years. These changes are mostly attributed to some environmental conditions such as economy, politics and cultural changes, which constantly influence the behavioural disposition of young people. According to Rego:

One cannot deny the influence the hectic pace of living is already having on young minds. Add to it the lack of much-needed parental guidance and the impact of the media and one has the answer to the questions regarding youth discipline.[14]

The second motivating factor for the inquiry into the impact of religious education in the lives of the youth is the zeal to discover the root cause of their indifferentism towards religious matters. In this instance a thorough look will be made into the contents and perspectives of the religious education they receive in the family, at school and in the Church as well as its development in the course of history. The motive is to find out whether the youth are not taught well in the above mentioned three places of religious education or whether they are environmentally not well disposed to learn. The discovery of these facts will help this work to achieve its aim.

0.5 Aim of the Work

The present study intends to investigate the problem of religious indifference among the youth from a pedagogical perspective. The central theme of this

12 Cf. Dillon M. (Trans.), Gravissimum Educationis (GE), 2, in: Flannery A., (Gen. Ed.), Vatican Council II, The Conciliar and Post-Conciliar Documents, Mumbai, 2007, 644.

13 Cf. Africae Munus (AE), 2011, 60, http://www.vatican.va/holy_father/benedict_xvi/apost_exhortations/documents/hf_ben-xvi_exh_20111119_africae-munus_en.html, 09.11.2012.

14 Rego A.J., How to Develop a Pleasing Personality, Mumbai, 2006, 7.

study will be reflected in the question of how far the youth are integrated into the life of the Church through religious teachings. What opportunities has the Church in Germany as well as in Nigeria created for a meaningful learning experience and an active youthful participation and involvement in her programmes? Does the Church in these two countries make some attractive offers to the youth to ensure their continued presence and the proliferation of her teachings? Do the youth here have a sense of belonging or do they feel estranged from the larger body of the Church? A first step towards the achievement of the goal of this work is the propagation of a sound religious upbringing of the child from the first instance of his or her religious studies. This upbringing will play a fundamental role in giving the child a formation devoid of religious indifference.

This study will also look at the education of the youth from the direction of their response to the efforts of the Church to bring them closer to her fold. Attention will be focused on the role of the youth themselves in religious education. Have they failed to utilise positively the opportunities offered them by the Church and the larger society? This study proceeds from the assumption that the level of religious education which the youth receive from the Church and the society will determine greatly how they integrate these teachings into their religious lives in the future. What of a situation whereby the youth are properly educated in the field of religion, yet they turn out to be totally irreligious? Will the blame be apportioned to the Church and the society or to the youth who failed to practice what they have been taught? Thus, the role of the peer group in religious education will be examined.

The problem of religious indifference among the youth is not peculiar to Germany and Nigeria. It has become a global issue in recent times. That is why it has received great attention in the field of academics. In many other countries, the attitude of young people towards religion is also a thing of great worry. This is why there is a global outcry against the problem of their neutrality towards religion and religious practices. However, the present research is limited to the religious learning and life of the youth in the diocese of Ahiara and the archdiocese of Munich and Freising. It intends to contribute to the ongoing and painstaking efforts of the Church in bringing the youth back to the practice of the faith.

Generally, this work is not only a furtherance of the already existing materials produced in the field of religious studies in proffering a solution to the indifference of the youth towards the practice of religion. Its uniqueness lies in the fact that it will discuss contemporary technologies as an ardent and effective means of bringing religious knowledge and liturgical celebrations to the youth. It intends to do this by bringing to light an aspect of this search for a solution which has so far not received adequate attention in religious studies. Thus, it intends to propagate the teaching of religion in relation to modern technology. This system of teaching encompasses the world of the contemporary youth. Any field of learning which neglects the use of post-modern technology may not gain the attention of the present day youth. This is because they spend a greater percentage of their time in the use of television, video games, mobile phone interactions, MP3 players, computers, Internet and web browsing. Hence, the use of post-modern technology in religious education will have a great impact on their lives. This approach, which will serve as a complementarity to the normal classroom teaching, will also be effective in presenting religious practice as an integral part of human life. Many publications have so far dealt with the issue of the religious education curriculum with regard to the analysis of its contents and planning. Others have treated religion in relation to its theories and principles in the field of learning. But its practicability in everyday life in connection with post-modern technology has not been adequately addressed especially with regard to the youth. This is why religious education in its present form makes less impact on them in the course of their maturity into adulthood. There is a need for a practical connection between the world view of the youth and the Christian message. Hence, the major thrust of this work is to establish why religious education of the youth should be a major concern of the larger society, to which the Church also belongs. This calls for team work, in which the family, the state and the Church will be able to cooperate with one another in achieving this all important goal.

Education in general is an inalienable right of the individual.[15] Children, therefore, have the right to receive a proper religious education; they have the right to know themselves, their God and their relationship towards Him. This knowledge should not be "half-baked" or incompletely presented. It should not be treated as a mere privilege, for it belongs intrinsically to them as a fundamental right. Taking cognisance of the "signs of the times", religious education should take place in relation to the environmental disposition and development of the individual human person. It is therefore the proper time to teach religion with the use of the post-modern technology so that the youth will see it as addressing their situation. In this way, religious education will be meaningful to both the German child as well as the Nigerian child, since technology has turned the world into "a global village".

15 Cf. Dillon M. (Trans.), Gravissimum Educationis, 1, in: Flannery A., (Gen. Ed.), Vatican Council II, The Conciliar and Post-Conciliar Documents, Mumbai, 2007, 634.

0.6 Delimitation of the Work

This work will be an investigation of the available religious educational materials in Germany and Nigeria, with the hope that such an investigation will reveal the loopholes that created the contemporary religious indifference of the youth. It will concentrate essentially on certain relevant teaching methods that will facilitate the achievement of its ultimate goal, which is bridging the gap of incompatibility between religion and the present day youth. Its primary pre-occupation therefore is the expository analysis of this indifference so as to see the need for its eradication. In this way, this work will be limited to the investigations that will be of relevance to the achievement of its set goal. The areas of coverage however will be the archdiocese of Munich and Freising in Germany and the diocese of Ahiara in Nigeria. The group being referred to here as the youth are young people between the ages of 18 and 25. This period is regarded as the post-school age of one's life time. However, their early religious learning in the family, in the school (primary and secondary) and in the Church (parish) will be treated in order to establish their religious background from infancy to adolescence. The work therefore will limit itself to how young people in the above mentioned areas (the archdiocese of Munich and Freising and the diocese of Ahiara) see the world around them, what characterises their world values and how these values can be used in their religious education. It will further look at the life of these young people after their primary and secondary school days and examine to what extent religious education has helped them in the religious aspect of their lives.

This work is intended to provoke interest, create awareness in the area of the limitations of religious education in the archdiocese of Munich and Freising, Germany, and in the diocese of Ahiara, Nigeria, and draw the attention of researchers to this topic. It does not claim any finality on this topic but only intends to offer useful suggestions in the area of religious educational research which can lead to the active participation of the youth in religious activities. The researcher is of the hope that the work will help the Church, especially in the two areas of investigation, to adopt new means of religious education which can attract the attention of young people not only to be involved in religious activities but also in the practice of the Christian faith.

0.7 Methodology

This work is a scientific inquiry into the religious learning and way of life of the contemporary youth. As such, the mode of its investigation will include both theoretical and practical aspects which will analyse, expose, describe as well as evaluate the available data. The theoretical aspect will trace the historical development of religious education in the countries (areas) of investigation. This historical overview helps to establish with concrete facts some revealing realities which have contributed to the development of the religious status of the youth in the two demographic areas. The practical aspect of the inquiry will focus on how the teaching of religious education in Germany and Nigeria is integrated into the lives of the youth in the archdiocese of Munich and Freising and in the diocese of Ahiara.

This research will however be chiefly based on qualitative methodology. According to Polkinghorne:

> *Qualitative research is inquiry aimed at describing and clarifying human experience as it appears in peoples' lives. Researchers using qualitative methods gather data that serve as evidence for their distilled descriptions. Qualitative data are gathered in the form of spoken word or written language rather than in the form of numbers... The focus of qualitative inquiries is on describing, understanding, and clarifying a human experience. It requires collecting a series of intense, full, and saturated descriptions of the experience under investigation.*[16]

Following Polkinghorne's caveats, there will be a collection of the data of relevant teaching materials and field work will carried out whereby some institutions (families, schools, and Churches) will be visited so as to find out how religion is taught and learned in these environments.

0.8 Structure of the Work

This work is made up of six major chapters. The first chapter deals with the approximation of the principal concepts contained in the title of the work. These include: religion, education, religious education, learning and youth. It describes the etymological meaning of these concepts as well as the scope in which they are used in this work.

The second chapter concentrates on Nigeria as a first step towards the description of the areas of investigation. This is done under nine sections. The first section presents Nigeria from the point of view of its location, vegetation, ethnicity, language and population. The second section traces the historical background of Nigeria as a product of the colonial conquest of the British invasion of Africa. It describes the Nigerian situation before, during and after

16 Polkinghorne D. E., "Language and Meaning, Data Collection in Quantitative Research", in: Journal of Counselling Psychology 52, no. 2, 2005, 137-139.

the colonial era. The third section is concerned with the history of religions in Nigeria. The religions involved are: African Traditional Religion (ATR), Islam and Christianity. Section four is dedicated to the youth in Nigeria. It is concerned with the categories of youth found in the Nigerian society and their involvement in religious and civil responsibilities. Section five contains a presentation of the types of schools in Nigeria. It takes a look at the primary school, the secondary school and the university. These schools are categorized into public or Government schools and private or confessional schools. Section six deals with religious education in Nigeria and concerns itself with the religions that are taught in the schools. These religions are Christianity and Islam, since the majority of Nigerians are adherents of these religions. In the seventh section, the current religious education curriculum in Nigeria is discussed. This is broken down into a nine-year basic religious education curriculum and the senior secondary religious education curriculum. The nine-year basic curriculum covers the teaching of religion from primary one to the third year of junior secondary education while the senior secondary curriculum contains the syllabus for the teaching of religion from the first year of senior secondary education to the third year. The chapter is evaluated in the eighth section and summarized in section nine.

The third chapter centres on Germany. It consists of nine sections. The first section is a brief description of Germany based on its location, vegetation, ethnicity and population as well as the languages spoken there. The second section traces a brief historical background of the country while the third section takes a look at the history of religions in the country. Section four presents the current religious situation in Germany beginning with Christianity and then with other religions. The fifth section deliberates on the concepts of religious education in Germany from the point of view of kerygma, hermeneutics, catechesis, problems, correlative concept and socialization. Section six focuses on the German school system by describing the types of schools that exist in the country. These include: the primary school, the grammar school, the intermediate secondary school, the general secondary school and the vocational school. Section seven, which is further broken down into five sub-sections, takes a detailed look at religious education in these schools with a summary of each school system. This is followed in the eighth section by an evaluation of the entire chapter and its summary in section nine.

Chapter four, which consists of four sections, deliberates on religious education in the family and in the Church. Section one is centred on religious education in the family. It traces the etymological meaning of the family and pinpoints the various roles of parents and children in religious education respectively. The second section discusses religious education in the Church. It states the meaning of the parish and gives a comprehensive analysis of parish catechesis in both the diocese of Ahiara and the archdiocese of Munich and Freising. This is followed in the third section by an evaluation and a summary of the chapter in section four.

The fifth chapter is the comparative and analytical presentation of the entire work. It consists of nine sections. Section one looks at some social phenomena affecting religious education ranging from the influence of religious pluralism, the influence of secularism to the influence of the media. Section two takes up the issue of some environmental phenomena affecting religious education. Attention is focused on the influence of parents, the influence of the religious education teacher and the influence of the peer group. Section three is a comparative analysis of the contents of religious education in the family. The fourth section is focused on some major contents of religious education in the schools within the diocese of Ahiara and the archdiocese of Munich and Freising. Section five is a comparative analysis of the contents of religious education in the Church within the two dioceses. The sixth section deliberates on some recommendations that can enhance the teaching of religion. These include the on-going formation of the agents of religious education (the teachers) and the use of the media in religious education. The seventh section focuses on the need for an inclusion of some African elements in the teaching of religion in the schools and families within the diocese of Ahiara. Section eight is the evaluation of the overall synthesis while the ninth section contains the summary of the chapter.

The sixth chapter is the general evaluation and conclusion of the entire work while chapter seven will contain the compilation of the materials used in the writing of the work.

1. Meaning and Understanding of the Key Concepts

Religious education is a young theological discipline[1] but it is not a completely new subject of learning. It concerns itself with the transmission of religious beliefs and how plausible these beliefs are to the contemporary human being. That is why the living situation of human beings, their needs, worries and culture are very important. Religious education tries to find out what meaning religion has for present-day human beings especially the youth, in whose hands the future of religion lies. This first chapter will try to broaden the meaning of some of the key concepts of religious education derived from the title formulation. It will first of all try to highlight the understanding of religion by stressing the need for it to be studied as an intellectual discipline. It will state the means for its study as well as pinpoint some underlying reasons why it should be studied. The next concept is education. The etymology of this word will be traced so as to find out its aim especially in relation to religion. By bringing the two concepts together under religious education, an attempt will be made to ascertain how education helps to make religion intelligible. This will help to discover its goals in human learning. The concept of learning has often been used interchangeably with that of study. The explication of this concept will give its meaning, when it begins and where it takes place.

1.1 Religion

Religion is understood from different perspectives and concepts. As a subject, it has been given different interpretations, meanings and definitions by scholars especially in its relationship with the human person. That is why some scholars have approached it either from its "root-meaning, its connotation, its origin or its definition."[2] From whichever angle of study it is viewed, the fact of its complexity has not been diminished. This complexity expresses itself in the many theories and principles of religion that have been formulated by scholars in the course of history. Such theories like Max Müller's science of religion, animism of E. B. Tylor, magic of James Frazer, religion and personality of Sigmund Freud, society as sacred of Emile Durkheim, religion as alienation of Karl Marx[3] and so many others indicate the various ways in which scholars

1 Cf. Kunstmann J., Religionspädagogik, Eine Einführung, 2. Auflage, Tübingen, 2010, 11.

2 Idowu E. B., African Traditional Religion, A Definition, London, 1973, 22.

3 Cf. Pals D.L., Seven Theories of Religion, New York, 1996, 10.

have understood religion in the course of time. These theories and principles postulate the aims and purposes of religion in the understanding of the human person. The close connection between humans and religion has made it necessary for human beings to inquire into the many roles which religion plays in their lives. This inquiry, understood as the study of religion is aimed at giving answers to the ultimate questions of human existence. Hence the questions: What is religion? Can and should it be studied? What is the essence of its study? The answers to these questions will be the focus of this section.

1.1.1 What is Religion?

A clear-cut definition of the word religion is a difficult task to undertake. This is because scholars have not been able to agree on a single definition of the word. From the Ancient Greek philosophers, through Roman writers, the long unbroken history of Hinduism, Judaism, Christianity, and Islam, to contemporary understanding, the etymology of the word, "religion" has remained a dichotomy. However, defining religion from its etymological perspective will help us to arrive at the original meaning of the word.

The word "religion" in its present sense originated from the Latin compound verb "religio".[4] Cicero for instance held that it came from a root 'leg-'– meaning 'to take up, gather, count, or observe, i.e. 'to observe the signs of Divine communication'.[5] Servius, on the other hand, held that it came from another root, 'lig-', 'to bind', so that 'religio' meant 'a relationship', i.e. 'a communion between the human and Super-Human'.[6] This etymological understanding was also traced by Lines:

The term "religion" is derived from the Latin compound verb "religio". The root is one of three possibilities: "ligo", to bind, tie, join together; "lego", to gather or collect; or "lig", to pay attention or give care. The prefix "re" means turning backward, restoration to original condition, or transition into the opposite state.[7]

The word religion according to Idowu came to embrace the above meanings either inter-changeably or in combination.[8] In this sense "religion" is understood to mean "to bind back", "to fasten up", or "join two or more things together". It is then the phenomenon which brings about the relationship between two entities. This is the understanding of Bouquet when he defined "reli-

4 Lines T. A., Systemic Religious Education, Birmingham, 1987, 143.

5 Cf. Idowu E. B., African Traditional Religion, A Definition, London, 1973, 23

6 Cf. Ibid.

7 Lines T. A., Systemic Religious Education, Birmingham, 1978, 143.

8 Idowu E. B., African Traditional Religion, A Definition, London, 1973, 23.

gio" as "a relationship between the human self and some non-human entity, the Sacred, the Supernatural, the Self-Existent, the Absolute, or simply 'God'".[9] Religion therefore has an anthropological connotation in the sense that it connects humans with the Supernatural in a series of sacred acts which are often expressed in the form of a pact between the two beings. It opens the search for a personal adherence to an ultimate and transcendental reality which gives authenticity to human life.[10] The *Webster's Third New International Dictionary* defined religion as:

> *... the personal commitment to and serving of God or a god with worship and devotion, conduct in accordance with divine commands especially as found in accepted sacred writings or declared by authoritative teachers, a way of life recognized as incumbent on true believers, and typically the relating of oneself to an organized body of believers.*[11]

For Allport, religion is "the audacious bid to bind oneself to creation and to the Creator".[12] Religion is understood here as the process of linking two (most often unequal) entities together. Each party assumes a duty towards the other which is often that of "worship" and "protection".

Tylor defined religion as "belief in spiritual beings."[13] According to him the essence of religion is animism – the belief in the living, personal powers behind all things. This belief in spirits is for Tylor the only characteristic shared by all religions, great or small, ancient, modern or post-modern.

1.1.2 Can and Should Religion Be Studied?

In the post-modern world, religion has become a private matter for many people. Upholding the view of Schleiermacher, they regard religion as a thing of the mind which can only be expressed with regard to one's feelings and perceptions.[14] Religion is no longer a thing of discussion for the post-modern person. It is to be handled as a matter of private responsibility. With such a

9 Bouquet A. C., Comparative Religion, 1945, 12f, quoted by: Idowu E. B., African Traditional Religion, A Definition, London, 1973, 23.

10 Cf. Buetow H. A., Religion in Personal Development: An Analysis and a Prescription 1991, 9.

11 Webster's Third New International Dictionary Vol. II, Chigaco, 1981, 1918.

12 Allport G., An Individual and his Religion, 16, quoted by: Lines T. A., Systemic Religious Education, Birmingham, 1987. 144.

13 Tylor E.B., Primitive Culture, 1:424, quoted by: Pals D.L Seven Theories of Religion 1996, 24.

14 Cf. Lines T. A., Systemic Religious Education, Birmingham, 1987, 135.

situation, doubts abound as to whether religion can and should be studied as a subject of human learning. In this section, attention will be focused on the means of studying religion under the title of religious education. This will be handled in two steps: articulating the means of learning the faith and giving some reasons why religion can and should be studied.

1.1.3 Means of Learning Religion

The learning of the Christian faith has always been associated with catechetical instructions. That is why the structure for the transmission of the faith in Christendom is catechetical. Under "Catechesis" the entire teachings of the church comprising the dogmas, sacraments and prayers are presented as elements of study. According to Murphy:

In the New Testament the word catechesis (κατηχεῖυ) is used to signify teaching or instruction in the law of God (Acts 18.25; Rom 2.18; Gal 6.6).[15]

The teaching of the Church, known as the Kerygma, is the announcement of the good news of God's kingdom[16] realised in the person of Jesus Christ. The "Catechism" is the book containing the summary of these teachings and is presented in a simple question and answer form so that the students known as "Catechumens" can understand these teachings without much difficulty. The word catechism was first used by St. Augustine in connection with the preparation for Baptism. This means that the basis for the use of this style of teaching lies with the early Church's preparation for the Christian life of which Baptism is the "opening door".[17] From their origin catechisms contained teachings on the New Testament's laws of love of God and love of neighbour, the Creed and the Our Father.[18] Sloyan says:

> *A catechism according to the English and German usage is a manual of Christian doctrine, often in question and answer form (German, Katechismus). In Romance languages, the term also signifies the act of catechising, the work of presenting Christian doctrine or an individual lesson, especially to the young.*[19]

15 Murphy F. X., Catechesis, I (Early Christian), in: Carson T., Cerrito J. (Eds.), New Catholic Encyclopedia, 2nd Ed. Vol.3, Detroit, 2003, 227.

16 Ibid.

17 Cf. Kalloch C., Leimgruber S., Schwab U., Lehrbuch der Religionsdidaktik, Für Studium und Praxis in ökumenischer Perspektive, Freiburg, 2009, 33.

18 Cf. Ibid.

19 Sloyan G. S., Catechisms, in: Carson T., Cerrito J. (Eds.), New Catholic Encyclopedia, 2nd Ed., Vol.3, Detroit, 2003, 239.

The teacher or catechetical instructor known as the "Catechist" helps the students to learn these teachings using the kerygmatic method of teaching. In a kerygmatic method of teaching, the teacher asks the students questions as well as provides the answers so that they repeat after him or her until they have memorised the answers. This method of learning which is currently no longer used in the schools is however limited to the parishes and Christian communities for catechetical instructions. In the schools, it has been substituted with the hermeneutic method, which is a system of teaching, whereby the teacher explains and analyses a text or topic and the students ask questions for clarification.

Catechisms as books have existed in the Church since the time of the Reformation.[20] Aquinas is known to have composed a catechism in 1273 containing teachings on elements such as: the Creed, the Decalogue, Prayers (such as Pater Noster and Ave Maria), and the Sacraments.[21] Before the Reformation, the humanist theologian, Erasmus von Rotterdam published the "Handbüchlein eines christlichen Streiters" in 1501. In the same year the Brothers of Böhm introduced the "Kinderfragen und Antworten", a work which was translated into the German language in 1521.[22] These transmitted the compressed summary of the articles of faith and the meaning of the entire Christendom. In the Catholic Church, there are as many catechisms as the many languages of the world. According to Sloyan:

> *With every passing year the number of catechisms grew so that already in 1742 Pope Benedict XIV recommended that Bellarmine's catechism become standard throughout the Catholic world.*[23]

The number of catechisms in the Catholic Church started increasing tremendously especially after the Council of Trent and the publication of "The Catechism of the Council of Trent" popularly known as "The Roman Catechism" (1566). Dioceses in numerous countries made some remarkable efforts to see to the production of catechisms for use within their various localities. This move came to a peak especially after the Second Vatican Council when the translation of the various liturgical books as well as the Bible from Latin into different languages escalated. Because of this quest for diocesan and national catechisms, many Church leaders, in the years following the Second Vatican Council, citing the precedent of the Roman Catechism, called for a new "conciliar Catechism"

20 Cf. Kunstmann J., Religionspädagogik, Eine Einführung, 2. Auflage, Tübingen, 2010, 35.

21 Cf. Ibid, 34.

22 Cf. Ibid.

23 Sloyan G. S., Catechisms, in: Carson T., Cerrito J. (Eds.), New Catholic Encyclopedia, 2nd Ed., Vol.3, Detroit, 2003, 244.

that would unify all the existing catechisms before it.[24] This quest resulted in the publication of "The Catechism of the Catholic Church" (CCC) in 1992. The need for catechisms in the Church is based on the fact that they form along with the Bible the primary materials for religious education.

In the Archdiocese of Munich und Freising as well as in the whole of Germany, the spread of catechism books after the Reformation was very rapid. This was as a result of the Protestant influence in the teaching of the faith at this time. The period of the Reformation coincided with the significant transition to the period in which the catechism manual began to play a dominant role in the formation of both the theory and practice of catechesis.[25] The first catechism to be used was "Der Kleine Katechismus für die gemeine Pfarrherrn und Prediger" written by Luther in 1529.[26] This catechism had as its contents: the Ten Commandments (Decalogue), the Creed (Credo), the Lord's Prayer or the Our Father, (Pater Noster), and the Sacraments of Baptism and the Eucharist. It also contains some prayers such as: Morning and Evening Blessings, Grace before and after Meals and some biblical instructions.[27] For Luther, Jesus instituted and willed only two sacraments namely: Baptism and the Eucharist.[28] This catechism was meant to be in the hands of the lower clergy as an instrument to instruct the uneducated laity.[29] The second catechism was also written by Luther in the same year with the title: "Der Große Katechismus". This contained the Ten Commandments, the Creed, the Lord's Prayer and the sacraments of Baptism and the Eucharist as in the first catechism; however, this catechism was enlarged to incorporate the sacrament of Reconciliation through Confession.[30] According to Jegen:

> *It was only with Luther that the term catechism came to refer to a book, both to the manual used by the catechist and to the simpler text placed in the hands of a child. Until this time, the term catechism referred only to the content of the catechesis.*[31]

24 Cf. Ibid., 245.

25 Cf. Jegen M. E., Catechesis, III (Reformation), in: Carson T., Cerrito J. (Eds.), New Catholic Encyclopedia, 2nd Ed., Vol.3, Detroit, 2003, 233.

26 Kalloch C., Leimgruber S., Schwab U., Lehrbuch der Religionsdidaktik, 2009, 35.

27 Ibid.

28 Cf. Kunstmann J., Religionspädagogik, Eine Einführung, 2. Auflage, Tübingen, 2010, 35.

29 Cf. Sloyan G. S., Catechisms, in: Carson T., Cerrito J. (Eds.), New Catholic Encyclopedia, 2nd Ed., Vol.3, Detroit, 2003, 241.

30 Cf. Kalloch C., Leimgruber S., Schwab U., Lehrbuch der Religionsdidaktik, 2009, 36.

31 Jegen M. E., Catechesis, III (Reformation), in: Carson T., Cerrito J. (Eds.), New Catholic Encyclopedia, 2nd Ed., Vol.3, Detroit, 2003, 233.

Other catechism books that appeared after Luther include: "Kurze schriftliche Erklärung" (1534), "Kurzer Katechismus" (1537), "Instruction et Confession de Foy" (1537), "Le Catéchisme de l'église de Genève" (1542) and "Der Heidelberger Katechismus" of 1563.[32] This catechism is divided into three parts: The Fall of Mankind, The Salvation of Mankind and the Gratitude of Mankind (for the work of salvation through the action of Christ). The first Catholic catechism written in reaction to Luther's was published in Augsburg in 1530 and was followed by a series of others in German and Latin.[33] The three catechisms of Peter Canisius appeared in 1555, 1556 and 1558 respectively as a remedy to many of the weaknesses of earlier Catholic efforts to produce a sound catechism with the authentic teachings of the Catholic Church after the Reformation.[34] These catechisms include: his large catechism "Summa doctrinae christianae", his small catechism "Catechismus minimus" and his middle catechism "Parvus catechismus catholicorum". The three catechisms were written in the same order. They are divided into two parts comprising teachings on Faith, Hope, Prayer, the Ten Commandments, the Sacraments, Sin, Good Works and Eschatology.[35] According to Jegen:

The catechisms of Canisius were written to defend the faith against heresy, and therefore they necessarily had a strong intellectual quality. They were admirably devoid of polemics, however, and although they are written in question and answer form, they retained much of the spirit and even the language of Scripture and the Fathers.[36]

The catechisms of Canisius served as the basis for the development of further catechisms in the Catholic Church. Thus, in 1566 after the council of Trent, the "Roman Catechism" was published. This catechism, which was not in the question and answer form, was primarily composed for the bishops and priests for the teaching of the faith especially to those preparing for Baptism and also for their entire congregation.[37] It was divided into four parts namely: God's revelation of Himself in history and man's response through faith; the

32 Cf. Kalloch C., Leimgruber S., Schwab U., Lehrbuch der Religionsdidaktik, Für Studium und Praxis in ökumenischer Perspektive, Freiburg, 2009, 37-38.

33 Jegen M. E., Catechesis, III (Reformation), in: Carson T., Cerrito J. (Eds.), New Catholic Encyclopedia, 2nd Ed., Vol.3, Detroit, 2003, 233.

34 Cf. Ibid.

35 Cf. Kalloch C., Leimgruber S., Schwab U., Lehrbuch der Religionsdidaktik, Für Studium und Praxis in ökumenischer Perspektive, Freiburg, 2009, 42.

36 Jegen M. E., Catechesis, III (Reformation), in: Carson T., Cerrito J. (Eds.), New Catholic Encyclopedia, 2nd Ed., Vol.3, Detroit, 2003, 233.

37 Cf. Kalloch C., Leimgruber S., Schwab U., Lehrbuch der Religionsdidaktik, Für Studium und Praxis in ökumenischer Perspektive, Freiburg, 2009, 42-43.

healing works of the Church through the sacraments and sacramentals; the response to God's covenant in the Ten Commandments (Decalogue); and the Lord's Prayer (Pater Noster) and Hail Mary (Ave Maria).[38]

The Reformation brought about many other catechisms with very strong emphasis on ethics and a deeper awareness of the self-understanding of the Bible. Among such catechisms were the catechisms of Robert Bellarmine. Written at the order of Clement VIII, these catechisms were the most influential of all the others written shortly after the Council of Trent.[39] These included: "Dottrina cristiana breve" (1597), which was a short summary of Christian doctrine for pupils and "Dichiarazione piu copiosa della dottrina cristiana" (1598) which was written for the use of priests and teachers.[40] The "Dottrina cristiana breve" contained seven articles namely: the Creed, the Lord's Prayer, the Ten Commandments, the Sacraments, Sin, Eschatology and Theological Virtues (of faith, hope and love). Other works such as the "christliche Grundlagen und Lebensregeln zum Unterrichte der Jugend", (1775) by Johann Ignaz von Felbiger were very much used for catechetical instructions in the schools. The catechism of Benedikt Stattler, "Katechismus der katholisch-christlichen Glaubens- und Sittenlehre für Kinder der ersten zwo Klassen Deutscher Schulen" (1794) was greatly used in Munich. Stattler appealed for the unification of the Protestant and Catholic Churches. Worthy of mention here are Bernhard Heinrich Overberg and his "Katechismus für die größere Schule" of 1804; Michael Sailer and his two catechisms namely: "Die Sieben heiligen Sakramente" of 1809 and "Übungen des Geistes". Johann Baptist Hirscher authored two catechisms: "Geschichte Jesu Christi" (1839), and "Katechismus der christkatholischen Religion" (1842).[41] Through these works Hirscher exercised a strong influence on pastoral theology in Germany as well as in France.[42] The highly influential catechism of Joseph Deharbe "Katholischer Katechismus oder Lehrbegriff" (1848) was officially adopted for use in the whole of Bavaria in 1853.[43] This catechism, which was developed from the catechism of Canisius was arranged into sections on faith, the Commandments and the means of

38 Ibid.

39 Cf. Jegen M. E., Catechesis, III (Reformation), in: Carson T., Cerrito J. (Eds.), New Catholic Encyclopedia, 2nd Ed., Vol.3, Detroit, 2003, 234.

40 Cf. Ibid.

41 Cf. Ibid.

42 Cf. Lehner F. C., Hirscher, Johann, in: Carson T., Cerrito J. (Eds.), New Catholic Encyclopedia, 2nd Ed., Vol.6, Detroit, 2003, 861.

43 Cf. Koehler J. E., Deharbe, Joseph, in: Carson T., Cerrito J. (Eds.), New Catholic Encyclopedia, 2nd Ed., Vol.4, Detroit, 2003, 612.

grace.[44] Other catechisms by Deharbe include: "Katholischer Katechismus" (1847), "Kleiner katholischer Katechismus" (1847), "Anfangsgründe der katholischen Lehre für die kleinen Schüler" (1847), "Erklärung des katholischen Katechismus" (4 v. 1857-1864). In 1925 Theodor Mönnichs transformed the catechism of Deharbe ("Katholischer Katechismus" oder "Lehrbegriff") into a unified German catechism. The last official catechism for children written in the question and answer form was the "Der Katholische Katechismus der Bistümer Deutschlands" (1955). This catechism was popularly known as the "grüner Katechismus" because of its green coloured cover.[45] It treated among other issues: creation and redemption, the Church and the sacraments, Christian life and eschatology.

The "Der Holländische Katechismus" (1966) was the first among other catechisms which appeared as reference books after the publication of the green German catechism. This catechism was addressed primarily to adults because the bishops of Holland wanted to teach the "unchangeable" faith according to the signs of the time.[46] It echoed the mind of the Second Vatican Council by addressing itself to the joys and hopes, fears and anxieties of the human person. From an anthropological perspective it provided answers to the many existential questions of the human person in a language that was peculiar to the people of the time. This gave rise to the publication of the "Katholischer Erwachsenen-Katechismus" by the German bishops. This catechism was published in two volumes. The first volume, published in 1985 dealt with the proclamation of the faith of the Church while the second volume which was published in 1995 dealt with living the faith.[47] The last in the series of adult catechisms is the "Catechism of the Catholic Church" (CCC 1992). This catechism was modelled after the Roman Catechism of the Council of Trent.[48] According to Pollard and Kutys:

The Catechism of the Catholic Church, promulgated by Pope John Paul II on December 8, 1992, is a compendium of Catholic doctrine that serves as a reference text for teaching and particularly for preparing local catechisms. Modelled to the so called "Roman Catechism," promulgated in 1566 by the Council of Trent, the Catechism of the Catholic Church is divided into four parts of unequal length: the profession of faith, the celebration of the Christian mystery, life in Christ, and Christian prayer. Part one introduces the reader to

44 Ibid, 613.

45 Cf. Kalloch C., Leimgruber S., Schwab U., Lehrbuch der Religionsdidaktik, Für Studium und Praxis in ökumenischer Perspektive, Freiburg, 2009, 44.

46 Cf. Ibid 49.

47 Cf. Ibid.

48 Cf. Ibid, 43.

God's revelation and is organized around the tenets of the Creed. Part two explains how God's plan for salvation was made present in the sacred actions of the Church's liturgy, especially in the sacraments. Part three presents Catholic tradition on law and grace and the principles of Christian morality found in the Commandments. Part four outlines the meaning and importance of prayer in Christian life and explains the petitions of the Lord's Prayer.[49]

The arrangement of this catechism into the four pillars of the Church – Creed, Sacred Liturgy, Christian Way of Life and Prayer – was praised by John Paul II in the apostolic constitution "Fidei Depositum".[50] This is because it followed the traditional order found in "The Roman Catechism" and is therefore meant to encourage and assist in the writing of local catechisms, taking into recognition the various situations and cultures of peoples and at the same time preserving the unity of the Catholic faith.[51] That is why the various catechisms in the Church, though marked by variety in style and presentation, witness to the unity of faith transmitted by the Scriptures and proclaimed in the Church's liturgy.[52]

The latest universal catechism, which to the glory of God was addressed principally to young people is the "Youth Catechism of the Catholic Church" popularly known as "YOUCAT". This catechism was published in April 2011 and was described by Benedict XVI as an "instrumentum laboris" for young people to be able to "engage the challenges and temptations of this time with strength and determination".[53] YOUCAT was written in the same pattern with "Der katholische Katechismus der Bistümer Deutschlands", which appeared in 1955 in a question and answer form. This catechism therefore, with its 527 questions and answers is meant to provide answers to the questions of young people, so that they might understand what they believe, appreciate their faith and be able to defend it. It is an accessible, contemporary expression of the Catholic faith which Benedict XVI appraised as showing "what the Catholic Church believes today and how one can with good reason believe".[54] It is written in four parts. Part one contains a full illustration of what Catholics believe; part two deals with the Catholic celebration of the sacred mysteries; part three is all about how Catholics are to have life in Christ; while part four is concerned with how Catholics should pray. The simplicity of language, im-

49 Pollard J., Kutys D., Catechism of the Catholic Church, in: Carson T., Cerrito J. (Eds.), New Catholic Encyclopedia, 2nd Ed., Vol.3, Detroit, 2003, 237.

50 Cf. Ibid, 245.

51 Cf. Ibid.

52 Cf. Ibid.

53 Youcat, 2011, 9.

54 Ibid., 6.

ages as well as illustrations with Biblical references, quotations from the saints and some great teachers of the Church make this catechism a master-piece for young people to learn the truth of the Catholic faith.

In the diocese of Ahiara, there is a strong attachment to catechisms because of the deep theological impact they have on the transmission of the faith. The oldest catechism used in the teaching of the faith (Katikizim Nke Mbu) dates as far back as the advent of Christianity in Nigeria. This catechism, popularly known as "Yellow Catechism" (because of its yellow cover) formed part of the life of the people as many would be heard reciting it as an aspect of their daily exercise. It was a translation of the "Baltimore Catechism" (1885) which was revised in 1941.[55] Other catechisms especially in the post-modern times appeared in a more simplified language to suit the level of the understanding of children who now form the bulk of contemporary catechumens. Very popular among them are the "Katikizim Nke Abuo" (2000) and its English equivalent, "Doctrine for Adults" (2000) which were written in complementarity with "Katikizim Nke Mbu" and with adaptations from "The Catechism of the Catholic Church". Another faith deepening catechism in the Igbo language is the "Katikizim Nke Okwukwe Nzuko Katolik" which was originally written in 1937 and was revised in 1996 by J.A Nwosu. The revised edition followed the four-pattern formula of the universal Catholic catechism.

"Katikizim Nke Abuo" and "Doctrine for Adults" are the most loved and used of all the catechisms in the diocese of Ahiara. This is especially as a result of their simplicity in language and illustration with Biblical references. They contain a summary of the entire dogmatic teachings of the Church in line with the universal catechism of the Church. The use of images sets them out as masterpieces and endears them to the children to whom they are specifically addressed. Teachers grouped them among the best teaching manuals and best students' textbooks used in religious education. The teachers are given particular pedagogical directives which would help them in bringing the knowledge of a topic to the level of the children.

In each chapter of our present book an explanation precedes the question and answer. This should be read aloud and repeated by the class. The sentences are short. Questions should be asked of which these questions of the explanation are the answers.[56]

The parents and guardians were also enjoined to use them in teaching their children at home as part of their duty in contributing to their religious upbringing. This is all the more important because their children have been entrusted

55 Cf. Sloyan G. S., Catechisms, in: Carson T., Cerrito J. (Eds.), New Catholic Encyclopedia, 2nd Ed., Vol.3, Detroit, 2003, 244.

56 Unegbu M. O., Doctrine for Adults, Second Edition, Owerri, 2000, 3.

into their care by God. Apart from catechetical upbringing, parents are also encouraged to teach their children from the background of their personal conviction and belief. This will help the children not to see Christianity as a foreign religion but as an inherited tradition.

1.1.4 Some Reasons Why Religion Can and Should Be Studied

Although faith is God's free gift to humans,[57] the human response to it has to be given an intelligible approach in line with Thomas Aquinas' theory of "fides quarens intellectum"[58] (faith seeking understanding). Faith needs to be understood in order to be practiced. This intelligible approach to faith, according to Kunstmann, takes place only within a religion[59] and thus there is a need for religious education. The view of Kunstmann is based on the fact that faith belongs to religion and therefore cannot be studied outside of it. Faith does not come through intuition, it comes from hearing (cf. Rom 10:17). Faith does not originate from goodwill or good work. It also does not develop from religiosity or religious practices. These are rather the fruits of faith. They cannot be the means to faith. What builds up faith is what is heard and therefore what is taught. The fact that religion should be studied has its fundamental basis in this need for the intelligibility of faith.

In Germany and Nigeria, the study of religion is based on a number of factors that depend on the cultural and social dispositions of the people. Some of these factors include:

1.1.4.1 Constitutional Reason

In Germany the study of religion is enshrined in the constitution as one of the fundamental rights of all her lawful citizens. According to Riegel and Ziebertz:

The German constitution establishes religion as part of the standard school curriculum, to be taught in accordance with the principles of the religious communities (Article 7/3, Grundgesetz).[60]

In Nigeria the study of religion is also articulated in her constitution as an inalienable right of all Nigerian people.

57 Cf. Kunstmann J., Religionspädagogik, Eine Einführung, Tübingen, 2004, 37.

58 Cf. Shanley B. J., The Thomist Tradition, 2002, 22.

59 Cf. Kunstmann J., Religionspädagogik, Eine Einführung, Tübingen, 2004, 37.

60 Riegel U., Ziebertz H. G., Germany: teachers of religious education – mediating diversity, in: Ziebertz H. G., Riegel U. (Eds.), How Teachers in Europe Teach Religion, An International Empirical Study in 16 Countries, Berlin, 2009, 70.

> *Every person shall be entitled to ... freedom (either alone or in community with others, and in public or in private) to manifest and propagate his religion or belief in worship, teaching, practice and observance (Chapter IV, Art. 38/1).*[61]

In both countries every citizen is provided with the fundamental right to religious education.

1.1.4.2 Cultural Reason

Culture plays a significant role in the religious development of a people. This is because a people are identified in the context of their cultural views. To understand them, attention must be paid to their cultural values as expressed in their language and symbols. In Germany and Nigeria, religious education also has to take into recognition the cultural motives of the people. In this instance, the family, the school and the Church have to unite in offering a holistic religious upbringing through the use of the Holy Scriptures.

1.1.4.3 Social Reason

Religion is an intrinsic part of our society. This can be seen in the religious pluralistic nature of the two countries in question. In Germany, membership in three major religions can be noticed: Christianity, Islam and Judaism. According to Riegel and Ziebertz:

In percentages, 32% of the Germans do not belong to any denomination, 31% are members of the Catholic Church, and another 31% are members of the Protestant Churches. 4% of the Germans are Muslim, 0.1% are Christian Orthodox and 0.0025% are Jewish.[62]

In Nigeria three major religions are practiced. These include: Christianity, Islam and Traditional religion. Christians are predominantly in the South while Muslims form the major population of the North. A minor percentage of traditional worshippers reside alongside the Christians of the South.

This religious plurality in the two countries gives rise to some pluralistic attitudes in the form of sectarianism, fundamentalism and civil unrest. The series of religious conflicts in Nigeria for example which have claimed millions of lives attest to the above assertion. Central to these religious conflicts

---

61 http://www.nigeria-law.org/ConstitutionOfTheFederalRepublicOfNigeria.htm#Chapter_4, 12.11.2012.

62 Riegel U., Ziebertz H. G., Germany: teachers of religious education – mediating diversity, in: Ziebertz H. G., Riegel U. (Eds.), How Teachers in Europe Teach Religion, An International Empirical Study in 16 Countries, Berlin, 2009, 69.

is ignorance and lack of proper religious education. Hence, religious education plays the role of bridging the gap between the various religions that form an intrinsic part of our society. It also helps in uplifting the dignity of the human person. This dignity stems from the creation of human beings in the image and according to the likeness of God (cf. Gen. 1:26-27). The human person therefore needs to be understood from his natural background in order to be respected and cherished. The understanding of the human person from his nature as a bearer of God's image will play a significant role in eliminating the use of violence in the practice of religion.

1.2 Education

Education is a wide discipline which embraces the entire human search for knowledge and inquiry. Lee maintains that:

> *Education is the broad process whereby a person learns something.*[63]

It is the act of transmitting information which leads to new discoveries and orientations in the process of learning. Its aim is generally to maintain an organised system of information in order to permanently establish a link between the past and the present with the hope of creating a prospective future. Education manifests itself in every aspect of human endeavour ranging from the sociological, religious, linguistic and scientific areas of inquiry. It is concerned with the needs of human beings and the society and this according to Lines "includes physical, emotional, cognitive, and interpersonal experience".[64] In this section of inquiry, attention will be focused on stating the meaning of education and its relevance in human endeavour. This will be approached in two steps: giving the definition of education and outlining its aims.

1.2.1 What is Education?

Etymologically, the word education according to *Webster's Third New International Dictionary* can be traced to three Latin roots:

Educare, which means to bring up. It is therefore the act or process of providing knowledge, skill, competence, or usually desirable qualities of be-

---

63 Lee J. M., The Shape of Religious Instruction: A Social Science Approach 1973, 6, quoted by: Lines T. A., Systemic Religious Education, Birmingham, 1987.

64 Lines T. A., Systemic Religious Education, Birmingham, 1987, 185.

haviour or character or of being so provided especially by a formal course of study instruction or training.

Educere, which means to lead forth, to draw out. It is then to bring into manifestation (as a form, quality or law conceived to be present in a latent, potential or undeveloped state).

Ducere, which means to lead.[65]

Lines summarised education as:

> *The derivation of the English word "education" is directly from the Latin compound verb "educo." The stem is "duco": lead, conduct, draw, guide, or direct. The prefix "e" is a form of the preposition "ex," meaning "out of" or "away from". "Educo," then, means to lead forth, to bring out of, (and) to direct away from. Education is that which leads out.*[66]

He further maintained that:

> *Education is the existential learning-adaptive process of leading out from past heritage into an idealized future.*[67]

Education is also understood as the learning process which moves from past discoveries and projects into the future using the present available experimental disposition. Another definition of education which traces present knowledge as the enhancement of the past for the purpose of creating a future one came from Dewey who claims that:

> *Education is that reconstruction or reorganization of experience which adds to the meaning of experience and which increases ability to direct the course of subsequent experience.*[68]

In this definition "past experience" is used to develop the "present experience" and this gives rise to the possibility of arriving at a better "future experience". Dewey's definition can be called the process of education. It is not meant to be stagnant but progressive. This explains also why there are new discoveries and inventions. Education opens the individual person to the new

65 Webster's Third New International Dictionary Vol. I, 1981, 723.

66 Lines T.A., Systemic Religious Education, Birmingham, 1987, 185.

67 Ibid.

68 Dewey J., Democracy and Education: An Introduction to the Philosophy of Education 1916, pp 89-90, quoted by: Lines T.A., Systemic Religious Education, Birmingham, 1987, 185.

waves of knowledge, to new ideas, to new horizons and prepares the mind to adapt to these changes.

1.2.2 Aims of Education

Dewey in *Democracy and Education* illuminated greatly the aims of education. Although his treatment of this concept has been faulted because he regarded "aim" as an equivalent of "purpose"[69], he contributed significantly to the development of this theory. According to Peters, it is quite indubitable that "aim" belongs to the same family of concepts as does "purpose" as well as "intention" and "motive" in the sense that they are conceptually connected with actions and activities, but there are subtle differences between them in the ways in which they are so connected.[70] To identify an action or activity reference has to be made to what exactly the agent conceives it to be.

For example the October beer feast is organised in Munich by the mayor of Munich (Oberbürgermeister) as a yearly activity. One might say that he does that just to convoke people from all parts of the world in Munich so that they might see its beauty, perceive its wealth or simply see that it is a mega city. It can also be said that this feast is organised for breweries, especially in Bavaria, so that they might be able to produce more beer, make more sales as well as profits and exhibit their new inventions in the production of beer. One can also take it to be an occasion for people to drink more beer and get drunk. Or it may as well be meant to offer psychologists the ample opportunity to observe human behaviour under the influence of alcohol. This yearly event can be identified as representing any of the above cases. But to be sure, it could be quite expedient to ask the mayor which of the cases he intends to portray in the staging of this feast. He could be asked, "Are you bringing people to Munich to show them your city?" Or simply, "What is your purpose or motive in organising this feast?" But if he is asked, "What are you aiming at in the organisation of this feast?", then he needs to specify the precise objective of the feast. This question places the responsibility on him to state exactly the objectives underlying the convoking of the feast. "Aim" in this sense is understood to mean the specification of the goal of an action. It states the direction of a particular discipline and pinpoints what distinguishes it from others. This is the view of Peters when he says:

69 Cf. Peters R. S., Woods J., Dray W. H., Aims of Education – A Conceptual Inquiry, in: Peters R. S. (Ed), The Philosophy of Education 1975, 12.

70 Ibid.

To ask a person what he is aiming at is not primarily to demand an explanation for what he is doing ... It is, as it were, putting the onus on him to specify his objective more precisely and to concentrate his efforts accordingly.[71]

"Aim" is associated with social and humanitarian institutions and organisations such as the association of religious education teachers, political parties and social clubs. Here some individuals come together for the purpose of achieving a common goal. The precise articulation of their aims will help them to focus their attention towards realizing them. It is also applicable to some scientific disciplines of human inquiry such as philosophy, education, psychology, etc. That is why such questions can be raised as "What are the aims of education?" The answers to this question are meant to focus the impact of education in a specific direction. The demand for the aims of education "is a salutary request for teachers to survey what they are doing, get their priorities right, concentrate their attention on them, and discard irrelevancies".[72] Education in this sense is all about the human person. The aims of education therefore are meant to conform to the improvement of the living standard of the individual. The development of a person's physical, mental and spiritual faculties is central in any educational pursuit. Here emphasis is laid on the acquisition of the capacities of understanding, appreciation and self-expression. According to Peters:

Education ... picks out a family of processes culminating in a person being better; education picks out a family of processes culminating in a person having an outlook and form of life that is in some way desirable.[73]

Education has a reformative value. Before being educated a person may be said to be pursuing a way of life that is not in conformity with the demands of the environment. But after having acquired education he assumes a better sense of perception and assimilation, an improved level of judgement and assessment of the "why" of things which characterize him as "a better person". Hence through the process of education he has improved his past by advancing into a better present with the possibility of having a refined future. His outlook

71 Ibid 13-14.

72 Ibid 14.

73 Ibid 15.

has been transformed by what he knows because "it is through education that mere living is transformed into a quality of life".[74]

Education is also aimed at securing the political growth and self-realization of the individual.[75] Here attention is focused on the political and technological advancement of the society. Education should enable each individual to conform to the changes in the post-modern times so as to move along with current trends. Especially in the developing countries like Nigeria, education is meant to help a person in handling political issues such as state failure in the provision of essential social amenities due to corruption and deep social or religious upheavals.[76] Peters comments:

> *Aims of this sort have their natural homes within an individualistic system of thought and they draw attention to the claims of the individual to pursue his own bent.*[77]

Education aims at creating an atmosphere of freedom and personal initiative which allows the individual to express his thoughts without restraint and make discoveries that are original to him. It encourages the system of learning from individual experience by instilling self-confidence, self- dependence and self-help into an individual. This makes a person the master of his field and gives rise to the development of a new thesis and hypothesis which will help to constantly improve the impact of education in the life of every individual human person.

Another important aim of education which is peculiar to both Germany and Nigeria is nation building and sustainable development. Every individual lives in the society and therefore has his or her obligations towards his or her nation. Education should achieve its goals and contents in the interest of nation building and social progress. Through education, students should be made aware of their commitment towards democracy, social justice, equality of opportunity, a sense of secularism, national identity and poverty eradication. These should be reflected clearly in the educational policies and programmes so that education will retain its position at the heart of sustainable development.[78]

74 Ibid 19 – 20.

75 Cf. Ibid 21.

76 Cf. Vogt M., Zur Rolle der Ethik im Programm "Bildung für nachhaltige Entwicklung", in: Münk H. J. (Hg.), Wann ist Bildung gerecht? Ethische und theologische Beiträge im interdisziplinären Kontext, Bielefeld, 2008, 270.

77 Cf. Peters R. S., Woods J., Dray W. H., Aims of Education – A Conceptual Inquiry, in: Peters R. S. (Ed), The Philosophy of Education 1975, 22.

78 Cf. Vogt M., Zur Rolle der Ethik im Programm "Bildung für nachhaltige Entwicklung", in: Münk H. J. (Hg.), Wann ist Bildung gerecht? Ethische und theologische Beiträge im interdisziplinären Kontext, Bielefeld, 2008, 270.

1.3 Religious Education

Religious education is the co-ordination of two different disciplines: religion and education.[79] Its formulation indicates the possibility of inter-disciplinary learning. As a subject it is all about the teaching of religion. The goal of religious education is to make religion meaningful in its transformation of the past for present use and to make religion operational as a growing, evolving process of integration, interconnection, and interrelationship. The previous sections of this inquiry have so far concentrated on explaining the meaning of religion and education as two separate subjects. In this section, attention will be focused on the role of education in the understanding of religion. This will be done in a two fold presentation. The first step will be to define religious education while the second will be to state its aims.

1.3.1 What is Religious Education?

A definition of religious education is not an easy task to undertake. This is because religious education is a field which almost everybody claims to understand. According to Moran:

> *Scholars often do assume that they know whatever is to be known about religious education even if they have never investigated the matter.*[80]

This claim makes it even more difficult for scholars to agree on a universal acceptance of a definition of religious education. Some scholars like Lee have preferred to call it, "religious instruction"[81] which however limits it to a particular religious denomination. Others like LeBar used the term "Christian education"[82] interchangeably with religious education. Although many scholars have approached religious education from different perspectives, some succeeded in treating it as holistic, non-particularistic, inclusive and unifying discipline which embraces the teaching of all religions. One of such is Chave who defined religious education as:

79 Cf. Hilger G., Leimbruber S., Ziebertz H. G., Religionsdidaktik, Ein Leitfaden für Studium, Ausbildung und Beruf, München, 2010, 13; 17-40.

80 Moran G., Religious education As A Second Language, Birmingham, 1989, 2.

81 Lee J. M., The Shape of Religious Instruction: A Social Science Approach, 1971, 6, quoted by: Lines T. A., Systemic Religious Education, Birmingham, 1987, 214.

82 LeBar L., Education That Is Christian 1981, 20, quoted by: Lines T. A., Systemic Religious Education, Birmingham, 1987, 214.

...a systematic, planned procedure for making religion meaningful and operative in individual and collective living.[83]

From this definition, religious education explains the meaning of any particular religion and makes it approachable to non-adherents of that religion. This means that one does not need to belong to any particular religion in order to study it. From this stems the inter-connectivity of religion. In religious education people of diverse beliefs come together for the purpose of discovering the teachings of a religion and its orientation to the human situation. Hence a Christian can now study Islam without necessarily being a Muslim and vice versa.

In Christianity, religious education comprises the learning of the Christian teachings through Bible stories, the profession of faith, morals, ethics, sacraments, prayers and the Christian tradition. Ethics and morals are two special disciplines which are concerned with the norms of human behaviour. However, in religious education emphasis is laid especially on the religiosity of the individual. The central theme is the religious awareness of the learner about the tenets of the Christian teachings. Its goal is the propagation of the Christian faith as well as the winning of many converts to her fold.

1.3.2 Aims of Religious Education

Before undertaking any venture, attention is always given to the question of the aim of that venture. This aim forms the focal point of that undertaking because efforts will always be made to accomplish it. For example the aim of a football team is always to score more goals than the opponents so as to win the match. The aim of a politician is to convince electorates to vote him into office. This is also applicable to religious education. What is the aim of this field of study? Although some of the aims of religious education have already been indirectly referred to in this work, it will be of great benefit to itemize them here for the purpose of clarity. The aim of religious education according to Nwele:

... is making education more religious and making religion more educational through praxis, critical reflection and experience rather than speculations.[84]

83 Chave E. J., A functional Approach to Religious Education 1947, 126-127, quoted by: Lines T. A., Systemic Religious Education, Birmingham, 1987, 214.

84 Nwele C., Fatherhood and Child's Education: Exploring the Effects of a Father's Absence on the Social, Moral and Religious Lives of Children, New York, 2010, 199.

Religious education in this instance is concerned with the intelligibility of religion and instilling the spirit of religion into the field of learning. The two therefore are not to be separated from each other. It is also aimed at infusing moral values and the spirit of religiosity into its recipients. This creates the awareness of a religious life and appreciation of religious beliefs and principles. Religious education therefore is not only concerned with making education more religious and making religion more educational but also fosters religious praxis.

Moran identified two aims as follows:

(1) to teach people to practice a religious way of life and

(2) to teach people to understand religion.[85]

The first of these aims is limited to a particular religion. One learns nothing other than the practice of that religion. A particular religious way of life is simply the way for both the teacher and the learner. Every other religious way of life is totally excluded. It is all about monopoly. Here the emphasis is for instance on Christian religious education or Islamic religious education or Buddhist religious education. The teaching is either on Christian practice or Islamic practice or Buddhist practice. The movement is on a parallel or horizontal line but never both.

The second aim involves a multiplicity of religions. Here one can talk about the didactic of many religions. One can learn about African religion, Christian religion or Islamic religion. This second aim leads us to the study of comparative religion. There is no limitation to any particular religion. Here the term "religion" is used in the post-modern times to involve plurality. The learner begins from the consolidation of his or her own religious background to study other religions thereby discovering similarities and differences. From a Christian background one learns that Islam and Buddhism have different but equally valuable lessons to teach. This discovery is possible when one compares his or her religion with others so that one is not restricted only to the teachings of his or her own religion. Religious ways differ and the recognition of these differences is an important issue in religious education. This recognition widens the religious horizon of the particular individual learner. It throws light on one's native religion and gives rise to an appreciation of other religions.

These two aims are summed up in the *Cambridgeshire Agreed Syllabus* which says:

85 Moran G., The Aims of Religious Education, in: Harris M., Moran G. Reshaping Religious Education, Conversations on Contemporary Practice, Kentucky, 1998, 30.

The aim of religious education is to enable pupils to understand the nature of religion, its beliefs and practices.[86]

Understanding here is used in a variety of ways. Firstly it is used to denote a correct and precise articulation of a concept as in the saying: "I understand that Isaac Newton developed the law of gravity". That means, I know it and can also prove that he was the inventor of this law. Understanding can also be used to indicate the sharing of a common experience. For instance, when one says: "I understand what my father went through when he had malaria because I too suffered from it". This empathetic mode of understanding is based on the fact that he or she was able to put himself or herself into the position of his or her father to really know the psychological trauma associated with malaria.

Understanding can also be used in an imaginative sense as in the statement: "I understand how Obama felt when he was accused of being a Muslim". Here understanding is used in an analytic mode which stems from the ability to separate, discriminate and label a situation correctly.[87] Another mode of understanding is based on the motives of human behaviour. Here attention is paid to the psychic norms which regulate and guide a particular mode of life. This is well expressed in the statement: "I understand why David refused to kill Saul".[88] Understanding in this sense pinpoints David's disciplinary life which regulates his behaviour. His refusal to kill "the Lord's anointed" is here appreciated.

Religious education then has the fundamental aim of fostering an overall human development. According to Webster:

It strives to achieve this by encouraging an openness to those disciplines within the sciences and the arts which speak of the humanity of men and women.[89]

These sciences and arts have concerned themselves with the fears and failures as well as the hopes and aspirations of the human spirit. Religious education therefore co-ordinates them and asks about the mystery which lies within

86 A Framework for Religious Education in Cambridgeshire, (the Agreed Syllabus of Cambridgeshire County Council), 1982, 1, quoted by: Webster D. H., Religious Education and the State School, in: McCelland V. A. (Ed.), Christian Education in a Pluralist Society, London, 1988, 57.

87 Cf. Webster D. H., Religious Education and the State School, in: McCelland V. A. (Ed.), Christian Education in a Pluralist Society, London, 1988, 57.

88 Ibid.

89 Ibid, 59.

persons so that an understanding of the human person and his or her relationship with that mystery can lead to his or her development.

Heckman made reference to three other aims of religious education. According to him:

> *Religious education is to help people of all ages 1) to develop and maintain a linkage with the past, 2) to anticipate the future, and 3) to participate responsibly in decision-making about their lives in the present.*[90]

This understanding makes religious education a growing and an on-going adaptive process. The past is not separated from the present and the future. The present is used to anticipate the future and not to determine it. The events of today for instance can help us to expect tomorrow with enthusiasm. But these events cannot determine those of tomorrow. The future is uncertain and unknown but it is anticipated that it will evolve positively. Religious education links the past with the present experience and projects this experience into the future. It consults the past, evaluates the present and predicts the future so that the learning process is uninterrupted. In this sense religious education helps to preserve the heritage of a particular religion so that its tradition is not lost. It sees to the handing-on of the religious teachings of a particular religion from one generation to the other without losing the centrality of her teachings.

1.4 Learning

Learning is a psychological and pedagogical concept which is concerned with the process of acquiring and seeking knowledge as well as the interpretation of experience. As an act it is attributed to both humans and animals. In this work, attention will be limited to human learning which characterises the mental development of a person. The human learning-process begins at the cognitive stage when the brain begins to recognise and form images. The brain interprets these images and thereby denotes their meanings. Learning then is brought about by external impulse. It takes place in the brain and manifests itself externally through adaptive behaviour.[91]

Learning can occur as a result of observation and imitation and deepens itself through habituation and personal experience. It is the ability of a living system or organism to acquire new knowledge as a result of external influence.

90 Heckman S. J., On the Wings of a Butterfly: A Guide to Total Christian Education 1981, 13 quoted by: Lines T. A., Systemic Religious Education, Birmingham, 1987, 217.

91 Cf. Leimgruber S., Interreligiöses Lernen, Neuausgabe, München, 2007, 18.

This means that learning takes place as part of education, teaching and personal experience. The *Webster's Third New International Dictionary* defined learning as follows:

> *Learning is a process of acquisition and modifications in existing knowledge, skills, habits or action tendencies in a motivated organism through experience, practice or exercise.*[92]

It is therefore the process of gaining knowledge or understanding of a skill by study, instruction or experience. It gives rise to the development of an ability to act in a particular way and gives a person the awareness of something new. Learning opens and widens the horizons of a particular scope thereby giving room for the acquisition of in-depth knowledge and experience.

92 Webster's Third New International Dictionary Vol. II 1981, 1286.

2. Nigeria: Cultural and Historical Contexts for Religious Education

A people do not evolve from a vacuum.[1] They are known as inhabitants of a particular area of land either by virtue of ancestral heritage or migration. The understanding of a people's geography, history, culture, religion and values often forms one of the first steps towards categorising the development and perceptible changes that characterise a particular group of people. In the second chapter of this work, the goal is to survey Nigeria, one of the two countries under investigation. This will be undertaken in *seven steps*. The *first step* will be a descriptive analysis of the country. A considerable examination will be given to its geographical location and vegetation. Its position on the global map as well as its climate and temperature will be brought into the limelight. A more detailed study of the various people who make up the country will be found under ethnicity, language and population.

In a *second* historical analytical *step*, the background of the people occupying the current land mass known as Nigeria will be evaluated with regard to the pre-colonial times, the colonial era encompassing the amalgamation of the people of the south and the north, and the post-colonial period which witnessed independence and the Civil War. This historical approach will give a relative picture of the life of the people before they were forced to endure external influences as well as their life after having contact with foreigners.

The religiosity of a people denotes to a large extent their cultural as well as anthropological values. This will form the framework of the *third step* in which an historical approach to the religions in Nigeria will be undertaken. Here care will be taken to exhume the religious situation of the country before any foreign influence. Thus the traditional religion which characterises the entire African populace will be presented as the original religion of the people. This traditional religion also plays a significant and influential role in the life of many Africans even to the present time, Nigerians inclusive. This will be followed by a coherent presentation of the two major world religions practiced by the majority of Nigerians namely, Islam and Christianity.

Because this work is limited to a particular theme, the description of the various categories of Nigerians will be limited to the youth so as to pay particular attention to the subject matter under discussion. Thus, the *fourth step* of this chapter will examine the types of youth in Nigeria according to their

1 Cf. Jawoniyi O., "Rethinking the Religious Education Curricula in Nigerian Schools", in: Chidester D. (Ed.), Journal for the Study of Religion Vol. 22, Nr. 2, 2009, Cape Town, 64.

environmental and religious backgrounds. The aim here will be to determine whether the youth have been positively integrated into the society especially after their secondary school education. This is because the dispositions of the individuals involved will determine whether or not they will become involved either in the religious and/or social life of the society. It is therefore necessary to consider the type of influence the society has on them and their contribution to the building of their society through religious education.

The attention given to religious education in Nigeria especially since the end of the Civil War has given rise to an increase in the number of schools in the country. In the *fifth step* of this chapter, the types of schools existing in Nigeria today as well as the religious educational system will be considered. The aim is to determine where the young people of Nigeria are being instructed and from which conditions they will emerge to take up their roles as future religious leaders. Thus their religious educational journey which begins officially from primary one will be described as taking place in the schools where they are meant to also acquire Western education. These schools will be itemised under public or Government schools and private or confessional schools. This will then lead to the subjects taught in these schools and thus to the theme of this inquiry, religious education. Moving from this background, the aim in the *sixth step* will be to pinpoint how religion is being taught in the schools. This section will also be limited to Christian religious education in recognition of the limited scope of the theme of this work. In the *seventh* and last *step*, a breakdown of the Christian religious education curriculum in the nine-year basic education programme in Nigeria will be presented. This will give rise to the roles of the various resource people – the teacher and the pupils – in the achievement of the goals of this programme with particular reference to religious education. This chapter will then be evaluated and summarised.

2.1 Brief Description of Nigeria

Although this work is not strictly about Nigeria, a brief description of the country will help to elaborate the background of the demography of this study as well as the environment in which religious education occurs. To properly understand the geo-political entity currently known as Nigeria, it is optimal to take a look at her characteristics and features. The aim of this section is to describe Nigeria in terms of land mass and structure. This will help to acknowledge its exact position on the equator and thus determine its landscape and atmospheric conditions. This will also be a pre-condition for the type of agricultural heritage of this area, its livestock, the human beings existing there as well as their spoken language(s).

2.1.1 Location

Nigeria is a West African country located on the Atlantic Ocean. She is officially addressed as the "Federal Republic of Nigeria" and comprises a total of thirty-six states plus the Federal Capital Territory (FCT), Abuja. She lies at the extreme inner corner of the Gulf of Guinea, formerly known as the Bight of Biafra and is the largest geo-political unit in West Africa. Nigeria is located between latitudes 4° and 14° north of the Equator.[2] That means that she is entirely within the tropical zone, exactly at the meeting point of the Western parts of the African Continent and the Equatorial Africa.[3]

Nigeria shares land borders with a total of four countries. She is bounded in the west by the Republic of Benin; in the east by the Republics of Chad and Cameroon; and in the north by the Niger Republic. In the south she is bounded by the Atlantic Ocean where its coast lies on the Gulf of Guinea (or the Bight of Biafra).[4] Eluwa, described the size of Nigeria as follows:

Nigeria extends northward from the coastline for some 1,170 kilometres. From the western border to the east, there is a distance of 1,260 kilometres at the widest part. The country extends in the south from the Atlantic Ocean (which is known variously along the West Coast as the Gulf of Guinea or the Bight of Benin and the Bight of Biafra... now known as the Bight of Bonny) which washes the coastline for about 900 kilometres to the Sahara Desert in the North.[5]

From the above description, it can be noted that Nigeria is located on the West African Coast. The map is structured like the letter **"Y"** due to the two large rivers, Niger and Benue, which run through the country with their courses toward the Atlantic Ocean. According to Okonkwo:

The natural geographical territory of the present political entity called Nigeria is artistically mapped outwards in the form of a 'trapezium' and marked beautifully inwards by a big naturally shaped letter **'Y'**. This topographic masterpiece is an endowment of the combined natural courses of the two great rivers – the Niger (running south-eastwards), and the Benue (running south-westwards).[6]

2 Cf. Udo R. K., Environments and Peoples of Nigeria, A Geographical Introduction to the History of Nigeria, in: Ikime O. (Ed.), Groundwork of Nigerian History, Ibadan, 2004, 7.

3 Cf. Eluwa G. I. C., Ukagwu M. O., Nwachukwu J. U. N., Nwaubani A. C. N., A History of Nigeria, For Schools and Colleges, Onitsha, 2005, (ix).

4 Cf. Ibid.

5 Ibid.

6 Okonkwo P.I., Minorities and the Problem of Fairness – A Social Ethical Enquiry, Aachen, 2002, 52.

The river Niger is the third longest river out of the seven great rivers of Africa (Nile, Niger, Congo, Senegal, Orange, Limpopo and Zambezi). It is also the most prominent physical feature of Nigeria. Ranking after the Nile and the Congo, it begins its course in the Fouta Djellon Mountains of North-east Sierra Leone and enters Nigeria in the Northwest for the last one third of the 4,200km course. The Niger flows south-easterly, then due south and again south-easterly to Lokoja, where it converges with its principal tributary, the Benue and then flows south into the Gulf of Guinea.[7] These two rivers (Niger and Benue) form the 'Y' curve with which Nigeria is identified. According to the *Britannica World Language Dictionary*, the Niger is:

A river of Western Africa, flowing 2,600 miles from near the Sierra Leone border through French West Africa and Nigeria to the Gulf of Guinea.[8]

2.1.2 Vegetation

Nigeria has a variety of land forms. The greater percentage of the country is a plain, generally less than 609.5 metres above sea level. The eastern border with the Republic of Cameroon is marked by an almost continuous extent of mountains which rise to about 2,420.5 metres in the Chappal Waddi, the highest known point in Nigeria.[9] In the North there are a number of elevations generally called "Rocks" which also form part of the country's prominent features like the "Aso Rock" in the Federal Capital City, Abuja and the "Oluma Rock" among others. The Jos Plateau (also in the North) rises abruptly from a general level of about 609.5 metres to an average level of some 1,219 metres. It reaches 1,781.6 metres in Shere Hill (in the Plateau).[10]

Nigeria has two official seasons, the rainy season and the dry season. The rainy season is regarded as the agriculturally fertile period which favours the cultivation of crops. This is why farming is at its peak in this season. Udo described rainfall as the most important element of climate in so far as agriculture, the main occupation of the people, is concerned.[11] With the use of irrigation, farmers (in the north) also produce huge quantities of food crops and other agricultural products during the dry season. Because of its location

7 Mabogunje A.L., Physical and Social Geography, in Africa South of the Sahara 1997, 26th Edition, 1996,724, quoted by: Okonkwo P.I., Minorities and the Problem of Fairness, Aachen, 2002, 52.

8 Britannica World Language Dictionary, Vol. I, Part I, A-P, Chicago, 1964, 856.

9 Cf. Eluwa G. I. C., Ukagwu M. O., Nwachukwu J. U. N., Nwaubani A. C. N., A History of Nigeria, For Schools and Colleges, Onitsha, 2005, (ix).

10 Cf. Ibid.

11 Cf. Udo R. K., Environments and Peoples of Nigeria, A Geographical Introduction to the History of Nigeria, in: Ikime O. (Ed.), Groundwork of Nigerian History, Ibadan, 2004, 10.

within the temperate region, the atmospheric temperature is at an average of 30 to 32 degrees centigrade. This means that the air is dry as a result of intensive sunshine but very conducive to normal human breathing. This is also the view of Ikein when he says:

> *There are only two well-defined seasons [in Nigeria], the dry season (from November to March) and the rainy season (from April to October).The average temperature is about 32 degrees centigrade.*[12]

There is however a special period within the dry season known as the harmattan, which lasts between November and January with an average low temperature of 15 to 20 degrees centigrade. The harmattan is the coldest period in the country. The air during this time is extremely dry and causes much discomfort. According to Eluwa:

> *During the dry season the harmattan wind blows in from the desert, causing extreme dryness and carrying with it the fine dust particles that form the haze ... all over the country (though with greater intensity as one moves south to north) from November to January.*[13]

2.1.3 Ethnicity

Nigeria has more than 250 ethnic groups, most of whom have distinct cultures, traditions and languages.[14] According to Okonkwo:

> *Nigeria's Federal Information indicates that the Nigerian government officially attests to the existence of 250 ethnic groups whose existence as independent cultural groups all precede the new political territory.*[15]

He, however, questioned the authenticity of this official government figure because of the controversies surrounding the statistical accuracy that have

12 Ikein A. A., The Impact of Oil in a Developing Country, The Case of Nigeria, New York, 1990, 59.

13 Eluwa G. I. C., Ukagwu M. O., Nwachukwu J. U. N., Nwaubani A. C. N., A History of Nigeria, For Schools and Colleges, Onitsha, 2005,(x).

14 Cf. Udo R. K., Environments and Peoples of Nigeria, A Geographical Introduction to the History of Nigeria, in: Ikime O. (Ed.), Groundwork of Nigerian History, Ibadan, 2004, 14.

15 Okonkwo P.I., Minorities and the Problem of Fairness, Aachen, 2002, 54, quoting Federal Information Service, 100 Facts about Nigeria 1958, 3.

haunted Nigeria's official government claims about many issues.[16] As a result of this, ethnologists and political analysts have variously challenged this official figure by providing alternatively variable estimates.[17] Hence Meek claims an estimate of about 300 ethnic groups in Nigeria.[18] Mabonguje goes for even a larger estimate of up to 416 groups.[19] The above conflicting statistics confirm that Nigeria is a multi-ethnic society.

The ethnic groups are classified into two categories: major and minor. The major ethnic groups are: Hausa/Fulani, Igbo, Yoruba, Edo, Ibibio, Ijaw, Tiv, and Kanuri.[20] According to Okonkwo:

Statistically, the first major group is the Hausa/Fulani, typically grouped together because of their substantial cultural and political integration. This group inhabits the Northern part of Nigeria and form [sic] the largest ethno-cultural category. Together they constitute an estimated figure ranging from 28 to 29% of Nigeria's total population. The Igbo ethnic group forms the second largest group (including the Ika Igbo). The Ethnic Igbo lives in southern Nigeria and constitute between 16 and 18% of the population of Nigeria. With 14% of the entire population, the ethnic Yoruba forms the third major group in Nigeria, being located in the south-western part of the country.[21]

The ethnic or tribal distribution in Nigeria is based on the tribe with the highest population in each of the three regions originally created by the colonial administration: North, South and West. The Hausa/Fulani are the most populous in the North, the Igbo in the South and the Yoruba in the West. These three dominant ethnic groups collectively make up two-thirds of Nigeria's population (about 60%).[22] They also have their various characteristics, due to the influence of their religious and cultural backgrounds.

16 Cf. Okonkwo P.I., Minorities and the Problem of Fairness, Aachen, 2002, 54.

17 Cf. Meek C.K., The Northern Tribes of Nigeria, Vol. 1 1925, 19 quoted by: Okonkwo P.I., Minorities and the Problem of Fairness, Aachen, 2002, 54.

18 Temple O., Note on the Tribes, Provinces, Emirates and States of the Northern Provinces of Nigeria, 2nd Ed. 1965, also cf. Chukwuma M., Nigerian Politics and the Role of Religion: An Analysis of the Role of Religion in Nigerian Politics at the Early Stages of National Integration 1985, 39 quoted by: Okonkwo P.I., ., Minorities and the Problem of Fairness, Aachen, 2002, 54.

19 Mabonguje A., Land, People and Tradition in Nigeria, in Blitz L.F., (ed.), The Politics and Administration of Nigerian Government 1965, 7, quoted by: Okonkwo P.I., Minorities and the Problem of Fairness, Aachen, 2002, 54.

20 Cf. Ikein A. A., The Impact of Oil in a Developing Country, The Case of Nigeria New York, 1990, 60.

21 Okonkwo P.I., Minorities and the Problem of Fairness, Aachen, 2002, 55-56.

22 Ibid., 55.

The Hausa/Fulani are known for their central administrative system with the Sarki at the head. The Sarki is the king and is not contrasted with the Emir who is the religious leader. Every political power and influence centred on the king.[23] The Igbo on the other hand exhibit an uncentralised political tradition which is referred by some scholars as stateless system of administration.[24] The idea of a centralised kingship is both alien and repugnant to the Igbo people.[25] An Igbo proverb summarises this assertion as follows: "*Igbo enweghi eze*" (The Igbo have no king). Their political administration is carried out through the kindred and age grades. The Yoruba have a centralised system of administration in which the Oba is the head of the government.[26]

2.1.4 Language

Languages in Nigeria are identified with the ethnic groups. This means that there are as many languages in Nigeria as the number of ethnic groups. However three languages: Hausa, Igbo and Yoruba have been adopted as the major languages based on the three colonial regions. English is the official language of the country and is taught in all the schools. The choice of English as the lingua franca is as a result of colonial influence and as an administrative convenience for the colonial masters.[27] Before this time, the Nigerian people had organised and handled their affairs in their various native languages. The inability of the British colonial Government to develop and integrate the already existing languages of the native people into their administrative network remains a matter of consternation. Through Western education the various ethnic groups are able to communicate with one another in the English language. This communication has to some extent helped to diffuse the rivalries existing among these ethnic groups. In addition to the English language, one of the major languages of the country: *Hausa*, *Igbo* or *Yoruba* has to be taught in the schools. This is determined by the language of a particular area. However, because of the fear of cultural extinction and linguistic liquidation, some minor ethnic groups insist on teaching their own native language in the schools within their locality.

---

23 Cf. Imoagene O., Know Your Country Series, Handbooks of Nigeria's Major Culture Areas Vol. 1, The Hausa and Fulani of Northern Nigeria, Ibadan, 1993, 31.

24 Cf. Imoagene O., Know Your Country Series, Handbooks of Nigeria's Major Culture Areas Vol. 3, The Ibo of East Central Nigeria, Ibadan, 1993, 20.

25 Cf. Ibid.

26 Cf. Imoagene O., Know Your Country Series, Handbooks of Nigeria's Major Culture Areas Vol. 2, The Yoruba of South Western Nigeria, Ibadan, 1993, 23.

27 Cf. Eluwa G. I. C., Ukagwu M. O., Nwachukwu J. U. N., Nwaubani A. C. N., A History of Nigeria, For Schools and Colleges, Onitsha, 2005, 228.

The diversity of ethnicity and language implies that Nigeria is a heterogeneous society. This diversity was also recognised in the Nigerian National Anthem of the First Republic in the phrase: "Though tribe and tongue may differ…"[28] This heterogeneity is seen in the clash of different worldviews and traditions that have been brought together under the umbrella of Nigeria.

2.1.5 Population

Nigeria is the most populous country in Africa.[29] It is a racially homogenous society because it has the highest conglomeration of "black people" in the world. This black colour of its inhabitants is as a result of its position on the equator which places the people in a close contact with the sun. It has an estimated current population of more than 148 million people.[30] Young people between the ages of 10 and 24 make up one third of Nigerian population.[31] A large percentage of the Nigerian people live under abject poverty. This is why the life expectancy of Nigerians was projected to be 48.4 years between 2010 and 2015.[32] According to the National Economic Empowerment and Development Strategies (NEEDS):

> *More than two-thirds of the Nigerian people are poor, despite living in a country with vast potential wealth. Although revenues from crude oil have been increasing over the past two decades, our people have been falling deeper into poverty. In 1980 an estimated 27 percent of Nigerians lived in poverty. By 1990, 70 percent of the population had income of less than $1 a day – and the figure has risen since then.*[33]

Under the British colonial administration Nigeria was (before the amalgamation of 1914) divided into four provinces: the northern, western and eastern provinces as well as the colony of Lagos. The Northern Province comprised the entire present-day northern Nigeria. The Western Province included all parts of post-modern western Nigeria as well as the Edo area and the Delta area except Lagos, which was administered as a separate colony. The Eastern

28 Cf. Okonkwo J.I., Nationalism, 117, in Okonkwo P.I., Minorities and the Problem of Fairness, Aachen, 2002, 57.

29 Cf. Okonkwo P.I., Minorities and the Problem of Fairness, Aachen, 2002, 59.

30 Cf. World Population Prospects, The 2006 Revision, Highlights, New York, 2007, 47.

31 Cf. http://www.nigeria.unfpa.org/youngpeople.html, 07.02.2012.

32 Cf. World Population Prospects, The 2006 Revision, Highlights, New York, 2007, 82.

33 National Economic Empowerment and Development Strategy, Meeting Everyone's Needs, Abuja, 2004, xiii-xiv.

Province covered the entire current eastern Nigeria as well as the Rivers and the Ibibio areas.

2.2 Historical Background

Nigeria exists today as one of the remnants of the colonial damages emitted to Africa by some external forces originating in Europe. Between the later part of the nineteenth century and the mid-twentieth century, some European forces invaded Africa due to an unrestrained ambition for the acquisition of colonial empires.[34] This move was initiated by the resolutions of the famous "Berlin Conference" of 1884[35] in which the Continent of Africa was divided and partitioned into European colonies under the heading "The Struggle and Partition of Africa" popularly known as "Pan Africanism". Hence boundaries were assigned and people of different origins were fused together irrespective of their cultural differences. Nigeria therefore happened to emerge from this fate as a British colony. According to J. O'Connell, Nigerian boundaries owed more to historical accidents of trading and political penetration and agreements at European conference tables than to social affinities between those peoples who found themselves within the boundaries.[36] This means that the borders created at the Berlin Conference run contrary to traditional tribal territories.

The name "Nigeria" has no direct identity with any of the historical cultural peoples that constitute it. This name was formulated in 1897 by Flora Shaw who later became the wife of the British colonial administrator, Lord Fredrick Lugard.[37] Before this time, there was no such place called Nigeria. The land-mass currently mapped as Nigeria was inhabited by people of different cultural backgrounds and beliefs. Daniels also identified Nigeria as a country of diverse cultures in the statement:

In what is now known as Nigeria, the British lumped together many neighboring cultures under one colonial administration, cultures that may have had little in common as far as customs and language. One of these cultures was the Igbo.[38]

34 Cf. Okonkwo P.I, Minorities and the Problem of Fairness, Aachen, 2002, 51.

35 Cf. Eluwa G. I. C., Ukagwu M. O., Nwachukwu J. U. N., Nwaubani A. C. N., A History of Nigeria, For Schools and Colleges, Onitsha, 2005, 179.

36 Cf. O'Connell J., Political Integration: The Nigerian Case, in: Hazlewood A., (ed.), African Integration and Disintegration 1967, 32, quoted by: Okonkwo P.I., Minorities and the Problem of Fairness, Aachen, 2002, 52.

37 Cf. Okonkwo P.I., Minorities and the Problem of Fairness, Aachen, 2002, 51.

38 Daniels P. J., The Voice of the Oppressed in the Language of the Oppressor. A Discussion of Selected Postcolonial Literature from Ireland, Africa and America, New York, 2001, 19.

The name (Nigeria) was coined after the great river Niger which runs through the territory and could be taken to mean "the land of the river Niger".[39] Three significant periods mark the bulwark of Nigeria's history namely: pre-colonial Nigeria, the colonial era which witnessed the amalgamation of the northern and southern protectorates into one single entity known today as Nigeria and the post-colonial epoch which is from the time of the independence to the beginning of the present Third Republic. These will be handled in the sub-topics of this section.

2.2.1 Pre-Colonial Nigeria

Like many countries in Africa, the history of pre-colonial Nigeria is faced with many problems especially those arising from the lack of written records. Before the colonial times, the administrative system of the various people that now form the present Nigeria was in the form of empires, kingdoms and communities. An organised Western system like the type that was present during the colonial era was not yet in existence. However some of the people who were ruled under the same Government were separated from one another and ascribed to different countries by the colonial masters. This attests to the reason why some people of a common language and culture are seen in two separate countries. The most prominent political entities of this period will be examined in this section.

The oldest empires were the first and second Kanem-Bornu founded by the Kanuri people between 700 and 800 A.D.[40] According to G.I.C. Eluwa:

> *The first empire, Kanem, existed east of Lake Chad, in the present Chad Republic, while the second empire, Borno, existed west of Lake Chad in what is now part of Nigeria.*[41]

The second political unit that existed before colonialism was the Hausa City-States. This political entity covered a large part of the present Northern Nigeria and was governed by the King known as Sarkin Karsa – Kings of towns and suburbs.[42] These States were assessed by Eluwa as follows:

None of the Hausa States grew into an empire of the rank of … Kanem Borno. They were essentially city-states with widely dispersed surrounding villages which they protected in time of trouble and exploited as the demand

39 Cf. Okonkwo P.I., Minorities and the Problem of Fairness, Aachen, 2002, 51-52.

40 Cf. Eluwa G. I. C., Ukagwu M. O., Nwachukwu J. U. N., Nwaubani A. C. N., A History of Nigeria, For Schools and Colleges, Onitsha, 2005, 18.

41 Ibid.

42 Cf. Ibid., 35.

arose. None of the States of Hausaland was powerful or extensive enough to achieve political, economic and moral authority for the entire area.[43]

Other political entities that existed in Nigeria before the colonial epoch were the Jukun Kingdom of the Middle Benue Region, the Nupe Kingdom, The Benin Empire, the Oyo Empire, the Igboland, the Ijo City-States, the Ibibio and Efik People of Cross River Basin, the Urhobo Community and the Itsekiri Kingdom. These flourished as independent political powers between 15th and 19th centuries.[44]

2.2.2 The Amalgamation of the Southern and Northern Protectorates (1914)

According to the *Webster's Third New International Dictionary*, amalgamation is the process of merging two separate societies into one single body.[45] In the Nigerian context it means the joining of the northern protectorate with the colony and protectorate of the south in 1914 to form the present day Nigeria. According to Ikein:

> *Modern Nigeria as a country was born in 1914 when the two British protectorates of north and south were amalgamated by Sir Frederick Lugard.*[46]

The process of this amalgamation was fully initiated in 1912, when Frederick Lugard was appointed the Governor of the two protectorates.[47] A number of factors led to this amalgamation and they were summarised by Eluwa as follows:

Firstly, the Protectorate of Northern Nigeria was so poor that it had to be given a subsidy by the government of the Colony and Protectorate of Southern Nigeria. This area had a budgetary surplus and also a grant-in-aid of £300,000 from the Imperial Treasury. Secondly, some of the Southern Nigerian surplus came from goods exported from Northern Nigeria through Southern Nigeria. In the circumstances, it was only fair and advisable to pool resources and share revenue. Thirdly, if the trade of the North was to expand rapidly, it would need an outlet to the sea which was open all the year round, as against the Niger River traffic which was seasonal. Fourthly, amalgamation would not only unite

43 Ibid.

44 Cf. Ibid., 37-79.

45 Webster's Third New International Dictionary, Vol. I, Chicago, 1981, 65.

46 Ikein A. A, The Impact of Oil in a Developing Country, The Case of Nigeria, New York, 1990, 60.

47 Cf. Eluwa G. I. C., Ukagwu M. O., Nwachukwu J. U. N., Nwaubani A. C. N., A History of Nigeria, For Schools and Colleges, Onitsha, 2005, 208.

the railway systems of the protectorates but also aid such other vital common services as the posts and telegraphs, currency, transport, army and police.[48]

This amalgamation had been flawed by a number of factors. What really took place was an amalgamation of the administration of the Southern and Northern Protectorates and not the amalgamation of the people of the South and the North. The people were groomed to see themselves as those of distinct ideologies and as such should crave only for things of their distinctive interests. Eluwa also identified this problem in his complaint:

However, in amalgamating Southern and Northern Nigeria, Lugard failed to fully unite the country. He retained the division between the two Nigerias as separate administrative units. He installed a Lieutenant-Governor in Kaduna to administer Northern Nigeria and a Lieutenant-Governor in Enugu to administer Southern Nigeria. The Governor-General, who was Lugard himself, coordinated the two governments in Lagos. As it was, however, the administrations of the Northern and Southern Provinces continued to exercise most of the functions they had under the old Protectorate days. They continued to operate as if there were two different countries… Lugard and his officials discouraged real union of the North and South. They emphasised the differences between the two Nigerian areas and encouraged the divisions that were to plague Nigerian politics in latter years.[49]

These two protectorates had nothing in common with each other due to the fact that they differed socially, culturally, religiously and linguistically. This amalgamation took place without the expected "Principle of Accord" as seen in many countries like the United States of America and Germany to mention but a few. Hence, the people of the two protectorates were not brought together to establish the terms of their union. It was only executed by the British for their own administrative convenience and economic interest.[50] This "strange union" made Nigeria a completely pluralistic society.

The administration of Nigeria after the amalgamation was carried out through an indirect rule system. In this dispensation the local heads of the people were used as administrative bodies. This proved successful in the North but did not work easily in the South. According to Eluwa:

> *Although Lugard had under his amalgamation scheme preserved the separate identities of Northern and Southern Nigeria, he proceeded to impose the system of indirect rule he and his successors had devel-*

48 Ibid.

49 Ibid., 208-209.

50 Cf. Ikein A. A., The Impact of Oil in a Developing Country, The Case of Nigeria, New York, 1990, 63.

oped in the North on the Southern Provinces. This policy proved by and large a failure in the South.[51]

This system of indirect rule was greatly opposed by the people of the Southern Protectorate because it was foreign to their traditional system of governance. In 1916 the people of the South revolted in Ibadan and in 1918 in Egba.[52] In the Delta areas and Warri demonstrations against it took place in 1927 and 1928 respectively.[53] In the East the women especially rioted against the indirect rule in Aba, Umuahia and Calabar in 1929 and 1930.[54] In some parts of the North, this new system of administration did not gain the acceptance of the people especially in Makurdi and Igbirra. This rejection led to a rebellion against it in 1915 at Bussa.[55] However, despite the people's rejection of this administrative measure, it remained an imposition on them until the dawn of independence.

2.2.3 Independence of Nigeria from Great Britain (1960)

The establishment of British rule in Nigeria took place with very strong resistance from the people because they saw it as a foreign measure to disintegrate them from their cherished sense of African brotherhood.[56] Their aim therefore was to free themselves from this rather strange entanglement. This led to the formation of political associations which empowered them in their agitation for independence. The first of such associations was the "Nigerian National Democratic Party" (NNDP) which was formed by Herbert Macaulay in 1923.[57] This gave rise to yet another party in 1938 known as the "Nigerian Youth Movement" (NYM).[58] This body could not function effectively because of the Second World War which greatly disrupted its activities. As a result another political party, the "National Council of Nigeria and the Cameroons" (NCNC) was formed on 26th August 1944 by Nnamdi Azikiwe.[59] Other political parties ensued. 1951 saw the formation of "Action Group" (AG) and the "Northern Peoples Congress" (NPC) by Obafemi Awolowo and Ahmadu Bello respec-

51 Ibid., 209.

52 Cf. Ibid.

53 Cf. Ibid., 210.

54 Cf. Ibid.

55 Cf. Ibid., 209-211.

56 Cf. Ibid., 232.

57 Cf. Ibid., 234.

58 Cf. Ibid., 235.

59 Cf. Ibid., 237-238.

tively.[60] On the eve of independence in 1959, four political parties were featured in the December elections namely: the NCNC under Nnamdi Azikiwe, the NPC under Abubakar Tafawa Balewa, the AG under Obafemi Awolowo and the "Northern Elements Progressive Union" (NEPU) under Aminu Kano.[61] After the elections, no party won the absolute majority to gain the control of the House of Representatives. The NPC won the highest vote seconded by the NCNC. As a result a coalition government of these two parties was formed with Balewa as the Prime Minister and Azikiwe as the President.[62]

The Nigerian Federal House of Representatives passed a motion in January 1960 requesting Her Majesty's British Government to grant independence to Nigeria from 1st October 1960. The two Houses of the United Kingdom Parliament passed an Independence Act in July 1960 and on 29th July of the same year the Act received the Royal Assent. The Nigerian Independence Constitution Order also received the approval of the Queen on 12th September to come into operation from 1st October 1960. In this Order the Independent Federation of Nigeria comprising Northern Nigeria, Western Nigeria, Eastern Nigeria and the Federal Capital Territory, Lagos, was established. Hence on 1st October 1960 Nigeria became an independent sovereign state within the Commonwealth of Nations.[63]

2.2.4 The Civil War in Nigeria (1967-1970)

The realization of independence gave rise to a period of rapid social, economic and political changes.[64] Prominent among these were the attainment of the status of a Republic on 1st October 1963, the first military coup d'etat on 15th January 1966 and the out-break of a Civil War in 1967. The new leaders embraced their task of governance with great zeal and enthusiasm, optimistic about achieving convincing goals. They did not fore-see that the above changes would lead to the devastation of the country through the loss of a countless number of lives including some of their own. This is because in their quest

60 Cf. Ibid., 239.

61 Cf. Eluwa G. I. C., Ukagwu M. O., Nwachukwu J. U. N., Nwaubani A. C. N., A History of Nigeria, For Schools and Colleges, Onitsha, 2005, 252.

62 Cf. Ibid.

63 Cf. Ibid.

The term Commonwealth of Nations refers to an international non-political organisation comprising of the United Kingdom and the other 53 sovereign nations that were once under the British colonial empire but gained independence at various stages of their national history. This organisation is headed by the Queen of England.

64 Cf. Eluwa G. I. C., Ukagwu M. O., Nwachukwu J. U. N., Nwaubani A. C. N., A History of Nigeria, For Schools and Colleges, Onitsha, 2005, 255.

for independence they made compromises which did not consider the issue of their differences and the problem of the minorities.[65] No accord was reached on issues of equal opportunities and the sharing of the wealth of the nation popularly known as the "National Cake".

After the attainment of independence, some of those political changes which took place in Nigeria resulted in a situation of economic, ethnic, cultural and religious tensions in various parts of the country. The first military coup of January 15th 1966 produced an Igbo leader, Aguiyi Ironsi, against the expectations of the northerners. Consequently it was interpreted as an Igbo coup. Because of this, the northerners resorted to massacring the Christian Igbo people living in the Muslim dominated areas of Northern Nigeria. The situation gave rise to a counter coup on 29th July 1966 with Yakubu Gowon, a northerner emerging as the head of state. Even after this second coup, the killing of the Igbo people would not stop. This situation of genocide gave the Igbo people no protection in any part of the country outside of their homeland. They were therefore forced to leave their various places of residence for their native land. This move earned them the title of "displaced people" and their property was declared abandoned. "This more than anything else, polarized the Nigerian crisis into an Eastern Region-Federal Government conflict."[66]

To curb the tense situation in the country, to restore peace and to discuss the position of the displaced people, (the Easterners), a meeting of Nigerian leaders was held in Aburi, Ghana, between 4th and 5th January 1967. Aburi was chosen for the venue of this meeting because the Eastern leaders could not participate in any meeting held in other parts of the country for security reasons. The resolutions reached at this meeting popularly known as the "Aburi Accord" took care of the re-organisation of the army, the drafting of a new constitution, appointments in the civil service and the problem of the displaced persons.[67] The failure of the then military government to implement these resolutions due to the different interpretations given to them by the Government of the Eastern Region and the Federal Government led to an increased tension in the country and the killing of the Christian Igbo people in the North did not stop. The matter was worsened when on 27th May 1967 the then head of state, Gowon, promulgated a decree which divided Nigeria into twelve states – six in the North, three in the East, the West and Mid-West remained the same and Lagos became the twelfth.[68] This action was interpreted by the Easterners as an

65 Cf. Ibid.

66 Igbokwe J., Igbos 25 Years after Biafra, Enugu, 1995, 13.

67 Cf. Ibid, 265-266.

68 Cf. Uwalaka J. N., The Struggle for an Inclusive Nigeria: Igbos: To Be or not to Be?, A Treatise on Igbo Political Personality and Survival in Nigeria, Enugu, 2003, 12.

attempt to weaken them and put them in the minority. As a result, the Easterners lost confidence in the Nigerian Government and were compelled to set up a way that would guarantee their safety by declaring on 30th May 1967 a country of their own (the Republic of Biafra) through their then governor, Odumegwu Ojukwu. The reasons for this declaration were outlined by Ojukwu as follows:

Fellow countrymen and women, you, the people of Eastern Nigeria: Conscious of the supreme authority of Almighty God over all mankind, of your duty to yourselves and posterity; Aware that you can no longer be protected in your lives and in your property by any government based outside Eastern Nigeria; Believing that you are born free and have certain inalienable rights which can best be preserved by yourselves; Unwilling to be unfree partners in any association of a political or economic nature; Rejecting the authority of any person or persons other than the Military Government of Eastern Nigeria to make any imposition of whatever kind or nature upon you; Determined to dissolve all political and other ties between you and the former Federal Republic of Nigeria; Prepared to enter into such association, treaty or alliance with any sovereign state within the former Federal Republic of Nigeria and elsewhere on such terms and conditions as best to subserve your common good; Affirming your trust and confidence in me; Having mandated me to proclaim on your behalf, and in your name, that Eastern Nigeria be a sovereign independent Republic, now therefore I, Lieutenant Colonel Chukwuemeka Odumegwu Ojukwu, Military Governor of Eastern Nigeria, by virtue of the authority, and pursuant to the principles, recited above, do hereby solemnly proclaim that the territory and region known as and called Eastern Nigeria together with her continental shelf and territorial waters shall henceforth be an independent sovereign state of the name and title of "The Republic of Biafra."[69]

Thus the secession from the Federal Republic of Nigeria and the origin of the "Republic of Biafra" were established. The Federal Government reacted to the secession of Biafra first with what she called "a police action" and later with a total declaration of war on 26th August 1967 against Eastern Nigeria. Describing the Federal Government action, Uwalaka said:

> *In reaction to the declaration of Biafra, the federal military government under Lt. Col. Gowon announced a "clinical police action" to end the rebellion in the east. Biafra's resistance overwhelmed the federal might that on August 26th, 1967, the Nigerian supreme military council declared total war against Biafra. Thus commenced a terrible fratricidal war which lasted for 30 solid months in which millions of lives were lost; a war in which everything was done to maximise the*

69 Igbokwe J., Igbos 25 Years After Biafra, Enugu, 1995, 18-19.

> *Biafran suffering; a war in which everything was fair means; a war in which one of the Nigerian political figures, Chief Obafemi Awolowo, was quoted to have said that "hunger is a means of warfare" in order to defend the total blockade of Biafra, which caused untold misery to the Biafran people and children.*[70]

The Biafran revolution lasted for a whole three years of severe hardship for the Easterners. During this period Biafran children suffered severely from a highly fatal epidemic outbreak known as "KWASHIOKO" as a result of hunger and malnutrition. This disease led to massive deaths among these children and also hampered their academic pursuits as well as their religious upbringing. Biafra received recognition as a sovereign state from only four African countries – Tanzania, Gabon, Ivory Coast and Zambia. The allied forces of Great Britain, Russia, USA and the Arab World fought for the Federal Government of Nigeria.[71] This made it impossible for Biafra to hold resistance beyond three years. Thus on 15th January 1970 Biafra made a formal surrender to the Nigerian Army through Philip Effiong.[72]

2.2.5 Post-Civil War to the Second Republic (1970-1983)

After the civil war, the Federal Government of Nigeria under the leadership of Gowon adopted a new policy which was popularly known as "the policy of the three R's" (policy of Reconciliation, Reconstruction and Rehabilitation).[73] It was fundamentally aimed at wiping out bad memories, reducing resentful and hostile feelings and integrating the various isolated parts of Nigeria into a united country.[74] A first step towards its achievement was the declaration of "general amnesty" by the Federal Government. Other measures adopted for the realization of this goal were:

1. The re-organization of the armed forces
2. The preparation and implementation of the Second National Development Plan (1970-74)
3. The eradication of corruption in the country's national life

70 Uwalaka J. N., The Struggle for an Inclusive Nigeria: Igbos: To Be or not to Be?, A Treatise on Igbo Political Personality and Survival in Nigeria, Enugu, 2003, 14-15.

71 Cf. Ibid., 15.

72 Cf. Eluwa G. I. C., Ukagwu M. O., Nwachukwu J. U. N., Nwaubani A. C. N., A History of Nigeria, For Schools and Colleges, Onitsha, 2005, 270.

73 Cf. Ibid., 272.

74 Cf. Ibid.

4. The creation of more states
5. The preparation and adoption of a new constitution
6. The introduction of a new revenue formula
7. The carrying out of a national census
8. The organization of genuine national political parties
9. The organization of elections and subsequent installation of popular governments at both state and federal levels[75]

A major step towards the realization of the policy of reconciliation was the establishment of the "National Youth Service Corp Programme" (NYSC) in 1973. This programme was aimed at giving Nigerian young people the opportunity to give a civil service year to the country after their graduation from the universities and other tertiary institutions. However, due to the inability of the Gowon administration to adequately implement the measures outlined for the achievement of the policy of the three R's, the government was overthrown in a bloodless military coup on 29th July 1975 which gave Murtala Muhammad the mantle of leadership.[76]

The regime of Muhammad embarked on a number of national projects namely: the establishment of the "Universal Primary Education" (UPE), the re-location of the federal capital from Lagos to Abuja, the creation of more states and the institution of democracy. Muhammad did not live to accomplish all his proposals because his administration was untimely ended. He was assassinated in a bloody abortive military coup on 13th February 1976. However, he was able to increase the number of states in Nigeria from twelve to nineteen. He was succeeded by Olusegun Obasanjo.[77]

The Obasanjo administration launched the "Universal Primary Education" (UPE) which gave many Nigerian children the opportunity of acquiring free primary education. This programme helped immensely in the eradication of illiteracy in Nigeria. He also organised elections and handed over the ruling of the country to a democratically elected government on 1st October 1979. The administration, which was headed by Shehu Shagari gave rise to the establishment of the "Second Republic".[78]

The Second Republic was a democratic system of government in which the three arms of government were fully represented and separated – the executive, the judiciary and the legislative. Education did not receive any special

75 Ibid.

76 Cf. Ikein A. A., The Impact of Oil on a Developing Country, The Case of Nigeria, New York, 1990, 68.

77 Cf. Ibid.

78 Cf. Ibid.

attention during this regime. The educational system was rather marred by incessant strikes by school teachers and university lecturers due to non-payment of salaries. This led to the deterioration of Nigerian educational standard. The regime rather occupied itself with such issues as housing, agriculture and relocation of the federal capital to Abuja. It was hence not surprising that its shortcomings attracted a military come-back through a bloodless coup on 31st December 1983. This military action brought about the end of the Second Republic and led Nigeria back to a military rule headed by Muhammadu Buhari.[79]

2.2.6 End of the Second Republic to the Beginning of the Third Republic (1983-1999)

The Buhari administration embarked on a War Against Indiscipline (WAI), especially in the schools, civil service and public life. It failed to invest much in education due to massive economic and social problems that ranked high in the Nigerian profile. During this regime, the constitution of the Second Republic was suspended and the country was ruled through the directives of a "Supreme Military Council" (SMC), which was the highest organ of government from which the state governors were excluded.[80] This administration did not succeed in providing solutions to Nigeria's problems and was therefore abruptly brought to an end through a bloodless military coup on August 27th 1985.[81] Buhari was succeeded by Ibrahim Babangida.

On assumption of office as the head of Nigerian government, Babangida gave himself the title of military president and chief executive.[82] He changed the name of the highest military governing body to "Armed Forces Ruling Council" (AFRC) and re-located the country's capital from Lagos to Abuja.[83] He increased the number of states from nineteen to thirty on 23rd September 1987. Under his administration, education also failed to receive the expected attention that should be accorded to it as the basis of the country's future. Many undergraduates of various levels indulged into some cultic practices due to educational laxity. After graduation many could not gain any meaningful employment. This situation brought about frustration on the part of many students

79 Cf. Ibid.

80 Cf. Eluwa G. I. C., Ukagwu M. O., Nwachukwu J. U. N., Nwaubani A. C. N., A History of Nigeria, For Schools and Colleges, Onitsha, 2005, 283.

81 Cf. Ikein A. A., The Impact of Oil on a Developing Country, The Case of Nigeria, New York, 1990, 68.

82 Cf. Ibid.

83 Cf. Eluwa G. I. C., Ukagwu M. O., Nwachukwu J. U. N., Nwaubani A. C. N., A History of Nigeria, For Schools and Colleges, Onitsha, 2005, 283.

and even made some of them to drop their academic pursuit. This administration lasted till the 26th of August 1993, when Babangida resigned from office and handed over the ruling of the country to an interim government headed by Ernest Shonekan. The regime of Shonekan lasted only for three months and was untimely terminated through a bloodless palace coup on November 17th 1993. Sani Abacha emerged as the new military head of state.

The administration of Abacha was characterised by many ills among which was the lack of care for education. He created six new states on 1st October 1996, which gave Nigeria its current political structure of 36 states. He died on June 8th 1998 and was succeeded by Abdusalami Abubakar. The regime of Abubakar was a transition to the re-institution of democracy. He organized elections and handed over the leadership of the country to Olusegun Obasanjo[84] on 29th May 1999, thereby leading Nigeria to its current "Third Republic". On assumption of office, Obasanjo continued his style of leadership especially in the area of education. He introduced the current "Universal Basic Education" (UBE) programme which has guaranteed massive literacy to Nigerian children. He also re-designed the educational system in 2007, thereby leading to the establishment of the current "Nine-Year Basic Education Curriculum".

In the course of Nigerian history, the Church (both Catholic and Protestant) played a prominent role in establishing and later revising the educational systems. This was seen in the predominant efforts of the missionaries in building and running mission schools, organising catechism classes and educating parents on their role in the upbringing of their children. After the departure of the foreign missionaries at the end of the Civil War in 1970, Nigerian missionaries continued the painstaking effort of the early missionaries. Their apostolate however suffered a setback with the forceful take over of the mission schools by the Government. As recourse, they intensified their efforts in the organisation and promotion of family and parish catechesis.

2.3 Religions in Nigeria

"Religion is a basic reality in any African society and has as such to be considered in any development strategy relevant to Africa."[85] Religion is very much identified with development in Africa especially in art and music. Africans have expressed their beliefs in various contexts of their culture. It is from this

84 Olusegun Obasanjo served as the head of the Nigerian government at two different periods: first as a military person from 1976 to 1979 and as a civilian from 1999 to 2008.

85 Hallencreutz C. F., Preface, in: Petersen H.K. (Ed.), Religion, Development and African Identity, Uppsala, 1987, 7.

background that the presentation of religions in Nigeria will be discussed. In the context of contemporary Nigerian society, this section of will seek to survey the history of religions in Nigeria starting with African Traditional Religion. This is the indigenous religion of Africans which has a manifold of expressions.[86] Nigerians practiced this religion from their earliest history within their varied cultural backgrounds until contacts with foreigners brought about a change in their understandings and world views. These contacts introduced foreign religions namely: Islam and Christianity. The history of these two religions will be traced in sub-sections two and three respectively.

2.3.1 African Traditional Religion (ATR)

From pre-historic times, the geo-political area currently known as Nigeria has been a multi-religious society. According to Jawoniyi:

> *Before the earliest contacts with the outside world, Nigerians lived under the governance of their respective paramount religio-political monarchs. Together with their sovereigns, they were adherents of different African Traditional Religions (ATRs), worshipping very complex pantheons of local and/or regional divinities.*[87]

Although African Traditional Religion is mono-theistic, the various African societies worshipped the Supreme Being under different connotations and perspectives. Thus while he is referred to as "Amadioha" in one locality, he may be known as "Igwe ka ala" in another. The images of these "gods" also differ from one community to another. In Nigeria, these differences are recognised in the religio-cultural heritage of the respective ethnicities. God as the Supreme Being is worshipped under different approaches and understandings. The mode of worship is also differently designed in line with music and lyrics. There are always incantations and the pouring of a libation as a means of invoking the gods and the spirits of the ancestors. These ancestors, though dead, are still believed to be part and parcel of the community. This practice known as "belief in the-living-dead" is a sign of communion between the living and the dead. The ancestors represent and protect the living in the spiritual world, while the living will continue to uphold and maintain the tradition handed over to them by the ancestors. According to Okonkwo:

86 Cf. Hallencreutz C. F., Preface, in: Petersen H.K. (Ed.), Religion, Development and African Identity, Uppsala, 1987, 7.

87 Jawoniyi O., "Rethinking the Religious Education Curricula in Nigerian Schools", in: Chidester D. (Ed.), Journal for the Study of Religion Vol. 22 Nr. 2, 2009, Cape Town, 64.

African cosmology highlights the close interactive relationship, which exists between the individual person, his cultural community to which he belongs, and their departed ancestors in the spirit world.[88]

In any African Traditional worship, these two parties (the living and the dead) are always present especially in the eating of the sacrificial victim. The blood of the sacrificial animal is always poured out as an offering to the gods and the ancestors, while the flesh is consumed by the living amidst very solemn rituals. This practice is highly respected because it forms the apex of any sacrificial gathering in African Traditional Religion as well as fulfilling the spiritual hopes of the people. Affirming this position, Okonkwo remarks:

Within the traditional African context, the diverse religious beliefs of the various cultural groups, which the fore-fathers of the various traditional societies have identified with as part of their cultural property, naturally commands the highest loyalty of the people.[89]

The training of priests for the offering of sacrifices was performed through the rites of initiation – first into adulthood and secondly into the priesthood. To be admitted into the order of priests, one must learn the singing of the incantations which goes with the pouring of libations. The need for this is based on the fact that the priest acts as a medicine man, diviner, fortune teller, educator of the youth and presiding minister in a sacrificial worship. Above all, he appeases the anger of the gods whenever they are offended by the people by offering them sacrifice in accordance with their demands. This offence against the gods can be through immoral behaviour, theft, bullying, slander or killing any member of the community. The gravity of the offence will determine the victim for the sacrifice. If the offence is considered heavy by the gods they can demand a goat, a cow or even a human being. The priest is trained to mediate between human beings and the spirits. This form of training, which is indigenous to the African society, helps the priest to understand and interpret the language of the spirits. That is why he is able to know what the gods want whenever they are offended. This form of indigenous education, which is carried out orally, is not limited to the training of priests. It is also applicable to the upbringing of other young men and women as a means of ensuring a continued transmission of African cultural heritage. According to Jawoniyi:

88 Okonkwo P.I, Minorities and the Problem of Fairness – A Social Ethical Inquiry, Aachen, 2002, 58.

89 Ibid., 59.

> *Contrary to the notion that Nigeria had no education before the earliest contact with the outside World, Nigerians from time immemorial received indigenous forms of education. These indigenous forms of education prepared individuals to take up their roles as cultured members of their respective traditional societies. These included herbalism, midwifery, priesthood, blacksmithing and art.*[90]

Before the coming of other religions in Nigeria, Nigerians, as described above, worshipped different deities who were believed to have influenced their lives. This worship has a two-tier structure. The first or the lower tier is that of the lesser spirits, the second or higher tier is that of the Supreme Being.[91] According to Clarke:

> *The role of the lesser spirits is to underpin events and processes in the microcosm of the local community and its environment, while that of the Supreme Being is to perform the same function within the wider world, the macrocosm.*[92]

These deities differed according to the various ethnicities and tribal groups and are regarded as representatives of the Supreme Being. There was believed to exist a mutual understanding between the deities (the microcosm) and the Supreme Being (the macrocosm) through whom He manifested His powers. Clarke argues:

> *Since there were interactions between microcosm and macrocosm, the lesser spirits were understood to be manifestations of the Supreme Being or as entities ultimately deriving their power from him.*[93]

Religious education at this time was also organised by these ethnic groups in line with their different local modes of worship. The traditional Nigerian system of education was altered by two major contacts with the outside world, namely the coming of Islam and Christianity respectively.[94] These two religions which were carriers of literacy and a universal ideology are causes rather

90 Ibid.

91 Clarke P.B., Islam, Development and African Identity: The Case of West Africa, in: Peterson K. H. (Ed.), Religion, Development and African Identity, Seminar Proceedings No. 17 1987, 136.

92 Ibid.

93 Ibid.

94 Cf. Ibid.

than catalysts of change.[95] The changes that were associated with them were manifested in the course of their spread in the various parts of the country.

2.3.2 Islam

The advent of Islam in Nigeria in the 11th Century through the trans-Saharan trade routes brought about the first wave of change in the transmission of religious beliefs and teachings especially in the northern part of Nigeria.[96] Some Islamic merchants, (though uneducated in the Western sense), gained entrance and made many converts among the people living in northern Nigeria. They also acquired land and built nomadic mosques where their new converts were groomed into the norms and tenets of Islam. According to Braimah:

> *Wherever the Muslim religion found foot-hold it was invariably followed by the language of the Holy Quran and the Arabian sciences. The Holy Quran contained everything needful for a disciple of Muhammad. It gave laws to man and regulated his faith, whether religious or philosophical. It was a code in which everything was decreed, so much so indeed, that to elucidate it was to teach religion, philosophy and law. Grammar and literature were also found in it, for they were taught on the lines of the language employed in the Holy Quran and illustrated by examples taken from it.*[97]

As a result of this, Islamic schools were also established and featured the teaching and propagation of Islamic beliefs and morals. Wherever the Islamic merchants settled, Qur'anic schools were started and the beginnings of an Islamic society put in place.[98] Islam made significant and rapid progress in gaining converts to her fold in the sense that it adapted itself to the mentality and condition of the people.[99] It also identified with the culture of the people

95 Fischer H.J., Conversion Reconsidered: Some Historical Aspects of Religious Conversion in Black Africa, Africa, Vol. 43, No. 1, January 1973, 27-42, quoted by: Clarke P.B., Islam, Development and African Identity: The Case of West Africa, in: Peterson K. H. (Ed.), Religion, Development and African Identity, Seminar Proceedings No. 17 1987, 137.

96 Cf. Jawoniyi O., "Rethinking the Religious Education Curricula in Nigerian Schools", in: Chidester D. (Ed.), Journal for the Study of Religion Vol. 22 Nr. 2, 2009, Cape Town, 64.

97 Braimah B.A.R., Islamic Education in Ghana, in: Pobee J. S. (Ed.), Religion in a Pluralistic Society, Leiden, 1976, 202.

98 Ibid, 135.

99 Clarke P.B., Islam, Development and African Identity: The Case of West Africa, in: Peterson K. H. (Ed.), Religion, Development and African Identity, Seminar Proceedings No. 17 1987, 127.

especially in the practice of polygamy.[100] The Islamic missionaries did not in practice reject the most valuable elements of traditional African cosmologies as well as their predictive, explanatory and controlling dimensions of their everyday life.[101] This tolerant attitude helped Islam to gain acceptability among the people. "By the 15th century the Islamic system of education had already become fully entrenched in this part of the country".[102] The teachings in these schools included the recitation of the Qur'an, Islamic laws and morals among other topics. These teachings were based on the five basic pillars of Islam. The first of these pillars is the belief in only one God or Allah (and in his prophet Muhammad). This belief forms the first verse of the opening chapter of the Qur'an. The other pillars are belief in: prayer – five times a day (salat), fasting, alms giving (zakat), and the pilgrimage to Mecca (hajj). There is also a claim of belief in a sixth pillar, the jihad, which is binding on an Islamic community and not on the individual Muslim.[103]

2.3.3 Christianity

The second contact that brought about an alteration to Nigeria's traditional educational systems, and its social, cultural and religious landscapes was the coming of the Europeans, who brought with them Christianity and Western education. Upon arrival in Nigerian in 1842, the Christian missionaries from Ireland and England embarked on a grass root evangelization amongst the people. The Irish missionaries introduced Catholicism while the English missionaries introduced Protestantism. They acquired lands and built churches and schools in the midst of many tribulations. Such difficulties included the harsh weather of Sub-Saharan Africa, language and hostility accruing from the adherents of other non-Christian religions especially the indigenous African Traditional Religion worshippers. The introduction of Christianity and Western education was seen by such people "as disturbing and disorienting – as creating an unsatisfactory situation which must be mastered and overcome".[104] They

100 Cf. Eluwa G. I. C., Ukagwu M. O., Nwachukwu J. U. N., Nwaubani A. C. N., A History of Nigeria, For Schools and Colleges, Onitsha, 2005, 229.

101 Ibid, 137.

102 Jawoniyi O., "Rethinking the Religious Education Curricula in Nigerian Schools", in: Chidester D. (Ed.), Journal for the Study of Religion Vol. 22 Nr. 2, 2009, Cape Town, 64.

103 Cf. Eluwa G. I. C., Ukagwu M. O., Nwachukwu J. U. N., Nwaubani A. C. N., A History of Nigeria, For Schools and Colleges, Onitsha, 2005, 130.

104 Bella R.N., Meaning and Modernization, Religious Studies, Vol. 4, No. 1, October 1968, 37-45, quoted by: Clarke P.B., Islam, Development and African Identity: The Case of West Africa, in: Peterson K. H. (Ed.), Religion, Development and African Identity, Seminar Proceedings No. 17 1987, 125.

strongly denounced a situation which would make them experience disorientation, alienation and loss of their cherished African identity.[105] In this instance, Christianity and Western education were considered to be degenerative and destructive of African traditional values. Their introduction into a traditional African society therefore would bring about a totally different way of thinking and acting, a completely different way of life, which for the fundamental African is unacceptable.[106]

There existed a great dichotomy between the Catholic missionaries and the Protestant missionaries. The Catholic missionaries did not allow their converts to associate with people who were not their members. Various punishments were mandated against defaulters. It was a taboo for Catholics to attend Protestant schools and vice versa. Participation in any Protestant Church activity was for Catholics a very serious sin and therefore material for sacramental confession. Children of Catholic parents were even prohibited from taking part in sporting events held on Protestant playgrounds. That was why religious education during the missionary era was to an extent marred by complicated divisions between Catholics and Protestants. This was based on the exclusivist theology of the Catholic missionaries that non Catholics would not be saved. In this way, the early missionaries used Christianity to sow a seed of discord among the people and established a situation of great rivalry among the members of the various Christian denominations. An Anglican document of 1950 entitled "What are we Anglicans doing?" was for instance a call to Anglicans to rise against the spread of Catholicism in Eastern Nigeria through the establishment of many schools.[107]

However, despite the numerous problems that existed among themselves, the missionaries made some painstaking efforts to establish Christianity amongst the people. They were able to establish parishes and mission stations. Thus they influenced a Christ-centred cleansing on the already existing religious practices and experiences of the local people. This was possible because there existed already a visible similarity between some Nigerian cultures and some cultures of the Jews; and Jewish cultures have significant influence on Christianity. Although this sanitization was not easy and smooth, those foreign

105 Cf. Clarke P.B., Islam, Development and African Identity: The Case of West Africa, in: Peterson K. H. (Ed.), Religion, Development and African Identity, Seminar Proceedings No. 17 1987, 125.

106 Cf. Ibid, 126.

107 "What Are We Anglicans Doing?" is a lecture presented at the teachers' week at Awka in August 1950 by Enemo E. O. He enumerated all the schools owned by the Catholics as against very few by the Anglicans and convinced his audience of Catholic dominance of the area. He therefore called his fellow Anglicans to the challenge of suppressing the rapid spread of Catholicism.

Christian missionaries were able to hold lessons in the schools and organize catechetical instructions in the parishes and mission stations. Through catechetical instructions the early Christian missionaries were able to prepare their new converts for the reception of the sacraments (rituals) and for the authentic life required of all Christians. Their teachings met the social and spiritual needs of the people. The new converts could practice their faith anywhere and were no longer restricted to one particular locality or to an immovable shrine. People from various places could refer to themselves as brothers and sisters because of the binding force of their new religion. In this way the missionaries brought a new phase of life to their new converts.

Some African religious educators claim that the primary aim of constructing institutions of learning was to use these schools as a means of converting the indigenes to Christianity and not necessarily to develop the cognitive ability of the people. Using the confessional mode of religious education which aimed at proselytizing pupils, the religious education curricula and collective worship in these mission schools focused exclusively on Christianity.[108] That was why the catechism was central in the Curriculum, although other fields of learning were also taught. This move yielded positive results especially in the eastern part of Nigeria where the people renounced their traditional religious practices and beliefs and accepted Christianity. They received Baptism and other sacraments in the quest for Western education. According to Eluwa:

> *By 1920, there were about 19,200 Christians in the Northern Region of Nigeria, 260,500 in the West and 514,395 in the East. By 1921, it was estimated that 284,835 out of 3,927,419 Igbo were Christians. By 1937 the number had increased to some 600,000.*[109]

The fruit of this missionary work can be seen in the entire Igboland especially in the diocese of Ahiara where Christianity is the major religion of the people. This was achieved through the efforts of many parents who sent their children to the mission schools for the sake of "prominence and prosperity".[110] Their children not only embraced Christianity, some of them also became missionaries.

108 Jawoniyi O., "Rethinking the Religious Education Curricula in Nigerian Schools", in: Chidester D. (Ed.), Journal for the Study of Religion Vol. 22 Nr. 2, 2009, Cape Town, 65.

109 Eluwa G. I. C., Ukagwu M. O., Nwachukwu J. U. N., Nwaubani A. C. N., A History of Nigeria, For Schools and Colleges, Onitsha, 2005, 229.

110 Cf. Isichei E., A History of Christianity in Africa: From Antiquity to the Present 1995, 270, in: Jawoniyi O., "Rethinking the Religious Education Curricula in Nigerian Schools", in: Chidester D. (Ed.), Journal for the Study of Religion Vol. 22 Nr. 2, 2009, Cape Town, 64.

The seven sacraments of the Church, which formed part of the school Curriculum, were presented as being closely connected to one another. With this teaching, the religious and sacramental life of the people at this time was something to be admired and appreciated. The catechetical instructions were carried out in such a manner that they were relevant both for the old and young. The evenings were used for adult religious education and sacramental education for those about to receive the sacraments. The people learnt the right morals both in the schools and in the parishes so that all were able to find meaning in the entire teaching of the Church irrespective of their age differences. Thus the missionaries were able to establish many schools as well as lively parishes and Christian communities.

However, in the establishment of Christianity in Nigeria and indeed in Africa, the missionaries did not respect the cultural heritage of the people. The tendency at this time was to eradicate African culture and replace it with Christianity. This is because the missionaries saw this culture as part and parcel of African Traditional Religion which they needed to displace.[111] For them, African Traditional Religion was primitive and pagan oriented. This is as result of some of the beliefs of this religion such as: the practice of polygamy, the killing of twins, belief in the (osu) caste system and superstition. But despite the rejection of African culture and tradition by the missionaries, a total displacement of this religion has no possibility of survival. This is because the traditional African religious practices still find a place in the heart of a good number of Africans, Nigerians inclusive.[112] They still consult the oracle to seek solutions to their problems. What the missionaries did not do was adapt of that which was inherent in the African Traditional Religion into Christianity through the theology of enculturation.[113] As a result of their rigid, dogmatic and rejecting approach they could not change African beliefs and practices in any profound way.[114] Christianity succeeded mainly in exposing the people to Western education and in harmonising their lives towards achieving it.

Since this work is on religious education, it will be pertinent to dedicate a section to the description of the youth in Nigeria, who are the direct recipients of religious teaching.

111 Cf. Eluwa G. I. C., Ukagwu M. O., Nwachukwu J. U. N., Nwaubani A. C. N., A History of Nigeria, For Schools and Colleges, Onitsha, 2005, 230.

112 Ibid.

113 Cf. Clarke P.B., Islam, Development and African Identity: The Case of West Africa, in: Peterson K. H. (Ed.), Religion, Development and African Identity, Seminar Proceedings No. 17, 1987, 136.

114 Ibid, 128.

2.4 Youth in Nigeria

The word "youth" has been given various understandings and interpretations by scholars. Some see it as a word surrounded by myth while others treat it as a relative terminology. According Laurentin, the mythical understanding of this term is based on the fact that the entire discourse on the human person seems to hover around the term "youth".[115] For instance it is often said: "Youth is the future". In this understanding "youth" is seen as a vague concept which evokes the consciousness of ideas that may not be realised. The identification of the youth with the future is only based on the fact that a youth is still at an early stage of life and is therefore perceived as living longer than the elderly. This projection is vague in the sense that it lacks any certainty as to the longevity of the youth over the elderly. It has often been the case that the elderly live to experience the demise of some of the youth. Again the youthful age is seen as an endangering stage of life that must be feared.[116] This is because the term youth is associated with vigour and strength. This strength which may sometimes be aggressive stands out as the main object underlying the attribution of fear to the youth. Hence, the youthful age is said to be a time of adventure and many possibilities sometimes culminating in violence.

As a relative terminology it is used to describe the young people of a group or family.[117] In this instance, a person may be identified as a youth all life long since he or she is the youngest in the group. This explains why some people attribute youthfulness to a thing of the mind and claim to be young as far as they are still useful to the society. Joe Barth captured this scenario:

In life one makes a distinction, experiences and observes as an individual or group, many adults who prefer behaving like youths, in so far as they are still bubbling with life, energetic, resourceful and adventurous [sic].[118]

The question here is the criterion for determining what qualifies a person as a youth. Is it based on age or on the ability to carry out useful activities in the society? The Young Men Christian Association of Nigeria (YMCA) for instance is a strong body which promotes Christian activities in Nigeria. This Association organises a yearly picnic on Easter Monday and holds a number of symposia aimed at enlightening the youth on the Christian teachings. Can it be said that all the members of this association are young people since some

115 Cf. Laurentin R., Ist Jugend definierbar?, Schröder B. (Trans.), in: Ahlbrecht A. (Ed.), Concilium, 21. Jahrgang 1985, Zürich, 1985, 307.

116 Cf. Ibid.

117 Cf. Ibid.

118 Abba J.C., The Need for Basic Pastoral Formation for Youths in Africa of the 21. Century, Aachen, 2005, 22.

of their youngest members are above the age of sixty years? How can the word "youth" then be defined?

2.4.1 Definition of Youth

According to Laurentin, this term can be defined in accordance with the understanding of various groups and human societies.[119] He ruled out the proportional definition of youth as for instance forming the half or third or fourth of the population of a people. This is because such an approach would not justify the social and traditional use of the word. Also defining the word from the health or dynamic point of view would not fully highlight its meaning despite the fact that these are some of the characteristics of the youth. No age is devoid of sickness or death. So defining the youth as a healthy and vibrant person does not rule out the fact that there are some sick youth who are not vibrant.

A better approach towards a deeper understanding of the term "youth" will be descriptive and chronological. Descriptively it is said to be the period of life between childhood and maturity.[120] This is the time when the life of a person is still in its early stage and has not yet exhausted its usefulness. A person therefore is said to be a youth when he or she has passed childhood and is attaining adulthood. This is why the word "youth" is sometimes used synonymously with puberty and adolescence. This is the understanding of the *Webster's Third New International Dictionary* where these terms were used as interchangeable words.

ADOLESCENCE, PUBERTY, PUBERSCENCE, YOUTH are frequently used interchangeably to refer to the period between childhood and maturity. YOUTH, the most inclusive of these terms, applies sometimes to the entire period from childhood to maturity, sometimes to the period only between the maturing of the sexual organs and attaining to other types of maturity; more than the other terms. YOUTH suggests the vigor, innocence, and ingratiating attributes generally associated with this early period of life and so has come to suggest vigor or fullness of life generally. ADOLESCENCE designates the same period of life as YOUTH in its most restricted sense, but carries a stronger implication of maturity, suggesting the inexperience or awkwardness or mental or emotional instability often characteristic of that period of life; in legal use it designates the period from puberty to full legal age or maturity. Strictly PUBERTY designates the age at which the symptoms of sexual maturing appear, as the growth of beard and alteration of voice range in boys or

119 Cf. Laurentin R., Ist Jugend definierbar?, Schröder B. (Trans.), in: Ahlbrecht A. (Ed.), Concilium, 21. Jahrgang 1985, Zürich, 1985, 307.

120 Cf. Webster's Third New International Dictionary volume III 1981, 2654.

breast development in girls; legally this age is fixed at fourteen for boys and twelve for girls. More broadly, PUBERTY covers the earlier period of adolescence. PUBESCENCE is sometimes used as the equivalent of PUBERTY or more specifically signifies the early years of sexual maturing.[121]

The sexual maturity of a person indicates that he or she is no longer a child. It designates an important stage of human development and is an indication that a person is undergoing normal growth. This period does not go without its characteristics of exuberance, instability, fear as well as hope for new horizons.[122] That is why it is often referred to as the turbulent age when juvenile delinquency is at its peak. At this period the struggle for identification overwhelms the activities of the individual person involved.

The interchangeable use of the word "youth" with "adolescence" refers to its chronological definition. The youth is then said to be a person who is between the age of adolescence and adulthood. This general understanding of the term youth helps us to ascertain the age at which a person is said to have attained adolescence. An adolescent is no longer within the age of childhood. He or she is one who is maturing towards adulthood. The youth age then is the period of time between the expiration of adolescence and the attainment of adulthood. The specific ages between these periods vary. According to the *Chambers Dictionary*, "most Western societies consider a person as an adolescent from about 13 to 18 years of age".[123] It is then at the attainment of the 18th year of age that a person becomes a full-grown adult. However opinions on the age limit of a youth vary among scholars as well as societies. But there seems to be a consensus in this case in the two countries under consideration. The youth age in Germany does not vary from that of Nigeria. This is because the two countries accord their citizens the right of enfranchisement at the attainment of the age of 18. This categorization of the youth age will form the basis for the discussion of the types of youth in Nigeria.

2.4.2 Types of Youth in Nigeria

The classification of the youth age in the Nigerian context may differ from its global application. The Nigerian National Youth Development Policy categorised Nigerian youth as young people between the ages of 18 and 35. This is also the case in the diocese of Ahiara where a person is regarded as a youth at the age of 18. This understanding has both economic and social implications.

121 Ibid.

122 Cf. Abba J.C., The Need for Basic Pastoral Formation for Youths in Africa of the 21. Century, Aachen, 2005, 23.

123 The Chambers Dictionary, New Edition, 1993, 2032, in: Abba J.C. ibid., 22.

Economically they form the bulk of those not yet absorbed into the labour market. A good number of people within this age limit constitute the biggest threat to economic stability. This is as a result of some of the problems affecting such youth. Some of these problems are: illiteracy, poverty, unemployment and violence.

Illiteracy is a great setback to the development of potentialities among Nigerian youth. Among other things, it generates abject poverty and dwindles away the progress of any society. The high level of illiteracy in Nigeria is attributed to the uneven chances of education among Nigerian children. In some Nigerian societies, male children are given more educational chances than their female counterparts. According to the United Nations Population Fund (UNFPA), girls are discriminated against in the enrolment into Nigerian schools.[124] This discrimination stems from both social and economic backgrounds. This is why there are more female illiterates in Nigeria than male. Young people between the ages of 15 and 19 years have a literacy rate of 79 percent for the boys and 61 percent for the girls.[125] In the sub-urban areas, girls are even more disadvantaged. This is especially the case in Northern Nigeria, where girls are not given educational opportunities due to religious reasons. In some other parts, girls are sent into various kinds of trade as a result of poverty. Early marriage also mars the educational chances of many Nigerian girls.[126]

The problem of unemployment among the youth of Nigeria has resulted in many negative tendencies in many Nigerian societies. Some of these negative activities are seen in the many cases of armed robbery operations and touting carried out by such young people. These able-bodied people take to arms and violence as the only alternative means of survival. By so doing they constitute a tremendous threat to national security. This is why kidnapping has reached an alarming degree in many states of Nigeria. Another visible economic menace of the youth is migration to the urban cities and foreign countries. This venture is undertaken in the search for employment, steady education and a better life. By taking to this lazy approach, they label themselves as opportunists and gold diggers who have robbed themselves of their human dignity and national pride. This is why most Nigerians classify them as those who have not yet arrived, those who must depend on others for their survival. This dependency has contributed immensely to reducing some Nigerian youth to the status of agents trying to achieve specific goals for other people which may be politically and

124 Cf. http://nigeria.unfpa.org/youngpeople.html, 08.11.2012.

125 Cf. Ibid.

126 Cf. Ibid.

selfishly induced. Under this category these youth have been manipulated by some wealthy people of the society. They employ them as thugs for unleashing anti-social activities such as kidnapping and terrorism. Such youth are branded with names which signify that they are part of the ills of the society. In the North they are known as the "*Almageris*", in the East "*Ndi Akpu Obi*" and in the West (especially in Lagos) "*Area Boys*". This is why the youth age is seen by some Nigerians as a risky and rebellious period of life since some youth can be used to achieve vulnerable and ill-fated goals. This type of lifestyle creates a negative influence on the religious practices of some Nigerian youth. Their prerogative is mainly to satisfy the needs of those who provide them with the immediate means of livelihood and not necessarily to pay allegiance to their religious inclinations. That is why such youth will stop at nothing in parading themselves as agents of destruction and those who constitute the greatest menace to society building.

However another set of youth exists in Nigeria. These youth contribute positively to the maintenance and development of the society. They have integrated themselves into the mainstream of those who help in the building of the nation. They are often described as important sources of manpower for development as well as the leaders of tomorrow. Such youth are meaningfully working in various parts of the economy. They engage themselves in the areas of politics, science, economics, education and religion. As such, many of them belong to the government, others work as engineers, some work in various financial institutions, many are teachers and a great number of them are religious leaders. Many Nigerian youth are also self-employed. They work as businessmen and women who are daily occupied with buying and selling. Some others who are not as well educated also work as mechanics, electricians, carpenters and cobblers. It is not awkward to hear such slogans: "the youth are our future", "the youth hold our future" and "in a baby is a mother or father respectively". As a result of this understanding, the demise of a youth is seen as a great catastrophe by most Nigerian societies. For such societies, when a youth dies, the future dies also along with him or her because the youth form a prodigious part of the society. The Nigerian youth themselves have come to realize this fact and are laying claims to the nation's leadership. They prepare themselves to take up some leadership roles in various sectors by participating actively in some preparatory leadership programmes designed for them by the Federal Government. One of such programmes is the "National Youth Service Corp". With the establishment of this programme, the Nigerian people placed the destiny of the country into the hands of their youth with a great amount of reliability and expectation. Thus this programme ushered in fresh goals and objectives aimed at establishing Nigeria as:

- a united, strong and self-reliant nation;
- a great and dynamic economy;
- a land of bright and full opportunities for all citizens; and
- a free and democratic society.[127]

The National Youth Service Corp Programme (NYSC) in Nigeria illustrates the positive contribution of the Nigerian Youth to the building of the nation. This Programme, which is assigned to every Nigerian youth after graduation from the university and polytechnic institute, has remained one of the vital prerequisites for employment in Nigeria. Through this programme the youth have distinguished themselves in para-military training, teaching assignments and services in many vital sectors of the Nigerian economy. Founded in 1973 under the then military Government of Jakubu Gowon, this programme has offered many Nigerian youth the ample opportunity of discovering their potentials and utilising them for the common good. It has as its ultimate goal, the reconstructing, reconciling and rebuilding of the nation after it was torn apart by the Civil War.[128] Above all, it is meant to serve as a bridge between the many different geographical areas, ethnic groups and religions in Nigeria. Furthermore, it offers Nigerian young people the opportunity to know themselves and to share ideas of national development. Thus it was established to enhance unity in Nigeria under the "Second National Development Plan" of the Federal Government which came into force in 1970. Under this Plan, Nigerian youth are posted to various states and parts of the country outside those of their immediate origin to serve in the different sectors of the economy for a period of one year. A detailed list of the objectives of the NYSC is contained in the Decree No. 15 of 16th June 1993 as follows:

> *2.4.1 To inculcate discipline in Nigerian youths by instilling in them a tradition of industry at work, and of patriotic and loyal service to Nigeria in any situation they may find themselves*
>
> *2.4.2 To raise the moral tone of the Nigerian youths by giving them the opportunity to learn about higher ideals of national achievement, social and cultural improvement*
>
> *2.4.3 To develop in the Nigerian youths the attitudes of mind, acquired through shared experience and suitable training which will make them more amenable to mobilisation in the national interest*

127 Federal Government of Nigeria, National Youth Service Corps, About NYSC, http://www.nysc.gov.ng/history2.php, 09.06.2011.

128 Cf. Ibid.

> *2.4.4 To enable Nigerian youth acquire the spirit of self reliance by encouraging them to develop skills for self employment*
> *2.4.5 To contribute to the accelerated growth of national economy*
> *2.4.6 To develop common ties among the Nigerian youths and promote national unity and integration*
> *2.4.7 To remove prejudices, eliminate ignorance and confirm at first hand the many similarities among Nigerians of all ethnic groups*
> *2.4.8 To develop a sense of corporate existence and common destiny of the people of Nigeria.*[129]

This service programme has remained a living memorial to the sacrifice of Nigerian youth to the growth, progress, development and unity of Nigeria. This is because the members of the youth service corps are equitably distributed where their skills are effectively utilised in areas of national needs. In this way they are exposed to the different modes of life of their fellow Nigerians. This is why they have often been described as "Nigerian ambassadors within Nigeria". By participating in this programme the Nigerian youth demonstrate their patriotic zeal and love for their fatherland. This is because this programme prepares them for a sound and patriotic leadership which is a pre-condition for the rapid social and economic development of the country.

As a prelude to the realisation of the goals of the NYSC, there exist in some Nigerian Universities and tertiary institutions organisations which aim at offering Nigerian young people an interactive forum for healthy nation building. One of such organisations is the "Nigeria Federation of Catholic Students" (NFCS). This association was formed in 1956 by Ambrose Ali. Its membership is open to all Nigerian Catholic students in any Nigerian University, tertiary institution and Catholic seminary.[130] Its aim is primarily to promote the practice of the Catholic faith and student apostolate among Nigerian youth in the Universities and higher institutions. Members of this Federation see themselves as members of one big family and also as the hope of the Church in the evangelization of the World through their exemplary lives.[131] This Federation helps them to identify themselves as people of one faith who are called upon to help in building a united and strong Nigeria.

In the Church the youth distinguish themselves in promoting the growth of their faith. They show their passage from the age of inquiry to that of full acceptance of their faith by involving themselves in some leadership roles to

129 Federal Government of Nigeria, National Youth Service Corps, About NYSC, http://www.nysc.gov.ng/history2.php, 09.06.2011.

130 Cf. http://nfcsuniben.wordpress.com/about/brief-history/, 08.10.2012.

131 Cf. Ibid.

accentuate their commitment to the promotion of the Christian faith. They take up such assignments as voluntary catechists, choristers and lectors. As voluntary catechists, they help in the teaching of catechism and preparing candidates for the reception of the sacraments especially the sacraments of Baptism, Holy Communion and Confirmation. In this way they manifest their vigour and poise to take up their future responsibility as leaders of tomorrow.

From the above description, two categories of youth (male and female) are to be identified among Nigerian young people: Those who present themselves as agents of negativism and those who contribute positively to the demands of the society. These two groups form their characteristics (positive or negative) mostly based on the type of school they attended and the kind of influence they had from their peer groups. The category of schools which exist in Nigeria will now be presented as places where these youth are groomed and from where they develop their moral and religious skills.

2.5 Schools in Nigeria

In Nigeria, two categories of schools are to be distinguished: the public or Government schools and the private schools. These schools have the same educational system that has been provided by the Federal Ministry of Education. This is the so-called six-three-three-four system of education. This system consists of primary school (six years), junior secondary school (three years), senior secondary school (three years), and university education (four years). In this section, the schools and school system in Nigeria will be presented as having the holistic goal of contributing towards national unity and development. This will be undertaken under the primary school, junior secondary school, senior secondary school and the university in the first to the fourth sub-sections. Because Nigeria operates a capitalist economy, the running of schools is also not limited to a government monopoly. Hence the type of schools operational within the Nigerian society will be presented under government or public schools and private or confessional schools in sub-sections five and six. The word "confessional" is used to distinguish those schools which are under the ownership of the Church. In such schools, denominational religious education is taught in addition to the government approved religious education curriculum which is mainly based on Biblical stories. Private ownership of schools exists from the primary school to the university. The aim of the last sub-section will be to indicate that individuals and cooperate bodies can obtain the right to build and manage schools under the guidelines of the government.

2.5.1 The Primary School

The acquisition of primary education occupies a position of greatest importance in the minds of many Nigerians. Derived from the two Latin words "primarius"[132], which means "basic", and "primus"[133], which means "first", it is used to denote the first level or stage of formal basic education in one's life, especially in the Western sense. The *Webster's Third New International Dictionary* defined the primary school as:

> *...a school at which children receive their first formal education usually comprising the first three grades of elementary school but sometimes also including kindergarten.*[134]

In Nigeria, primary education gained an unprecedented level of importance and awareness after the Civil War with the introduction of the "Universal Primary Education" (UPE) which offered every Nigerian child a free primary education. This programme which was launched in 1976 brought about an educational boom in many states of Nigeria. Its introduction and implementation marked the dawn of an educational expediency which witnessed the enrolment of many Nigerian children into the various primary schools of the country – owing to proximity and place of residence. With this development, the problem of the illiteracy rate in the country was controlled. The problem of the unbalanced educational level of the various states was to an extent solved. The South was no longer seen as playing a dominant role in the areas of educational and economic development. The urban areas no longer claimed educational superiority over the rural. Enrolment into the primary school was open to both male and female children, so that the male predominance over the female in the area of education no longer "came into play". The Federal Government embarked upon this policy of education – the UPE – because it looked upon education as the key instrument for the realisation of rapid national development, economic and social changes as well as uniting the nation once more after having been split by the Civil War. In this way, the country as a whole placed great expectation on education's unifying and developmental potential. A child is enrolled into the primary school at the completion of the sixth year of age. It is expected that a child completes his or her primary education at the completion of the age of childhood or the age of twelve. At the completion of primary education, the pupils are admitted into the junior secondary school to

132 Webster's Third New International Dictionary Vol. II, Chicago, 1981, 1800.

133 Ibid.

134 Ibid.

continue their academic pursuit which is based on a continuous assessment system. The subjects offered in the primary school are:
- English language
- Nigerian language (Igbo language)
- Mathematics
- Christian religious knowledge (Christian religious education)
- Agricultural science
- Civic education
- Social studies
- Physical and health education
- Home economics
- Basic science
- Creative arts
- Writing
- Moral instruction

2.5.2 The Secondary School

The word "secondary" is derived from two Latin words "secundarius" and "secundus" which are used to denote the second position in a countable series.[135] The secondary school was defined by the *Webster's Third New International Dictionary* as:

> *...a school more advanced in grade than an elementary school and offering general, technical, vocational or college-preparatory courses.*[136]

In Nigeria, some secondary schools are only for boys while some are only for girls but many are unisex. Secondary education takes place in two phases: in the junior secondary school (JSS) and in the senior secondary school (SSS).

2.5.2.1 The Junior Secondary School (JSS)

At the completion of primary education, Nigerian children are encouraged to further their level of education in the junior secondary school. It forms the final part of formal basic education in Nigeria. A child is expected to be in the JSS between the ages of twelve and fifteen. This is the beginning of puberty. The JSS provides students with a broad-based general education which will enable them to cope in the secondary school. This is why there is no choice of subjects

135 Cf. Webster's Third New International Dictionary Vol. III, Chicago, 1981, 2050.

136 Ibid., 2051.

at this educational level. The subjects offered at this level are compulsory for all students. These subjects are also meant to enable those who may like to continue their educational career in vocational or technical institutes fit into the educational system of such institutes. They also provide them with the basic technical-know-how to earn a living if they can no longer continue with the educational career. A choice of subjects is only possible in the senior secondary school. At the end of JSS all students are mandated to take the "Junior West African School Certificate Examination". The subjects offered in the junior secondary school are:

- English language
- Nigerian language (Igbo language)
- Mathematics
- Basic/integrated science
- Social studies
- Christian religious knowledge (Christian religious education)
- Fine arts
- Introductory technology
- Home economics
- Agricultural science
- Civil education
- Physical and health education
- Business studies
- Foreign languages (French)
- Moral instruction

2.5.2.2 The Senior Secondary School (SSS)

At the completion of JSS, all successful candidates in the "West African Junior School Certificate Examination" are automatically promoted to the senior secondary school (SSS) which is the completion of secondary education. No further entrance examination is required. A child is expected to be in the SSS between the ages of 15 and 18 which is the age of adolescence. At this level of education a child is expected to indicate his or her area of specialization. Subjects offered at this level are meant to prepare the students for studies in the university or in other institutes of study after the secondary school. There are basic or compulsory subjects: English language, mathematics and one of the three Nigerian major languages – Igbo, Yoruba or Hausa. In general students are allowed to choose their subjects according to their various areas of competence. With the help of their guidance counsellors and parents they are advised to choose those subjects that would enable them to study meaningful courses in the university or other tertiary institutions in the areas of basic or social sciences. At the completion of their secondary education students are required to take the “West African Senior School Certificate Examination”. A student’s grade at the examination will determine his or her continuation of the educational carrier at the university level. The subjects learned in the senior secondary school are:

- English language
- Nigerian language (Igbo language)
- Mathematics
- Biology
- Chemistry
- Physics
- Computer science
- Agricultural science
- Geography
- Home economics
- Home management
- Literature in English
- Economics
- Government
- Christian religious knowledge
- Commerce
- Accountancy
- Business studies
- French
- Moral instruction

2.5.3 The University

The word “University” is derived from the Latin word “universus” which means “entirety” or “whole”.[137] It was defined by the *Webster’s Third New International Dictionary* as:

> *...an institution of higher learning providing facilities for teaching and research and authorized to grant academic degrees.*[138]

In Nigeria, there are three categories of universities: the federal universities, state universities and private universities. The federal universities are all universities that are funded by the Federal Government. These are relatively

137 Cf. Ibid, 2502.

138 Ibid.

affordable by most of the populace because the fees are charged at a considerably low rate when compared with the state universities. The state universities are all universities that are under the sponsorship of the State Government. The cost of studies is higher in the state universities than in the federal universities. This is because the states cannot afford the same subsidy which the Federal Government gives for the running of her universities. On the third level are the private universities which are funded by individuals and parastatals. In these universities very high fees are charged so that the cost of studies is almost prohibitive.

Under the six-three-three-four system of education, a person is expected to enter the university at the age of 18 and finish at the age of 22. This is the beginning of the youth age as defined by the Nigerian National Youth Development Policy. Admissions into the universities are preceded by an examination conducted by the "Joint Admissions and Matriculation Board" (JAMB). Successful candidates of this examination are offered automatic admission into the various universities of Nigeria, depending on their choices of entry. Students in the universities of science and technology are expected to run a five-year programme of studies. In this case they are meant to graduate at the age of 23. University education in Nigeria is designed in such a way that at the completion of the 24th year of age, a person is supposed to have completed the National Youth Service Programme. In addition to the universities, Nigeria has other institutions of higher learning such as colleges of education and polytechnics. These also offer a four-year programme courses after which students are awarded national certificates of education and national diploma respectively. The universities and other higher institutions of learning are primarily meant to be training grounds for future leaders and responsible citizens.[139] At the age of 25, one is expected to have been fully absorbed into the national labour force. Although these set goals are yet to be realized, it must be acknowledged that the Nigerian educational system is designed to offer prospects of a successful future to every Nigerian child irrespective of age, sex, religion or ethnicity.

2.5.4 Public or Government Schools in Nigeria

These are all schools (primary or secondary) that are been funded by either the Federal or State Governments. No schools in Nigeria are under the direct sponsorship of the Local Government. The Federal or State Governments rather uses the Local Governments to administer the schools within their jurisdiction.

139 Cf. Federal Government of Nigeria, National Youth Service Corps, http:/www.nysc.gov.ng/history2.php, 09.06.2011.

The origin of the word public school is traced by *The New Encyclopaedia Britannica* as follows:

> *The term public school emerged in the 18th century when the reputation of certain grammar schools spread beyond their immediate environs. They began taking pupils whose parents could afford residential fees and thus became known as public, in contrast to local, schools. In the early 1970s the term applied to about 200 fee-paying schools for boys and to a lesser number of girls' schools.*[140]

Some states in Nigeria offer free primary education while others do not. In this case some state-owned schools charge school fees to help in the funding of these schools. In these schools only the officially Government approved subjects are taught. These include: (in the primary schools) English language, Mathematics, Christian Religious Knowledge (CRK) or Islamic Religious Knowledge (IRK), Science and three Nigerian languages – Igbo, Yoruba and Hausa.

2.5.5 Private or Confessional Schools in Nigeria

The private or confessional schools are those schools (primary or secondary) which are funded by individuals or voluntary agents like the Church. The *Webster's Third New International Dictionary* defined a private school as:

> *...a school that is established, conducted, and primarily supported by a nongovernmental agency.*[141]

In these schools the proprietors have the right to introduce some subjects which they consider important in the upbringing of children. In the mission schools for instance such subjects like religion in addition to CRK and Latin may be introduced. Under religion the pupils learn about the sacraments of the Church, prayers and songs. In the Catholic minor seminaries other subjects like liturgy, table ethics and catechetical instructions are allowed.

The mission schools established by the missionaries were classified as confessional schools. This is because the pupils are offered denominational catechesis. These schools were forcefully taken over by the Federal Government after the Civil War in 1970. Such schools belonged to some Christian denominations like the Roman Catholic Church, the Anglican Church, the Methodist Church, the Presbyterian Church and the Baptist Church. In these schools

140 The New Encyclopaedia Britannica Vol. VIII, Chigaco, 1984, 286.

141 Webster's Third New International Dictionary Vol. II, Chicago, 1981, 1805.

denominational religious education is no longer allowed. All the students learn only CRK as provided in the national curriculum for primary and secondary education.

2.6 Religious Education in Nigeria

Although Nigeria is religiously pluralistic, the right to teach religion in the schools is accorded only to Christianity and Islam. This is why the learning of religion in the schools is done under "Christian Religious Studies" (CRS) and "Islamic Studies" (IS) respectively. The inclusion of religion in the school curriculum is based on the fact that religion forms a basic element of human existence and social interaction in Nigeria.[142] One may wonder why African Traditional Religion (ATR) is not included in the school curriculum. This is as a result of missionary as well as colonial influence which wrongly saw African Traditional Religion as a merely fetish religion. The missionaries even went to the extreme of making an opprobrious and degrading remark towards ATR as "ancestral worship" and "downright animism".[143] However some private and confessional schools have included the study of this religion in their curriculum so as not to lose the rich religious and cultural heritage of this noble religion. Apart from the schools, religious education is also undertaken by the various religious denominations in the country. For the Christians, the exercise is reserved for the various Christian Churches and sects under parish catechesis and pastoral care of the youth. Each Church or sect has the duty of educating her young ones in the areas of her sacraments, prayers, songs and other practices which are peculiar to her faith. Religion is also taught in the families under the guidance of the parents. In Nigeria, religious education in the family, in the school and in the Christian community, needs to be exercised in a language and manner which are meaningful to Nigerians. Such a religious education should have the aim of contributing to the social development of the people as well as assigning them the responsibility of maintaining their society in equity and social justice. It should therefore take cognisance of the social ethics and cultural heritage of the Nigerian people. In this instance, such a religious education will contribute immensely to the political development of the country and also play a role in the sustenance of her current nascent democracy. The religious language needed for such education is to be expressed in the

142 Cf. Okonkwo P.I, Minorities and the Problem of Fairness – A Social Enquiry, Aachen, 2002, 58.

143 Cf. Ibid., 59.

forms of rites and symbols, narrative traditions and ways of life.[144] Such language should also include religious genre like parables, legends, myths, doxology, prayer and blessing realized stylistically through the use of metaphor and oxymoron.[145] The use of religious concepts such as God, Saviour, salvation and Divine healing should also be integrated into the language of religious education in Nigeria. Because of the limited scope of this work, attention will be focused only on a detailed overview of CRS in the primary and secondary schools in Nigeria in this section. The learning of religion in the Church and in the family will be treated in chapter four of this work. This present section will give the true picture of how the practice of Christianity is encouraged in the Nigerian schools. Islam will also be introduced as another religion that is also taught in the schools in Nigeria. This will be done without much detail because this work is basically a study on Christian religious education.

2.6.1 Christian Religious Studies (CRS)

The term "Christian Religious Studies" (CRS) has been adopted by the "National Council on Education" (NCE) for the study of Christian religion in the primary and secondary schools in Nigeria. This term will be used interchangeably in this work with "Christian Religious Education" (CRE) and "Christian Religious Knowledge (CRK). Under this terminology, there is a deliberate and conscious attempt to inculcate spiritual and moral values into Nigerian children by reference to biblical stories which highlight these spiritual and moral principles.[146] This field of study according to Odiaka concerns itself with the relationship between God and man (humans), the universality of the Christian faith, discipline in the youth, character and moral training and the development of sound attitudes in the pupils. Furthermore, God is presented as the Creator of all mankind, the One who sustains lives and the source of Christian belief, joy, love and hope.[147] The Bible stands as the primary material for the study of Christian religion in Nigeria. Biblical illustrations are used among other things:

144 Cf. Niehl F. W., Sprache / religiöse Sprache, in: Bitter G., Englert R., Miller G., Nipkow K. E. (Hg.), Neues Handbuch religionspädagogischer Grundbegriffe, 2. Auflage, München, 2009, 232.

145 Cf. Ibid.

146 Cf. Quarcoopome T.N.O, Obinna A. J. V., Daudu M., Ilori J. A., Christian Religious Education and Moral Instruction for Junior Secondary Schools I, 3rd Ed., Ibadan, 2005, 5.

147 Odiaka M. O., Garba A. M., Fadeyi Y., Udom M., Basic Primary Christian Religious Knowledge, Pupils' Book 2, Onitsha, 2002, 3.

- To present God to the Nigerian children as well as help them to develop their faith and love in Him,
- To give them an idea of the wonderful works of God before the birth of Jesus Christ,
- To enable the children to know why God sent His only Son, Jesus Christ to us,
- To enable them to accept Christ as friend and Saviour whom we should imitate in our daily lives,
- To enable the children to recognize Jesus as the founder and the one who sustains the Christian Church,
- To encourage them to accept the guidance of the Holy Spirit and to apply it in their daily lives and activities,
- To help them to understand the basic teachings of Christ and to apply it in their daily lives and works,
- To develop in the children good attitudes, Christian virtues and moral values like honesty, humility, respect for others, love, kindness, justice, fairplay, spirit of forgiveness, obedience, devotion to duty, orderly behaviour and life of prayer.[148]

The need for the use of the Bible as the basic source for materials in Christian religious knowledge is to make religious education non-denominational and ecumenical. This is also because of the fact that the Christian teachings are drawn primarily from it. Christ is the centre of the Christian message and He is to be presented as the model for every Christian, especially the children, whom He loves so much. Every Christian denomination uses the Bible to inculcate her teachings. The Bible therefore stands as the principal unifying factor of the Christian religion. Its use in the teaching of Christianity in the schools is mainly to lay emphasis on the oneness and universality of the Gospel of Christ. Denominational or doctrinal teachings are not meant to be handled in the schools but rather in the homes, catechism classes and Sunday schools.[149] This means that they are to be reserved for the various Christian Churches and sects within their communities and parishes.

Christian Religious Knowledge has as a primary objective the contributing to nation building in Nigeria. The Biblical pictures are therefore meant to help the children in their dealings with other citizens at home, in the school and the community as a whole. The application of the Christian teachings in their lives will help them to grow in faith, virtues, good citizenship, character training,

148 Ibid.

149 Cf. Ibid.

a sense of responsibility, a spirit of voluntary service and brotherly/sisterly love.[150] Quarcoopome summarised it thus:

> *The Bible stories are no longer studied for their own sake, but for their relevance to the spiritual and moral development of our country.*[151]

The relevance of Christian religious knowledge in the schools is determined by its translation into the objectives of education in Nigeria. Central to these objectives are unity and national development (nation building). This is why Quarcoopome identified the relevance of Christian religious knowledge to the spiritual and moral principles of Nigeria as:

> *The universal brotherhood of mankind, which is very essential for the unity of Nigeria,*
> *Honesty, which is very vital for the moral integrity and credibility of the individual and our nation,*
> *Loyalty to God and patriotism to our fatherland, which is indispensable for the spiritual and moral growth of our nation,*
> *Hard work, which is highly important for the success of all our spiritual and material endeavours.*[152]

From the spiritual and moral perspectives, the achievement of these goals will identify Christian religious knowledge as one of the most potent instruments for nation building. It will help in creating a disciplined Nigerian society marked with unity, peace, progress and prosperity.

2.6.2 Islamic Studies

Islamic religion is taught in the schools where the population is predominantly Muslim. This is the case in many parts of Northern Nigeria. In this demography, Islam is not only taught in the schools but also in the Mosques and families. Some Mosques are used as Qur'anic schools where some Imams explain the tenets of Islam to their young ones. This is often done in the form of memorizing the Qur'an and reciting the Islamic beads. The sacredness of the Qur'an as the revealed word of Allah through his prophet Muhammad is emphasized.[153]

---

150 Cf. Ibid.

151 Quarcoopome T.N.O., Obinna A. J. V., Daudu M., Ilori J., A Christian Religious Education and Moral Instruction for Junior Secondary Schools 1, 3rd Ed., Ibadan, 2005, 3.

152 Cf. Ibid.

153 Cf. Federal Ministry of Education, 9-Year Basic Education Curriculum, Islamic Studies for Primary 1-3, Lagos, 2007, iv.

The Qur'an guides and governs Muslims in their belief, including social, economic and political affairs.[154] It therefore serves as the first source of book for a Muslim. Its recitation serves as a source of inspiration to Muslims and guarantees their spiritual growth.[155] The Qur'an is also the primary resource book in Islamic religious education. Since this work is based on Christian religious education, attention will now be focused on some new developments in the teaching of the Christian religion in Nigerian schools.

2.7 Current Christian Religious Educational Trends in Nigeria

Christian Religious Education in Nigeria has undergone some transitional processes from the time of its inception to the present day. These processes are due to a series of changes in the educational systems and policies. From the time of the missionaries until the end of the Civil War, Christian religious education in the schools was purely denominational and confessional. The missionaries built their schools and organised an educational system that enhanced the propagation of their religious beliefs and teachings. The Nigerian Government took over these schools in 1970 and introduced a non-confessional religious educational system. This system runs concurrently with the educational policies that have been established for Nigerian education. Under the "Second National Development Plan", Nigeria had a six-five-four system of education. This means: six years in the primary school, five years in the secondary school and four years in the university. For the achievement of this educational system, the "Universal Primary Education" (UPE) programme was introduced by the Federal Government in 1976.

Presently, Nigeria is running a six-three-three-four system of education. To ensure the realization of the objectives of this system, the "Universal Basic Education" (UBE) programme had been introduced by the Federal Government in 1999. The UBE is Nigeria's response to the United Nation's declaration of "Education for All" (EFA) in 1990.[156] This programme (UBE) has as its motto: "Education for all is the responsibility of all".[157] This programme is aimed at providing greater access to, and ensuring the quality of basic education throughout Nigeria. Furthermore; it is set to drastically reduce the rate of

154 Cf. Ibid., iv-v.

155 Cf. Ibid., v.

156 Cf. Universal Basic Education Commission, http://ubeconline.com/index-2.html, 07.11.2012; World Education Forum, The Dakar Framework for Action, Education for All: Meeting our Collective Commitments, Dakar, 2004, 2, http://unesdoc.unesco.org/images/0012/001202/120240e.pdf, 08.10.2012.

157 Universal Basic Education Commission, http://ubeconline.com/index-2.html, 07.11.2012.

school drop-outs by improving the relevance, quality and efficiency of education. Above all, it is to ensure the acquisition of literacy, numeracy, life skills as well as the ethical, moral and civic values needed for lifelong education and useful living. Among these values for lifelong education and useful living is the introduction of the rudiments of computer literacy in the schools.

Religious education has been primarily assigned to ensure the realisation of these values from the ethical, moral as well as civic perspectives. Under this scheme, every Nigerian child of school-going age has been offered an ample opportunity to have an uninterrupted access to a nine-year formal basic (religious) education from the primary school to JSS one. This is called the "Nine-Year Basic (Religious) Education Programme", which is free and compulsory for every Nigerian child. A new curriculum for this programme has been developed by the "Nigerian Educational Research and Development Council" (NERDC) under the direction of the "National Council on Education" (NCE). The need for a new curriculum is to meet the targets of this Nine-Year Basic (Religious) Education Plan in the context of the "National Economic Empowerment and Development Strategies" (NEEDS) and the "Millennium Development Goals" (MDGs).[158] These targets are: "value re-orientation, poverty eradication, job creation, wealth generation and using (religious) education to empower the people".[159] These are contained in the "Compulsory, Free Universal Basic Education Act 2004" of the Federal Government. The key issues in this Act are:

- The Federal Government's intervention shall provide assistance to the States and Local Governments in Nigeria for the purposes of uniform and qualitative education throughout Nigeria.
- Every Government in Nigeria shall provide free, compulsory and universal basic education for every child of primary and junior secondary school age.
- Every parent shall ensure that his/her child or ward attends and completes primary school education and junior secondary school education.
- The stakeholders in education in a Local Government Area shall ensure that every parent or person who has the care and custody of a child performs the duty imposed on him/her under the Universal Basic Education Act, 2004.
- Transition from Primary to Junior Secondary School (JSS) should be automatic; as basic education terminates at the Junior Secondary School level. Thus entrance examination may no longer be necessary. Emphasis should be placed on effective continuous assessment, while final examination and

158 Cf. Federal Ministry of Education, 9-Year Basic Education Curriculum, Christian Religious Studies for Primary 1 – 3, Abuja, 2007, i.

159 Ibid., ii.

certification will now be done at the end of the nine-year basic education programme.

- The Secondary School system shall be restructured so as to ensure that the JSS component is disarticulated from the Senior Secondary School (SSS) as stipulated in the National Policy on Education (NPE).[160]

The presentation of a detailed breakdown of the nine-year basic Christian Religious Education and its curriculum is the goal of this section.

2.7.1 The Nine-Year Basic Christian Religious Education (2007)

The improvement of the quality and standard of (religious) education has remained the primary concern of many Governments in Nigeria. This is seen in the numerous painstaking efforts of many Nigerian Governments in ensuring that (religious) education retains her status as a social process in capacity building and skill acquisition aimed at national development. The newly introduced "Universal Basic Education" (UBE) programme (since 2007) is an example of such efforts. The curriculum designed for this programme especially in Christian Religious Education offers Nigerian children the opportunity of benefiting from Christian religious educational materials that would help them to meet their basic learning needs. This curriculum further helps to bring the benefits of Christian religious education to every Christian Nigerian child within the Nigerian society. It is structured to offer a basic Christian religious educational foundation that would help in guaranteeing the success of the entire Nigerian educational system. The curriculum is further meant to serve as a motivating factor for all involved in the educational sector to contribute towards realizing a sustainable Nigerian society in the future. This curriculum provides basic educational guidelines for the Lower Basic Education (Primary one to three), Middle Basic Education (Primary four to six) and Upper Basic Education (JSS one to three) in the Christian religious perspective.

2.7.1.1 Lower Basic (Religious) Education (Primary One to Three)

Primary one to three form the first block of formal (religious) educational pursuit in Nigeria. This block is expected to be a basic foundation of religious education that can guarantee a functional basic education for the Nigerian child (in line with today's realities) from the first year in the Primary School to the completion of Junior Secondary School. The themes for learning have been carefully selected to suit the learning capacity of the Nigerian child as follows:

160 Universal Basic Education – Free Primary Education, About UBEC, http://ubeconline.com/about_ubec.html, 07.11.2012.

Primary One: God's Goodness; Jesus, My Brother and Friend; God Our Father.

Primary Two: Talk to God through Jesus Christ; The Life of Jesus Christ; God the Creator and Father of All.

Primary Three: God fulfils His Promises; Faith in Jesus Christ my Saviour; Knowing God through our relationship with others.[161]

In Nigeria "primary one" denotes the official first step of formal (religious) education. Although some of the pupils may have attended nursery school or kindergarten, they are said to begin their school years with admission into the primary school at the attainment of 6 years of age. This is because formal learning begins with the attainment of the age of reason which is the sixth year of age. This is also reflected in the curriculum in the sense that learning is designed to be discursive and interactive.

In the religious education curriculum for the lower basic education, three themes are to be learned in each academic year. This is because there are three terms in each school year. Each theme in the curriculum is expected to run throughout a particular term. The teacher is encouraged to further work on these themes and bring them to the level of the understanding of the pupils so that they will be relevant to them in the future. This is why each theme is further broken down into series of sub-topics in the detailed curriculum. In primary one there are eight topics for the first theme, seven for the second and eight for the third. Primary two contains eight topics for the first theme, seven for the second and also seven for the third. The curriculum provides eight topics for the first theme in primary three, nine topics for the second and seven for the third. The curriculum also gives directives about the performance objectives of the pupils, the contents of the theme of learning, the activities for both the teacher and the pupils, the teaching and learning materials that are required and the evaluation guide for the teacher.

2.7.1.2 Middle Basic (Religious) Education (Primary Four to Six)

Primary Four to Six indicates the second block of formal basic (religious) education in Nigeria. It serves as the continuation of the first block and an introduction to the last block which will be undertaken in the junior secondary school. This block also completes the first phase of the child's educational pursuit which is the primary education. In the religious education curriculum the themes for learning do not follow the same pattern as in the first block in the

161 Federal Ministry of Education, 9-Year Basic Education Curriculum, Christian Religious Studies for Primary 1 - 3, Abuja, 2007, vi-vii.

sense that there are only two themes for learning in each academic year. These themes are outlined by the NERDC as follows:

Primary Four: God as Father Guides His Children; Jesus the Way to the Father and Our Guide

Primary Five: God wants to Save All Men; Holy Spirit Working in Us

Primary Six: Paul the Apostle; Nigerian Christian Leaders and Leadership.[162]

These themes are to be handled holistically from the first to the third term by the teacher. In the detailed curriculum, they are divided into sub-topics in order to give room for proper specification in the course of the three terms which form each academic year. As in the first block, the curriculum specifies the performance objectives of the pupils, the contents of the themes, the activities for the teacher and the pupils, the teaching and learning materials that are required and the evaluation guide for the teacher. The first theme in primary four is divided into five topics while the second is divided into six. In primary five there are six topics for both the first theme and the second. Primary six contains five topics for the first theme and nine for the second.

2.7.1.3 Upper Basic (Religious) Education (JSS One to Three)

The Junior Secondary School is the beginning of the second phase of formal (religious) educational pursuit and the completion of the nine-year basic (religious) education programme in Nigeria. From Primary One to this level of learning, there is a continuous assessment of the pupils' performance. Under this system the usual common entrance examination that characterised the transition from the primary school into the secondary school has been proscribed. This is to give the pupils an uninterrupted access to the benefits of the current nine-year basic (religious) education programme. According to the Universal Basic Education Act 2004 of the Federal Government:

> *The transition from Primary School to Junior Secondary School (JSS) should be automatic; as basic education terminates at the Junior Secondary level thus an entrance examination may no longer be necessary. Emphasis will be placed on effective continuous assessment, while the final examination and certification will now be done at the end of the nine-year basic education programme.*[163]

162 Federal Ministry of Education, 9-Year Basic Education Curriculum, Christian Religious Studies for Primary 4 - 6, Abuja, 2007, vi-vii.

163 Universal Basic Education – Free Primary Education, About UBEC, , http://ubeconline.com/about_ubec.html, 07.11.2012.

The continuous assessment will later be used as the major criteria for promotion into the Senior Secondary School (SSS). The religious education curriculum follows the same pattern as in the lower basic education by providing three themes of learning for each academic year so that each theme can be handled in each of the three terms respectively. It also stipulates the performance objectives for the pupils, the contents of the themes, the activities for the teacher and the pupils, the necessary teaching and learning materials and the evaluation guide. These themes are outlined as follows:

Junior Secondary One (JS ONE): God and His Creation; Relationship with God and Man; God's Call.

Junior Secondary Two (JS TWO): The Early Life of Jesus Christ; The Ministry of Jesus Christ; The Passion, Death and the Resurrection of Jesus

Junior Secondary Three (JS THREE): The Beginning of the Church; The Life and Teaching of Paul; The Christian Church Today.[164]

As in the previous two curricula, the curriculum for JSS One to Three forms the conclusive block of the curriculum for the nine-year basic religious education programme. The themes are also divided into sub-topics as in the curricula for the lower classes. The first theme in JSS One is divided into five topics while the second and the third are divided into four respectively. In JSS Two there are five topics for the first and second themes, and four topics for the third. The three themes in JSS Three are divided into four topics each so that these themes can be properly explained to the pupils for their adequate understanding of them.

2.7.2 Senior Secondary (Religious) Education (SSS One to Three)

The Senior Secondary School (SSS) is the second phase of secondary education in Nigeria. It is a three-year educational programme which completes secondary education and prepares the students for various careers or further educational pursuit in the university and other tertiary institutions. A student must complete the nine-year basic education (Primary One to Junior Secondary School) before being admitted into the Senior Secondary School. Although the Senior Secondary School is not part of the current "Universal Basic Education" (UBE), its religious education curriculum contains a "repetition of some Old Testament and New Testament passages already covered in the Junior Secondary School."[165] This is to enable the students to have a better under-

164 Federal Ministry of Education, 9-Year Basic Education Curriculum, Christian Religious Studies for Junior Secondary 1 - 3, Abuja, 2007, vi – vii.

165 Federal Ministry of Education, Senior Secondary School Curriculum, Christian Religious Studies for SS 1-3, Abuja, 2010, ii – iii.

standing better when the same ideas are presented to them at higher levels of learning.[166] There are 16 themes for learning in SS One and SS Two respectively while twelve themes are to be learned in SS Three. This is completely different from the nine-year basic education curriculum. The reason for this change is "based on the belief that students are now staying in school longer than before."[167]

These themes are:

SSS One:

1. Jesus' teaching about Himself
2. Love
3. Justification
4. New life in Christ
5. Son-ship
6. Faith and works
7. Fruit of the Spirit
8. Spiritual gifts
9. Forgiveness
10. The family
11. Humility
12. Effectiveness of prayer
13. Christian living in the community
14. The Christian and persecution
15. Impartiality
16. The resurrection and the second coming of Christ[168]

SSS Two:

1. The sovereignty of God (as manifested in the creation stories)
2. The leadership of Moses, Joshua, Joseph and Deborah
3. God's care for His people
4. Parental responsibility
5. The consequences of obedience and disobedience
6. Forgiveness
7. Friendship
8. Submission to the will of God
9. Making decisions as a Christian

166 Cf. Ibid., iii.

167 Ibid.

168 Ibid.

10. Greed and its effects
11. The supremacy of God
12. Religious and personal reforms
13. Concern for one's nation
14. Faith in God
15. True religion and social justice (from Amos)
16. Divine love (from Hosea)[169]

SSS Three:
1. Baptism and temptation
2. Call to discipleship
3. Mission of the Apostles
4. The trial, death and resurrection of Jesus (all from the synoptic Gospels)
5. Communion and fellowship
6. The Holy Spirit and mission to the Gentiles
7. Stories of opposition to the Gospel (all from Acts of the Apostles)
8. Civic responsibility
9. HIV/AIDS
10. Skill acquisition and empowerment
11. Dignity of human labour
12. Dignity of human life (contemporary issues)[170]

These themes are selected from the Old and New Testaments of the Bible. This is because the Bible is the basic source of material for instructions in Christian religious studies.[171] In the detailed curriculum, these themes are broken down into topics to enhance a deeper understanding of the students and a thorough teaching by the teacher. The curriculum further contains guidelines on the performance objectives, Biblical references for further reading, activities of the teacher and the students, teaching and the necessary learning materials as well as an evaluation guide.

2.8 Evaluation

The attainment of Nigeria to the status of a united and strong Nation has remained a mirage. The inclination of many Nigerians towards ethnicity, religion and culture has made the goals of the Federation unrealizable. This is because

169 Ibid., iii – iv.

170 Ibid., iv.

171 Cf. Ibid., ii.

the idea of having an assembled country known as Nigeria originated from the British colonial administration. Before this time, the people who presently make up the Nigerian Nation lived as independent separate people with different ideological principles and beliefs. They did not intend to be identified as one political entity. They were only invited and compelled to participate in the creation of Nigeria for the benefit of colonialism. This is why Nigeria remains an unrealistic country. It was only fabricated and moulded to suit the administrative pattern of the British. It is now left for the people called "Nigerians" to decide whether to correct this mistake or to retain it. In this view a National Conference is necessary. Such a Conference has to be guided by honesty, probity, accountability and the spirit of Nationalism. Such a Conference should provide an atmosphere of reflection, to decide on the bond of unity or to declare a state of "to your tents O Israel!" (1 Kings 12:16). The struggle for supremacy after Independence led to the Civil War and later to marginalization which makes some Nigerians feel alienated in their own country. The youth find it very difficult to integrate themselves into the various streams of the Nigerian economy. This is why even after their graduation from the University and/or other institutes of studies, some of them remain jobless and are the prey of many politicians who use them to achieve some of their evil plots.

So far many laudable programmes have been drawn up for the youth in the many series of National Development Plans since the end of the Civil War. The National Youth Service Corp has remained pivotal among them. The realization of its goals however has remained a thing of the future. The cases of many Nigerian Youth Corp members killed in religious riots in the North have ignited the demand for the closure of the programme. For many Nigerians it is against the goals of the NYSC that a Nigerian youth could lose his or her life while serving the country just because he or she belongs to a particular religion or tribe. As a result of this development some Nigerians have advocated for the posting of National Corp members within their state of origin to avoid further loss of life.

The educational sector has also remained worrisome. Fifty-three years after independence from Britain, Nigeria has remained in the process of experimentation in the development of a standard religious educational school system worthy of enhancing nation building. Very praise-worthy religious educational policies and principles have been seen in her development plans but their proper implementation has remained questionable. The six-five-four system of the second National Development Plan and Universal Primary Education did not yield the expected results especially in the field of religious education. They produced many school drop-outs in the sense that many Nigerians stopped their educational pursuit at the secondary school level. Some even left the school system after the primary education while others discontinued at various levels of the secondary school. This situation leaves much to be admired. The current six-three-three-four system has come with its flaws. The automatic promotion from the primary to the secondary school and the abrogation of the Common Entrance Examination under Universal Basic Education is a thing of worry to many Nigerian elites. It does not provide for a proper evaluation of the pupils' performances in religious studies since the primary and the secondary schools are two different levels of academic pursuit. An examination at the end of primary education (as was the case under the six-five-four system) would have provided a better assessment of the pupils and guaranteed their promotion to the secondary school for further religious studies.

Christian religious knowledge in the primary and secondary schools is based more on the history of Christianity than the denominational teaching of the Christian faith. Its curriculum is designed to promote Christian unity and not denominationalism. Biblical references are used mainly to illustrate this unity as the basic teaching of Christianity. Denominational religious education is assigned to the various Christian Churches in their own environments and schools. These Churches can build denominational schools in which emphasis can be laid on the propagation of their denominational practices. The teaching of denominational religious education will be treated in chapter four under family and parish catechesis.

2.9 Summary

Nigeria is in West Africa and has a total population of more than one hundred and forty-eight million people. Three significant events – the Amalgamation, Independence and the Civil War – shaped Nigerian history. These gave Nigeria its present circumstances for they sowed the seeds of nepotism, ethnocentrism, religious conflicts and political rivalries. After the attainment of independence, ethnic interests gave rise to the neglect of "the provision for the various skills and competences needed for the building and development of a modern society".[172] Among these skills and competences are the development of science and technology, agricultural facilities and education. The foundation of these skills and competences was laid by the colonial administration through the establishment of Western education but was not enhanced by the pro-independence administration. As a result, education lost its position in the development of the people and religious education was replaced by religious conflicts and rivalries.

172 Eluwa G. I. C., Ukagwu M. O., Nwachukwu J. U. N., Nwaubani A. C. N., A History of Nigeria, For Schools and Colleges, Onitsha, 2005, 228.

Religious education in Nigeria was developed according to Western standard by the missionaries in the nineteenth century through the establishment of schools in which the teaching of Christianity was propagated using the confessional system of education. The Nigerian Government took over these schools after the Civil War in 1970 and introduced a non-confessional or non-denominational religious education. Though the Nigerian school system has undergone a series of changes, religious education has been included in the school curriculum in order to contribute towards nation building and the realization of African religious identity. The current religious education system in the country has been designed to offer the Nigerian pupils an uninterrupted nine-year acquisition of basic religious education in the primary and secondary schools which will guarantee "values of lifelong education and useful living".[173] Such a religious education has an orientation towards humanity and is realized in the nature of the human person, in his knowledge and in his expression of emotion.

The primary school introduces one into the field of formal education in the Western sense. It lays the foundation of academic pursuance. In Nigeria, it is used to denote the acquisition of basic education which gives room for further levels of learning. Without the acquisition of primary education, no further level of academics can be pursued. As such, its importance cannot be underestimated.

The secondary school forms the second level for the acquisition of basic education. It solidifies the educational foundation laid in the primary school by placing the students at a higher level of educational pursuance. Above all, it prepares students for university education and as such is a connection between the foundation of education in the primary school and graduation into professionalism in the university. The secondary school also provides the necessary knowledge required for self-employment and the acquisition of some skills.

173 Universal Basic Education – Free Primary Education, http://ubeconline.com/about_ubec.html, 07.11.2012.

3. Germany: Cultural and Historical Contexts for Religious Education

The aim of this chapter is to present Germany as a (Christian) country which encourages religious education in the schools. This will be undertaken in seven steps. The first step will be a brief description of Germany. The second step will be an attempt to give a short historical background of the country. This will be followed in the third step with the history of religious education in the country especially between 1945 and 1990. The fourth step will be an analysis of the concepts which emphasize the teaching of religion in the schools. This will lead to the fifth step which will be the presentation of the various religions and denominations that exist in Germany. The types of schools in Germany will be discussed in the sixth step as one of the places where religious education takes place. The religious education curriculum that will be discussed in this chapter is that of the state of Bavaria which controls the schools in the archdiocese of Munich and Freising. The presentation of a detailed content of religious teaching in the various classes of these schools will be the major concern of the seventh step which will then be followed by an evaluation and a summary of the chapter.

3.1 Brief Description of Germany

In this section, Germany will be described with regards to its location, vegetation, ethnicity, population and languages. This will help in determining its landmass and climatic conditions. Under ethnicity and population, the type of "people" dwelling in Germany will be discussed in relation to their multicultural backgrounds. This will give rise to a multi-nationalistic and religious situation where people of different beliefs and understandings come together in a co-habitational situation. The fact that the people currently living in Germany come from different nationalities means that they also have different linguistic backgrounds. The description of these languages will form the last part of this section.

3.1.1 Location of Germany

Germany is a Central European country sharing borders with nine neighbouring countries. It is officially addressed and known as "The Federal Republic of Germany". It has a total of sixteen states and lies between latitudes 47° N and

55° N and longitudes 5° E and 16° E. The country covers an area of 357,042 square kilometres.[1] It "is made up of the North German Plain, the Central German Uplands (Mittelgebirge), and the Southern German Highlands".[2] The Bavarian elevations have an average height of 1,600 feet or 488 metres above sea level and 9,721 feet or 2,962 metres in the Zugspitze Mountains which is the highest point in the country.[3] The capital is Berlin which is also a state and the largest city of the country with the highest population density. It is estimated that about 3.41 million people live in Berlin.[4] Munich which is the third largest city after Hamburg as well as the area of this study has a total population of about 1.31 million people.[5]

"Germany is bordered on the North by the Baltic Sea and Denmark, on the East by Poland and the Czech Republic, on the Southeast by Austria, on the Southwest by Switzerland and France; and on the West by Luxemburg, Belgium and the Netherlands".[6] Among the prominent features in Germany are these rivers: the Danube, the Elbe, the Oder, the Weser and the Rhine.

3.1.2 Vegetation of Germany

Germany has different types of terrain. The North is low while the Centre and the East are high. The South is mountainous and constitutes the highest elevated parts of the country. Like most countries of the West, Germany has a total of four seasons namely: spring (March – May), summer (June – August), autumn (September – November), and winter (December – February). The temperature is humid and often falls below the freezing point in winter and rises above 30°C in summer. Some of its natural resources are: coal, lignite, salt, natural gas, and iron ore. Germany also produces many agricultural products such as: potatoes, sugar beets, wheat, barley and grapes.[7]

1 Cf. Schwachulla, W. (Red.), Der Brockhaus in einem Band, Leipzig, 1998, 193.

2 Germany: History, Geography, Government, and Culture, - Infoplease.com, http//www.infoplaese.com/ipa/A0107568.html, 25.07.2011.

3 Cf. Germany: History, Geography, Government, and Culture – Infoplease.com, http//www.infoplease.com/ipa/A0107568.html, 25.07.2011.

4 Cf. Germany, http://www.state.gov/r/pa/ei/bgn/3997.htm, 24.08.2011.

5 Cf. Ibid.

6 Conzemius V., Germany, the Catholic Church in, in: Carson T., Cerrito J. (Eds.), New Catholic Encyclopedia, 2nd. Ed. Vol. 6, Detroit, 2003, 171.

7 Cf. Ibid.

3.1.3 Ethnicity and Population of Germany

Germany is made up of people of different ethnic groups which represent some nationalities whose people are either native to Germany, naturalised citizens of Germany or are temporarily residing there. These are:

Germans – making up about 91.5% of the entire population,

Turkish – representing about 2.4% of the German population,

Others – standing for about 6.1% of the population (This group is made up largely of other nationalities that are naturalised citizens of Germany through migration or birth).[8]

These groups make up the overall German population which according the United Nations is about more than 82 million people.[9] A good percentage of Germans live in affluence. This explains why their life expectancy is 77.2 years for men and 82.4 years for women.[10] This life of affluence plays a negative role in the religious life of the people especially the youth. Some of them do not see the need to go to Church or even to pray since all their needs have already been met. Most of them rely on their ability to work and earn their living and live a life that is devoid of religion.

3.1.4 Languages in Germany

The people in Germany speak a variety of languages. Each state and province has its own different dialect and also often, these dialects are completely different from one another. The official language is German and most of the people living in Germany use it as their first language for interaction, business and especially education. Other popularly spoken languages are: English, which is also taught in the schools as the second official language; Sorbian; North Frisian; Danish; Romani; Kurdish and Turkish.

- The German language as spoken today is a mixture of various dialects, culled from central, southern and northern districts. The Germans often speak the standard language with the accent that is typical of their native districts.
- The Danish language is mostly spoken in the Northern parts of Germany. Though spoken mainly in Denmark, it is also the tongue of many people

8 Cf. Germany, http://www.state.gov/r/pa/ei/bgn/3997.htm, 24.08.2011.

9 Cf. United Nations, World Population Prospects, the 2010 Revision, http//esa.un.org/unpd/wpp/Sorting-Tables/tab-sorting_population.htm, 29.08.2011.

10 Cf. United Nations, World Population Prospects, the 2010 Revision, http//esa.un.org/unpd/wpp/Sorting-Tables/tab-sorting_mortality.htm, 29.08.2011.

living in Schleswig Holstein. Also, it is one of the official languages of the European Union.
- The North Frisian language, spoken by the minority in North Frisia, has two dialectical divisions – the dialect of the mainland and the dialect of the insular districts.
- More than two million Turkish-speaking people live in Germany. The Turkish language is the native language of the Turks and has been carried to Germany by the immigrants.
- Kurdish language is an Iranian language and belongs to a place called Kurdistan. There are only a few people in Germany who speak this language.
- The Sorbian language is the native language of the Sorbs. There are again two varieties of Sorbian language: the Upper Sorbian and the Lower Sorbian. The people in Saxony mostly speak the Upper Sorbian.
- Romani is often referred to as the language of the Gypsies and consequently the speakers of this language are widespread and stateless. There are a very few people in Germany belonging to this tribe who use this language.[11]

3.2 Brief Historical Background of Germany

In around the year 1512 Germany existed as the "Holy Roman Empire of the German Nation".[12] It was then made up of "hundreds of petty principalities, free cities, and ecclesiastical and aristocratic states".[13] At this time it was still very far from being a formidable empire. It existed as a quiet pastoral enclave which had not yet been transformed into the highly industrialised nation that it had to become in the modern times. It was, according to Kitchen, "in a state of steady decline and was impervious to reform".[14] In his further description of the empire, Kitchen said:

> *It (the empire) was a threadbare patchwork of innumerable political entities from the European states of Austria and Prussia to the fiefdoms of the imperial knights, imperial monasteries, independent towns, and even villages.*[15]

---

11 Cf. Languages in Germany, Languages spoken in Germany, http//www.asiarooms.com/en/travel-guide/germany/-culture-of-germany/languages-in-germany.html, 30.08.2011.

12 Kitchen M., A History of Modern Germany 1800-2000, Malden, 2006, 1.

13 Ibid.

14 Ibid.

15 Ibid., 9.

That was why the empire was overrun by the armies of revolutionary France and was reorganised under Napoleon. Its political geography also underwent a series of transformations. Napoleon created the Confederation of the Rhine after the French seizure of all the territory on the left bank of the Rhine thereby enhancing Bavaria, Württemberg and Baden. This seizure resulted to the redrawing of the map of Germany and the secularization of the territorial possessions of the Catholic Church in 1803.[16] That is why Napoleon is regarded as one of the makers of modern political Germany and one of the destroyers of religious Germany especially by the Catholic Church.[17] The Holy Roman Empire of the German Nation collapsed in 1806 and gave rise to the reorganisation of the southern German states into the Confederation of the Rhine.[18]

This development had a devastating effect on the teaching and practice of religion especially for the Catholic Church. The attention of young people was no longer focused on religion but on the fighting of the Napoleonic wars. For instance, Napoleon forced the Confederation of the Rhine to provide him with 19,000 soldiers in 1808 to aid him in his war against the British.[19] These soldiers were made up of young German people whose life priorities had been diverted from those of religious practices to those of war combats. Also about one third of the 600,000 men in Napoleon's *Grande Armee* that fought against Russia in 1812 were Germans.[20] At this time, the Confederation was under the occupation of France and rigorous censorship was applied to the minutest details.[21] Religious or Church activities were neglected and many young people were recruited into the army. The schools were not encouraged to concentrate on the teaching of religion but on other secular subjects which tended to undermine the confidence of the Church.

The formation of the Confederation of the Rhine gave rise to the unification of most German States in 1871.[22] This new German empire turned out to be a secular state having no specific denominational affiliation despite the fact that the majority of the ruling elite were Protestants.[23] As a result, religious education at this time was more secular than denominational.[24] After the Ger-

16 Cf. Ibid., 9.

17 Cf. Carr W., A History of Germany, 2nd Ed., London, 1979, viii.

18 Cf. Kitchen M., A History of Modern Germany 1800-2000, Malden, 2006, 10.

19 Cf. Ibid., 11.

20 Cf. Ibid., 24.

21 Cf. Ibid., 11.

22 Cf. Ibid., 1.

23 Cf. Ibid., 140.

24 Cf. Ibid.

man revolution of 1918, the new empire came to an end and was replaced by the Weimar Republic which lasted till 1933. Between 1933 and 1945 Germany witnessed the greatest period of turmoil in its history. It was characterised by the Nazi dictatorship which culminated in the Second World War. During this period religious education was seriously suppressed as the Church could find no appropriate place of worship and could not talk about giving catechetical instructions to the young people due to the tense war situation. Secondly religious education found itself in a state of derision not only because priority was given to loyalty to the Nazi Regime, but also to survival and safety. All this however was to change after 1945 with the collapse of the Nazi Dictatorship and the end of the Second World War.

The end of the Second World War saw the division of Germany into two separate sovereign states: East Germany and West Germany respectively. At this time Germany was a pile of rubble with a starving population. The East German economy remained hopelessly stagnant and could not sustain the demands of the people. They were subjected to dictatorship, censorship, snooping and repression.[25] On the other hand, the economy of West Germany grew at an astonishing rate. This success was attributed to the determined efforts of the Western Germans to develop a parliamentary democracy and a liberal market economy.[26] These situations in the two German nations resulted from their unequal efforts to recuperate from the effects of the Second World War. The rate of development between them remained at a "yawning gap" because West Germany was made up of a generation of people determined to start anew while East Germany was mismanaged and virtually bankrupt by the early 1980s.[27] With the looming signs of the collapse of the Soviet Union in the mid-1980s, the regime of the East German Democratic Republic eventually crumbled and gave rise to the first free election after 57 years. In the mid 1980s also, the two independent nations started making moves towards a re-unification. This re-unification was achieved on November 9th 1989, but because of past events associated with this date such as, the proclamation of the Weimer Republic on November 9th 1919 and the Hitler putsch in Munich on November 9th 1923, this date could not be adopted as the national day.[28] The unification treaty was formally signed into law on August 31st 1990 with October 3rd set aside as the

25 Cf. Ibid., 5.

26 Cf. Ibid.

27 Cf. Ibid.

28 Cf. Ibid., 385.

German national day.[29] Thus on October 3rd 1990 the two German countries came together under the Federal Republic of Germany.

3.3 Brief History of Religious Education in Germany (1945-1990)

After the Second World War, East Germany remained under the occupation of the Soviet Union and was known as the German Democratic Republic. Christian doctrine was for decades the Church's substitute for professional religious education in the school.[30] This came to be the case because religious education was not allowed in the schools by the socialist Government which introduced ethics in place of religious education. This abrogation of religious teaching in the schools resulted in a non-integration into the life of the Church for most people in East Germany. Emphasis was laid on obedience to the state and not to God. As a result of this socialist influence, most East Germans became atheists and had no resolve to convert to any religion. In West Germany, where the reverse was the case, religious education was understood as the "Church event in the school".[31] It was designed in line with catechetical instruction and was aimed at the proclamation of the Gospel in the schools. Biblical instruction developed as a school subject in the late 1950s in which the cultural heritage of Christianity was emphasised through catechetical instructions.[32] This was introduced into religious education under the term "hermeneutic religious education". The central role of the education and training of young people in the schools was at this time transferred to the Churches as the moral authorities. The Churches in question are the Catholic Church and the Evangelical (Protestant) Church.

The Protestant or Evangelical Church[33] made some attempts to design religious education in the light of the revelation of God in Jesus Christ. The Bible was used as the dominant document of God's self revelation, which was written under the inspiration of the Holy Spirit. The Christian faith was made accessible to children and adolescents exclusively through biblical lessons. Christian teaching was at this time the epitome of the catechetical mission of

29 Cf. Ibid., 395.

30 Cf. Mette N., Rickers F., Religionspädagogik/Katechetik, in: Eicher P. (Hg.), Neues Handbuch theologischer Grundbegriffe, Band 4, München, 2005, 55.

31 Cf. Ibid.

32 Cf. Ibid.

33 In Germany, every Christian denominational Church, outside of the Catholic Church, is referred to as an Evangelical Church.

the Protestant Church. This claimed also to be the aim of all the fields of her educational work.[34]

The Catholic Church prepared the contents of religious education in such a way that they were oriented to the pupils, who in turn would be encouraged to make personal decisions of faith. As a result, a widely accepted fundamental clarification for religious education in the schools, which has remained valid until the present time, was achieved in the decision of the joint Synod of the Catholic Dioceses of the Federal Republic of (Western) Germany (1971-1974) under the heading "Religious Instruction in the Schools".[35] This decision proceeded consistently from the existential, social and ecclesial situation, developed a plausible and convergent argument for religious and theological education in the schools as well as outlined a realistic goal and task-oriented spectrum for these two subjects. It further articulates a comprehensive understanding of religious education that would address the previously developed school models and at the same time integrate itself with these models in a critical larger context.[36] The central themes contained in this decision can be summarised under five headings: discussion on the concept of kerygmatic religious education; discussion on the hermeneutic concept of religious education; discussion on the didactic concept of religious education; discussion on the problem-oriented religious education; and discussion on the socialization of religious education.[37] These concepts will now be articulated for a better understanding of their roles in religious education.

3.4 Religions/Denominations in Germany

Germany is known as a heterogeneous religious society. This is seen in the number of religions which peacefully co-exist among the people. From the ancient times, the people who occupy the present German demography used to worship a number of gods that existed in an anthropomorphic form.[38] The New Catholic Encyclopedia summarised it thus:

Although there was no uniform cult among the various (*German*) tribes, many of the same deities seem to have been known to all tribes. The central

34 Cf. Mette N., Rickers F., Religionspädagogik/Katechetik, in: Eicher P. (Hg.), Neues Handbuch theologischer Grundbegriffe, Band 4, München, 2005, 55.

35 Cf. Ibid., 57.

36 Cf. Hilger G., Leimbruber S., Ziebertz H. G., Religionsdidaktik, Ein Leitfaden für Studium, Ausbildung und Beruf, München, 2010, 58.

37 Cf. Ibid.

38 Cf. Selmer C., Germanic Religion, in: Carson T., Cerrito J. (Eds.), New Catholic Encyclopedia 2nd. Ed., Vol. 6, Detroit, 2003, 169.

figure of the cult, taking the highest place among all gods, was Wodan, the All-Father, (*and*) the Scandinavian Odin. Another important deity was Tiu or Ziu …, the Nordic Týr. Next to these male deities was Freya, Wodan's wife, the Scandinavian Frigga. The names Tiu, Wodan, Thor, and Freya are preserved in our days of the week: Tuesday, Wednesday, Thursday, and Friday.[39]

These deities were worshipped through prayers and the offering of sacrifices using fruits, animals and even human beings. Worship sessions were carried out in the open air in the forests and grooves. It was only with the later influence of the Romans that they were organised in houses and temples. The people believed in the magical power of nature and the spirits of the dead. Some natural elements which were perceived to be above human understanding were personified and worshipped as deities.[40] This natural religion was wiped out with the establishment of the Holy Roman Empire which introduced Christianity. This was the case especially in the old Roman cities such as Trier. By the end of the 3rd Century there were Bishops in this imperial city. Bishops were assigned to Cologne by the beginning of the 4th Century.[41]

3.4.1 Christianity

Christianity in Germany is recognised under two denominations: Roman Catholicism and Protestantism. The Catholics and the Protestants make up more than 34% of the entire population respectively.[42] Under the Protestants are the Lutheran Church, the Anglican Church, the Baptist Church, the Methodist Church and the free Pentecostal Churches. The two denominations (Catholicism and Protestantism) join efforts to expound the Christian teaching and by so doing contribute towards the building of the German nation.

3.4.2 Other Religions

Later religions include: *Judaism, Islam, Hinduism* and *Buddhism*. Islam is the second largest religion in Germany after Christianity. Its membership amounts to about 3.7% of the entire population.[43] It gained entrance into Germany after the Second World War through Turkish immigrants. Adherents of the Buddhist religion and Judaism make up about 0.3% of the German population respec-

39 Ibid.

40 Cf. Ibid.

41 Cf. Conzemius V., Germany, the Catholic Church in, in: Carson T., Cerrito J. (Eds.), New Catholic Encyclopedia, 2nd. Ed. Vol. 6, Detroit, 2003, 171.

42 Cf. Germany, http://www.state.gov/r/pa/ei/bgn/3997.htm, 24.08.2011.

43 Cf. Ibid.

tively. Hinduism has a membership that accounts for about 0.1% of the population. Germans with no stated religious affiliation make up about 34% of the population. This figure is attributed mainly to the former East Germans who were forbidden from any religious practice under the Communist Government.

3.5 Concepts of Religious Education in Germany

The concepts of religious education in Germany form the basis for the teaching of religion in the schools, especially from a Catholic background. They are the underlying principles for the development of the religious education curriculum. Their description here is meant to present the goal of religious education as forming the pupils into holistic individuals who can be properly integrated into the various sectors of the society.

3.5.1 Kerygmatic Concept of Religious Education

Under the discussion on the concept of *kerygmatic* religious education, the Synod ruled out the notion of religious education as catechesis in the schools.[44] This is because religious education is meant to be meaningful to both the believing and non-believing students. The situation of the teacher is especially taken into consideration here so that he or she may not have any difficulty while trying to explain the teaching of the Church of which he or she may not have sufficient knowledge. Hence there is need for a clear distinction between religious education in the school and catechetical instruction in the Church or Christian community. That was why the Synod out-rightly rejected the idea that religious education is "Church in the school".[45] With this stand, the Church or Christian community was requested to strengthen its catechetical efforts. However the Synod acknowledged the fact that religious education familiarises itself with the Christian faith and as such makes use of some kerygmatic materials. This applies in the formulation that religious education needs to understand the faith of the Church in its entirety. In this instance the religious education teacher should be ready to personalize the cause of the Gospel since much depends on him or her for a worthy witness to the Christian faith.[46]

44 Cf. Ibid.

45 Cf. Ibid.

46 Cf. Ibid., 58-59.

3.5.2 Hermeneutic Concept of Religious Education

On the discussion of *hermeneutic* religious education, the Synod expressed its conviction that religion and theology are very important in the understanding of the Scriptures and their fulfilment in the life and faith of the Church.[47] The reference to Scripture is not meant to suppress the hermeneutic problem of religious education. This problem is the "ugly ditch" existing between the Biblical Texts and the contemporary religious situation.[48] In this instance, there is the obligation to persistently question the meaning of past teachings and how these teachings are meant to be understood in the present times due to some social changes that have taken place in the course of history. From the hermeneutic point of view, the Synod made some efforts to classify religious education as a regular subject in the school.[49] This is based on the fact that religious education in the (public) school is clearly detached from religious instructions in the Church or Christian community. Religious education and religious instruction are therefore seen as two separate exercises having the common goal of the religious upbringing of the child. Religious education promotes, concretizes and supplements this goal in the school while religious instruction does the same function in the Church or Christian community.

3.5.3 Catechetical Didactic Concept of Religious Education

This concept is a move to use religious education as a means of passing religious information to the pupils irrespective of their religious status. This concept has also served as a source of useful suggestions for the reform of religious education. Under this concept religious education has been made open to all regardless of the fact that they are committed Christians or convinced atheists. This corresponds to the differentiation between the use of religious education as a means of transmitting the Christian faith and that of gaining knowledge. Hence the believing and searching pupils as well as those having doubts abouttheir faith and as such regard themselves as unbelievers can receive religious education not for the purpose of conversion or deepening of their faith but simply for the purpose of widening their religious horizon. Thus a non-Christian can be informed about Christianity without being involved in Christian practices and vice versa. That is why the Synod suggests that reli-

47 Cf. Ibid., 59.

48 Cf. Ibid.

49 Cf. Ibid.

gious education should be designed in such a way that all the three groups in this typology will find it useful and meaningful.[50]

A certain proximity to the realization of the didactic concept of religious education shows itself in the fact that the Synod distanced itself from any form of religious education which is aimed at conversion or manipulation of the pupils.[51] The Synod rather opted for a religious education that will promote the ability of the pupils to make a personal decision especially in matters concerning "religious inclination, worldviews and ideologies as well as understanding and respecting the decision of others".[52] This will create room for a self judgement and personal conviction in a broad concept of religious education. In this sense religious education is understood as a transcendental means of knowledge and enhancement of worldviews. Personal experience and disposition are to be taken into consideration in religious education. However it must be observed that religious education is not just meant to serve as a means of information but more to consolidate the faith of the Christian pupils in the school. The didactic concept is not to displace the main goal of religious education which is the teaching and practice of the Christian faith. That is why religious education has to embrace some confessional elements contained in theology as a means of deepening the faith of the pupils. Purely informative religious education therefore must be rejected.

3.5.4 Problem-Oriented Religious Education

With regard to the *problem-oriented* religious education, the Synod made some references to some situations of intense difficulty in religious education. This is particularly seen in the problem of where religious education should take place because of some educational and theological reasons, the duty of the school and the mission of the Church.[53] The co-operation of the school and the Church in the religious upbringing of the child is taken into consideration here. If religious education is limited to the school, then the confessional aspect of it is taken for granted and if only in the Church, then the non-believing pupils will not benefit from it. There is then the need to strike a balance owing to the correlation principle of the Synod that "faith is to be practiced in the context of life" and that "life is to be understood in the context of faith".[54] This principle indicates that faith and life experience are to be handled simultaneously in re-

50 Cf. Ibid.

51 Cf. Ibid.

52 Ibid.

53 Cf. Ibid., 60.

54 Ibid.

ligious education. That is why the school and the Church are to be recognised as official places of religious education.

3.5.5 Correlative Concept of Religious Education

The *correlative* principle raises another problematic situation in religious education in which the systematic teaching material no longer plays the major role but the life situation and faith of the pupils does. That is why their questions, problems and experiences form an "indispensable criterion for the selection of the objectives and contents" of religious education.[55] This change of perspective is underpinned by an anthropological theology for which a basic understanding of human phenomena has become a central concern of theological categories.[56] This change as well binds religious education to other sciences such as philosophy, history, sociology and psychology and as such gives religious education an interdisciplinary connotation.[57] This interdisciplinary aspect of religious education is seen in the fact that religion can be studied in relation to other disciplines.

3.5.6 Socialization Concept of Religious Education

The *socialization* concept of religious education is realized in the establishment of the goal of religious education which is to strengthen the pupils as well as motivate them to identify with the society.[58] Under this concept, religious education is used as a means of social learning. In terms of proximity to this concept, the Church has to carry out her mission in such a way that through her participation in religious education the socio-critical and humanising impulses of the Gospel can be made available to the understanding of the pupils for their subsequent use in the society. That is why the Synod established the task of religious instruction as the basic function of the Church which is to be realised in the pastoral dimension of her mission.[59]

Religious education in Germany has experienced a series of changes due to political and social instabilities as well as developments. These changes were marked by the development of religious educational concepts especially in the early 1970s.[60] With the publication of the decision of the German Bishops'

55 Cf. Ibid.

56 Cf. Ibid.

57 Cf. Ibid.

58 Cf. Ibid.

59 Cf. Ibid.

60 Cf. Ibid., 61.

Synod of 1974 under the theme, "Religious Instruction in the School", the era of concepts with regard to religious educational curriculum came to an end. This was replaced with didactic principles of religious education. Some of these principles include: fundamental or elementary principle, children's theology and performative religious education.[61] These principles have made important contributions in the development of religious education in the schools. They penetrate deep into the understanding of school systems and influence the decision making in the classification of the goal, content and method of religious education. The development and implementation of these principles have been currently assigned to the regions so as to meet up with the needs of a variety of targets due to the complicated differences existing among the regions.[62] The era of unification of religious education based on concepts has been phased out so that each region can develop its own workable religious educational principles that will serve the needs of the area. This system has so far worked out well taking cognisance of differences in weather, climate and culture.

Munich and Freising which are the areas of this study are located in Bavaria and as such make use of the Bavarian religious educational system. This system will be discussed in sub-section seven of this chapter. The different religions and religious denominations in Germany will now be handled.

3.6 Schools in Germany

Five categories of schools exist in Germany namely: the Primary School (*Grundschule*), the Grammar School (*Gymnasium*), the Intermediate Secondary School (*Realschule*), the General Secondary School (*Hauptschule*) and the Vocational School (*Berufsschule*). The primary school offers primary education which lasts for a period of four years while the grammar school, the intermediate secondary school and the general secondary school offer various levels of secondary education. The criterion for admission into any of them is based on the academic ability of the pupils. These schools operate various school systems which differ from state to state. According to the basic law or the constitution of the Federal Republic of Germany (die Grundgesetz), it is the responsibility of each of the sixteen states that make up the country to organise a school system that is suitable for its environment. This system is to take cognisance of the social needs and the religious adaptations of the people living within a particular state. Hence these sixteen states have various school

61 Cf. Ibid.

62 Cf. Ibid.

systems which do not necessarily run concurrently with one another. The vocational school offers technical skills of various professions to students who do not have the opportunity of studying in the university after their secondary education. In this section these schools will be discussed in connection with the quality of education they offer the pupils.

3.6.1 The Primary School (Grundschule)

In Germany, educational pursuit begins officially in the primary school known as the "Grundschule". Before this time, most German children must have attended the kindergarten (nursery school) which is not part of the official school system. At this level fees are charged according to the income of the parents and admission is based on the availability of space. The kindergarten is normally run by Churches, private companies and organizations. The primary school is compulsory and free for all German children. Between the ages of six and ten all children are to acquire primary education. Here they learn basic skills such as: reading, writing, speaking, mathematics and religion.[63] In addition they also learn the grammar of the German language as well as "Heimat and Sachunterricht" where they are acquainted with their local history, geography and biology.[64] Furthermore they learn music and physical education. The performance of the pupils in the primary school (Grundschule) determines where they will acquire their secondary education. This level of educational pursuit lasts for a period of four years.

3.6.2 The Grammar School (Gymnasium)

The grammar school (Gymnasium) enrols the most gifted children from the primary school (Grundschule) and offers the type of secondary education which prepares the pupils for studies in the university. The period of learning at this level is eight years (from the 5th class to the 12th class). Religion is included among the subjects offered at this level of educational pursuit. At the completion of the 12th class, students are required to take the "Abitur" examination through which they gain admission into the university.[65] Successful candidates of this examination are issued a maturity certificate which grants them automatic qualification for admission into any university of their choice.

63 Cf. http://library.thinkquest.org/26576/kindergartenpage.htm, 03.10.2011.

64 Cf. Ibid.

65 Cf. http://library.thinkquest.org/26576/gymnasiumpage.htm, 03.10.2011.

3.6.3 The Intermediate Secondary School (Realschule)

The intermediate secondary school (Realschule) counts as one the schools where children acquire secondary education. It enrols intermediate children from the primary school (Grundschule) and prepares them for a mid level job in business (for a period of six years).[66] Among the subjects taught in this school is religion. A student who performs very well in the intermediate secondary school (Realschule) can be transferred to the grammar school (Gymnasium) and thereby gains the opportunity of acquiring a university education.

3.6.4 The General Secondary School (Hauptschule)

The general secondary school (Hauptschule) is the lowest level of secondary education in Germany. It lasts for a period of four years. In this school, students are prepared for an occupational career that requires training. They learn the basic subjects including English and religion. Students who graduate from the general secondary school (Hauptschule) proceed to the vocational school known as the "Berufsschule" which lasts for a period of two to three years.[67]

3.6.5 The Vocational School (Berufsschule)

The vocational school (Berufsschule) is where young people are prepared for various professions. There are three types of this school namely: the Intermediate Technical School (Berufsfachschule), the Higher Technical School (Fachoberschule), and the Advanced Vocational School (Berufsaufbauschule).[68] The intermediate technical school is meant to offer young people specialty training in a particular skill. It is also known as "full-time vocational school".[69] This school is the most attended among the three vocational schools for skill acquisition.[70] Some untrained people who are already in the workforce can also attend this school in order to obtain an equivalent of the "Intermediate Secondary School Certificate" (Realschulezeugnis).[71] The higher technical school and the advanced vocational school are also designed to prepare young people for different kinds of vocational careers. They are attended by students

---

66 Cf. Ibid.

67 Cf. Ibid.

68 Cf. http://www.germanculture.com.ua/libraryfacts/bl_vocational_education.htm, 04.10.2011.

69 Cf. Federal Ministry of Education and Research, Germany's Vocational Education at a Glance, Bonn, 2003, 1.

70 Cf. Ibid.

71 Cf. http://www.germanculture.com.ua/libraryfacts/bl_vocational_education.htm, 04.10.2011.

who have graduated with an intermediate secondary school certificate from the Realschule or its equivalent.[72] In these vocational schools, "the method of teaching is called the dual system because it combines classroom study with a work-related apprenticeship system in a designated company."[73] According to the German ministry of education and research:

In the dual-system, a combination of learning and working provides the basis for teaching vocational skills. The system seeks to teach theory and practice, and to impart structured knowledge and active competence, in their proper context. The different learning sites involved, the company and the vocational school, interact in keeping with their different emphases, but their tasks are not rigidly divided: school is not reserved solely for teaching theory, and in-company training involves more than simply practice.[74]

After the vocational training in any of the vocational schools, the graduates are qualified to be employed as skilled workers in their area of specialisation. Their training is also meant to prepare them for further learning so as to improve and update their intellectual acumen. The German ministry of education and research summarised it as follows:

The great majority of graduates of dual-system training … work as skilled employees – and many later make use of opportunities for vocational further training. Under certain circumstances, graduates of such training can also acquire a university entrance certificate, in a year of full-time schooling, and then go on to university studies. And successful participants in vocational further training are also increasingly being admitted to university studies.[75]

Within this dual-system, the intermediate technical school prepares pupils for occupations or for vocational training. The higher technical school and the advanced vocational school teach specialised occupational skills and theory and confer university certifications within the dual-system.

3.7 Religious Education in the German Schools

Religious education is organised in Germany as a joint undertaking of both the State and the Church (res mixta). This is based on a long lasting co-operation between the State and the Church in building a corporate German society. The State provides the teaching staffs as well as a healthy learning environment and at the same time guarantees the educational qualification of the teachers.

72 Cf. Ibid.

73 http://www.germanculture.com.ua/libraryfacts/bl_vocational_education.htm, 04.10.2011.

74 Federal Ministry of Education and Research, 4.

75 Ibid.

The Church draws up the religious educational syllabus and also certifies the religious well-being of the teachers. This idea was represented by Ziebertz and Riegel as follows:

> *The Christian Churches and the state co-operate in religious education at school... The state's role is to provide the personnel, the organizational structure and the physical resources and to ascertain pedagogical and democratic standards. The religious communities determine the content of the religious education courses and establish the spiritual standards for teachers and instructors.*[76]

The Churches in question here are the Catholic and the Protestant or Evangelical Churches. The teaching of religion in the schools is organised by these two Christian denominations. This is because religious education in Germany is aimed at familiarizing the students with the life of a concrete religious society.[77] However religious education is not taught in all the States due to the religious background of some States in Germany. This is especially the case in some of the new States in Eastern Germany. In such States religious education is replaced with "Life Orientation – Ethics – Religious Knowledge" (LER).[78] This is the case especially in the State of Brandenburg. In the States of Mecklenburg-West Pomerania and Saxony-Anhalt students are free to choose between "Philosophy" and "Ethics" instead of Catholic or Protestant Religious Education.[79] Other subjects which are also taught in place of religious education in some States include: Biblical history (as in the State of Bremen), religious education for everybody (as in the State of Hamburg), and ethics (as in the State of Berlin). In some States, there is religious education for the Jews and the Orthodox Christians. In North-Rhine Westphalia, there is even Islamic religious education for Muslims.

In the State of Bavaria, which controls the schools in the area of this study, religious education is offered in all public schools in alliance with the Catholic and the Protestant Churches. In this State, "religion is equated with either the Protestant or Catholic faith and the two Christian Churches dominate religious education in the schools".[80] In the subsequent part of this section of this work, the teaching of religion in the above described schools in Bavaria will be discussed. This is because Munich and Freising which are the particular areas of

76 Ziebertz H. G., Riegel U. (Eds.), How Teachers in Europe Teach Religion, Berlin, 2009, 70.

77 Cf. Ibid.

78 Cf. Ibid.

79 Cf. Ibid.

80 Ibid., 71.

this study have no separate religious education system different from other parts of Bavaria.

3.7.1 Religious Education in the Primary School

Children of primary school age have the ability to be amazed at strange discoveries and want to be taken seriously with their questions and their desire for a meaningfully ordered world as well as developing a way to design playful rituals of life.[81] They come into the primary school with different religious experiences, ideas and understandings and are especially interested in religion and faith. In religious education, the pupils will be offered the clarifications of their religious needs, their ideas of God and of the world.[82] They will be encouraged to express their hopes and fears, to deal with their questions of meaning and value as well as those of their school mates in a mutual exchange to learn from and with one another. In this way, the pupils will experience support in their personal, social and religious development. The religious education curriculum for the primary school offers a four-year programme of materials which are mainly aimed at preparing the pupils for the reception of the First Holy Communion (in primary three) in collaboration with parish catechesis. These materials will be discussed in this section in accordance with the four classes of the primary school.

3.7.1.1 Religious Education in Primary One

Children are usually curious and highly motivated when they are admitted into the school.[83] The school promises an increase in knowledge, skills and independence. It also poses new challenges. In religious education and in other fields of learning, the pupils (boys and girls) have to get along with themselves, establish new relationships and render services to one another.[84] The sense of responsibility for one's actions grows with the acquisition of appropriate tasks. The realization of these goals is the central task of the religious education curriculum for primary one. It begins with basic rules of the principle of mutual respect, interaction and the practices of daily life. It is laid out in six topics which are:

---

81 Cf. Katholisches Schulkommissariat in Bayern, Lehrplan für Katholische Religionslehre an den bayerischen Grundschulen, München, 2000, 25.

82 Cf. Ibid.

83 Cf. Ibid., 32.

84 Cf. Ibid.

1. “Coming together in religious education
2. Jesus is good to the people
3. Experiencing Advent and Christmas
4. We are children of the same world
5. Celebrating Easter
6. Discovering God’s world in the senses”[85]

With their enrolment into the school, the pupils begin a new phase of life. They enter the school with many expectations and curiosities and also with feelings of insecurity and fear. The first topic of primary one is meant to guide the pupils in learning how to recognise their interests, recall their experiences and become aware of how to give and accept attention and affection from one another.[86] It begins with the self-introduction of the pupils so that they will get to know themselves as members of one class. It then proceeds to give them some tips on how to deal with their ideas of God and of the world as well as how to express some issues that are important to them. At this level of their academic pursuit, they will also become aware of how people experience God so as to be able to open up to the presence of God.[87]

In the second topic, the pupils will get to know Jesus, though some of them may have already heard of Him (in the family and in the Church). Based on their former knowledge and new questions, they will get to know more about Jesus and the people with whom He lived. From Biblical stories, they will also become aware of how He talks about God (e.g. the Good Shepherd: Lk. 15:3-6) and interacts with people (e.g. the healing of the blind man: Mk. 10:46-52).[88] In this way, they will become aware of how a relationship with Jesus changes the life of a person. This understanding can help them to gain a new or deeper access to Jesus.

The third topic will introduce Advent to the pupils as a special period which is associated with great expectations and desires expressed in the exchange of gifts, the use of Advent wreathes, Advent candles, Advent calendars and Advent songs.[89] This is also a time of preparation for a significant feast – Christmas. The pupils will gain a better knowledge of the diverse traditions of the Advent and Christmas seasons. They will be made to understand that people

85 Katholisches Schulkommissariat in Bayern, Lehrplan für Katholische Religionslehre an den bayerischen Grundschulen, München, 2000, 31.

86 Cf. Ibid., 35.

87 Cf. Ibid.

88 Cf. Ibid., 36.

89 Cf. Ibid, 37.

celebrate Jesus at Christmas as the one who brought "light" into the world.[90] By becoming familiar with the Biblical testimonies of the birth of Jesus (cf. Lk. 2:1-20; Mt. 2:1-12), the pupils will be encouraged to experience Christmas with more consciousness and be part of its celebration.

In the fourth topic, the pupils are to experience the existence of other children in other parts of the world. This happens especially in their encounter with people of other countries and cultures at home, at school and in the media. This experience will help them become conscious of other people and at the same time may arouse the feeling of insecurity. The lesson of this topic will expose them to the different life situations of other children in whom they can also experience familiar and strange situations.[91] They will be made to understand that it is an act of injustice when children are rejected because of different attitudes and habits of life.[92] From the Gospel narratives, they would become aware that Jesus interacts with children and protects them (cf. Mk. 10:13-16). This can encourage the pupils to meet one another with openness and helpfulness.

The fifth topic raises the issue of Easter, the celebration of the Resurrection of Jesus from the dead. Although children experience the awakening of nature in spring, many of them are not familiar with the Christian meaning of Easter which also signifies newness of life. This is why the lesson of this topic should be a testimony to the reality of the Death and Resurrection of Jesus to the pupils (cf. Lk. 24:1-12).[93] It is also meant to indicate that the message of Easter gives new courage, hope and joy.[94] By being introduced to the symbols of the Easter celebration and tradition (e.g. Easter fire, Easter candle, Easter eggs, Easter songs), the pupils can develop an understanding for the Christian meaning of Easter and discover the various forms of expressing Easter joy.

The sixth and last topic of primary one introduces the pupils to the reality of the world through sense perception. In our contemporary society, children grow up in a world dominated by technology and the media, in which a direct access to nature is often difficult.[95] The lesson of this topic is to help the pupils to become aware of their senses so as to understand themselves and the world more clearly.[96] In this way, they can be sensitive to the beauty and mystery of life. Above all, they should be aware of the fact that people view the world

90 Cf. Ibid.

91 Cf. Ibid., 39.

92 Cf. Ibid.

93 Cf. Ibid., 40.

94 Cf. Ibid.

95 Cf. Ibid., 42.

96 Cf. Ibid.

and all life as a gift from God. Songs and praises can therefore move them to express their joy and gratitude for God's creation.

3.7.1.2 Religious Education in Primary Two

In religious education, primary one and primary two are regarded as "the classes of initiation". They are meant to lay the educational foundation which will carry the learning capacity of the pupils in their subsequent academic pursuits. The teaching content of the two classes therefore perform an introductory role in the learning areas of the primary school.[97] This is why the materials of learning for the two classes are closely related. The curriculum for primary two comprises six topics which are:

1. "Praying in various ways
2. Living together
3. People wait for the One who brings peace
4. Accompanying Jesus in His way of life
5. Belonging to the communion of the Church
6. Living in God's creation"[98]

The first topic introduces the pupils to the theme of prayer. It begins by admitting the fact that children have different experiences with prayer.[99] The pupils will therefore learn different prayers and forms of praying so as to become aware that people express their thoughts and feelings before God in various ways. Using the Lord's Prayer as the model for all Christian prayers (cf. Mt. 6:9-13; Lk. 11:2-4), they will realize the trusting attitude of prayer.[100] In this way, they will be exposed to the major prayer points contained in the Lord's Prayer in order to be able to develop their own forms of prayer. This will help them to respectfully meet other people with different prayers and forms of praying.

The second topic is concerned with community life. It expresses the fact that children live in a variety of relationships with other people – in the family, school and the larger society. Using the story of Joseph (cf. Gen. 37:1-36), the pupils will learn how the relationships among Joseph, his father and his brothers eventually changed.[101] They would be encouraged to empathize with

97 Cf. Ibid., 32.

98 Ibid., 30.

99 Cf. Ibid., 44.

100 Cf. Ibid., 45.

101 Cf. Ibid., 46.

the persons whose feelings and relationships are expressed and linguistically illustrated in the story. In this way, they can deal with conflicts and contribute their own experiences. This story will help to make them aware of how God guides people in their lives and moves them towards reconciliation and peace. It will also encourage them to go about their lives, trusting in God and seeking the paths of reconciliation and peace.[102]

The third topic presents Jesus to the pupils as the one who brings peace into the world. Because of the hectic atmosphere associated with the pre-Christmas period, children often do not experience the season of Advent as a time of silence and the preparation for the feast of the birth of Jesus.[103] The lesson of this topic therefore is to make them become aware that the Christian desire for God and His kingdom of peace is expressed in various forms during Advent. Based on selected Biblical texts (e.g. Lk. 1:26-38; 39-56; 2:1-20; 21-40), they will deal with the message of Christmas and thereby realize through the Christian faith that the birth of Jesus brought the promised Messiah into the world.[104] This can make them become sensitive to the joy of Christmas and encourage them to open themselves to the Christian meaning of the seasons of Advent and Christmas.

In the fourth topic, the knowledge of the pupils about the person of Jesus and the people who trust Him is presumed. With the help of selected Gospel texts (e.g. Mt. 6:25-34; Mk. 2:1-12; 7:31-37), the pupils will learn how Jesus preached His message in words and deeds.[105] They will realize that Jesus shows the way of God's love for the people consistently until Death on the Cross (cf. Lk. 22-23; Phil. 2:6-8). By dealing with the Resurrection of Jesus (cf. John 20:1-21), they can develop a sense of joy and hope which emanate from Easter.[106] They will thereby learn about the celebration of Holy Week as well as how Christians celebrate Easter.

The fifth topic is on the membership into the communion of the faithful through the sacrament of Baptism. Many children were baptised as infants while some would only be baptised later (as adults) according the decision of their parents.[107] Some have also witnessed a Baptism ceremony in the circle of relatives and acquaintances. The lesson of this topic will help make the pupils aware that at Baptism, parents ask for God's help and blessing for their child

102 Cf. Ibid.

103 Cf. Ibid., 47.

104 Cf. Ibid.

105 Cf. Ibid., 49.

106 Cf. Ibid.

107 Cf. Ibid., 52.

and entrust the life of the child to the life style of Jesus Christ.[108] By learning the celebration of Baptism and the meaningful signs of the sacrament (e.g. Water, Sign of the Cross, anointing oil, Baptismal cloth and candle), the pupils can understand that people are received into fellowship with Jesus and the Church through Baptism. They would also be aware of how faith in Jesus is transmitted and lived through the communion of the baptised. This can encourage them to open themselves to the gift of Baptism and growth in the life of the Church.[109]

The sixth and last topic for primary two deals with the beauty of God's creation. The encounter with nature, plants and above all animals is of particular interest for children and gives them much joy.[110] Under this topic, they will be helped to understand the world as one big community and give attention to rhythms and regulations which carry and maintain life (such as sun and rain, night and day, summer and winter).[111] Testimonies of faith can stimulate them to thank God for the gift of life and our fellow creatures (e.g. Ps. 8). The lesson will also help the pupils to become aware of the destruction of the environment around them, and on the basis of the story of Noah, to understand that people fulfil an important mission of God when they are committed to the preservation of nature. This can encourage them to discover some ways through which they themselves can build protective "arks" in their immediate environment.[112]

3.7.1.3 Religious Education in Primary Three

The pupils know one another already in the school and are familiar with their various individual social potentials. In the third class of the primary school, they gradually come to a realistic assessment of their leadership abilities. They discover their capabilities and weaknesses and look for better ways of handling them.[113] The development and expression of individual ideas, which will culminate in the reception of the First Holy Communion, is the main goal of religious learning in primary three. This will boost their self-confidence and help them to identify themselves as "bona fide" members of their class and the Church. The adjustment to a new teacher, which is often necessary at the beginning of the third class, will support individual, flexible and independ-

108 Cf. Ibid.

109 Cf. Ibid.

110 Cf. Ibid., 53.

111 Cf. Ibid.

112 Cf. Ibid.

113 Cf. Ibid., 56.

ent learning.[114] It will also help the pupils to increasingly orientate themselves towards their peers. They will among other things learn how to co-operate with one another and at the same time how to manage conflicts in a constructive way. The religious education curriculum for primary three is divided into seven topics which are:

1. "Speaking about God
2. Meeting the Jewish faith
3. Learning forgiveness and reconciliation
4. Being together with Jesus and celebrating His banquet
5. Living in the parish
6. Longing for a just and peaceful world
7. The Bible tells about God and people"[115]

The first topic provides opportunity for the pupils to speak about God. As they develop their individual personalities, their image of God also changes and develops. The lesson of this topic will help them to conceive their own ideas of God in order to deal with some of their questions about God later in life.[116] With some Biblical references and interpretations of the life of other people (e.g. Gen. 12:1-9; 28:10-16), they can see that people experience God as faithful and dependable; but also as incomprehensible and mysterious.[117] This will encourage them to trace such experiences about God in their own lives.

The second topic introduces the pupils to the root of Christianity in Judaism. The pupils are already familiar with many stories from the Bible, but have little idea of the roots of the Christian faith.[118] They will therefore learn about the Passover and be aware that the commemoration of Israel's Exodus from Egypt as God's saving and liberating act belongs to the key experiences of the Jewish faith.[119] They should also gain an insight into how the Jews worship and express their faith in God (in the Synagogue). The lesson of this topic will also help them to realize that Jesus belonged to the Jewish people and lived as a Jew in order to discover how Christianity is strongly connected to Judaism.

114 Cf. Ibid.

115 Ibid., 31.

116 Cf. Ibid., 58.

117 Cf. Ibid.

118 Cf. Ibid., 59.

119 Cf. Ibid.

The third topic presents the pupils with the theme of forgiveness and reconciliation. In living with other people, children can experience joy and happiness, but also misconduct which disrupts and sometimes destroys togetherness.[120] Using concrete Biblical examples and pictures (e.g. 2 Sam. 12:1-15), the pupils will learn how people become guilty and live with experiences of guilt.[121] By becoming aware of how Jesus meets guilty people and grants them forgiveness (cf. Lk. 15:11-24; 19:1-10), they can realize that God accepts everyone and offers reconciliation and new beginnings.[122] They will learn the different forms of reconciliation and become familiar with how Christians celebrate the sacrament of Reconciliation. This plays a major role in their preparation for the reception of the First Holy Communion. The knowledge of this sacrament (Reconciliation) can also help them to accept themselves, to start over again and again and be ready for forgiveness and reconciliation.

The fourth topic handles the celebration of the Eucharist as a fulfilment of the Lord's will. God relates with His people like children who depend on the support and sympathy of others, especially their parents.[123] Through Jesus, God goes to the people and gives them companionship and attention in a meal. Children are known to grow up in a community, in which they acquire their identity and find friends and allies.[124] The Church as a community of believers offers them the opportunity of growing in their faith and celebrating the Eucharist with others. By learning about the Last Supper of Jesus with His Apostles, as part of their preparation for their Fist Holy Communion, the pupils will recognize the special significance of this celebration as bringing people together with Jesus. From the Emmaus story (cf. Lk. 24:13-35), they will be aware of the fact that the disciples meet the Risen Christ in the breaking of bread and that Christians come together under the injunction of Jesus to celebrate the Lord's Supper.[125]

The fifth topic highlights a typical Christian life in a parish setup. In the preparation for their First Holy Communion, children get to know their parish better.[126] The lesson of this topic will make the pupils become aware of the fact that Christians come together in their parish to live out their faith in Jesus Christ. They will thereby learn to understand the feasts of the liturgical year

120 Cf. Ibid., 62.

121 Cf. Ibid.

122 Cf. Ibid.

123 Cf Ibid., 63.

124 Cf. Ibid.

125 Cf. Ibid.

126 Cf. Ibid., 65.

and the celebration of Sunday as highest points of the Christian faith.[127] They should therefore experience a typical Christian worship and learn especially the parts of the Mass. They should above all be made to understand that communion with Jesus Christ is strengthened and deepened in the Eucharist.

The sixth topic takes up the social issues of justice and peace in the world. In their immediate environment and through the media, children often experience some situations in which they are confronted with suffering and misery, injustice and unrest.[128] The lesson of this topic should help the pupils to speak about some problematic situations they have experienced. Using the words of the prophets (e.g. Is. 1:16-17; Jer. 22:13-15; Am. 8:4-7) and the message of Jesus (e.g. Lk. 10:25-37), they should be encouraged to deal with injustice and to consider options for help.[129] They should pay attention to how Christians realize and handle this in their lives. This can energize them to seek the means of helping the situation in the spirit of brotherly love so as to make the world more just and peaceful.

The seventh topic is an introduction to the Bible as a special book which contains stories of God's dealings with human beings. In the school, parish and family as well as through the media, the pupils may have already encountered a number of Biblical stories.[130] They are therefore familiar with the Bible as a book and are aware that the writings of the Bible tell about faith in God's liberating action. The lesson of this topic will help them to remember some old Biblical texts and learn new ones so as to deepen their knowledge of the Old and New Testaments.[131] They should pay particular attention to the meaning of the Bible for all Christians as the book of faith and be able to find personal approaches to it.

3.7.1.4 Religious Education in Primary Four

In primary four, which is also the last level of primary education, the pupils are said to have attained the age of reason. Their contributions to school activities boost "school life" and make it an important phase of human development. They practice democratic ways of living together and learn how to act in solidarity and compassion.[132] They draw much moral inspiration primarily from the experience of friendship with one another. They increasingly acquire some

127 Cf. Ibid.

128 Cf. Ibid., 66.

129 Cf. Ibid.

130 Cf. Ibid., 68.

131 Cf. Ibid.

132 Cf. Ibid., 70.

critical skills and tolerance as well as develop and deepen their interest in various fields of life. They are now confronted with the comparative performance of their abilities and potentials in view of the impending change to the secondary school.[133] From this background, the religious education curriculum offers them lessons that would facilitate their transition to the secondary school and widen their horizon for a broader socio-religious interaction. These lessons are divided into seven topics which are:

1. "God leads His people to freedom
2. Having confidence in life
3. Meeting people with other religions
4. Suffering and death trigger off many questions
5. Handing-on the Gospel message
6. Speaking in images and symbols
7. Christians live in different denominations"[134]

The first topic is on God's liberation of the people of Israel and the giving of the Decalogue (Ten Commandments). From previous lessons, the pupils are already familiar with the story of the liberation and its significance for the Jewish-Christian faith. The additional theme here is the handing over of the Ten Commandments to the people through Moses (cf. Ex. 20:1-11). With the help of Biblical texts, the pupils will learn that Israel lives with the memory of this liberation and knows that God accompanies her on her ways (cf. Deut. 6:20-24).[135] They will also learn that the Ten Commandments are aids for the preservation of our God-given freedom, the protection of God's dignity and fundamental human rights.[136] By learning the Ten Commandments, the pupils will discover their own approaches to these words of life and realize that the commandment of love is the centre of all Biblical teachings (cf. Mt. 7:12).

The second topic tries to situate the importance of each person in God's plan of creation. Every human being is unique and has abilities and potentials. The lesson of this topic is to help the pupils realize this fact and ask questions about themselves.[137] They should see the need to look forward to having a happy and meaningful life. They should also be aware that people have differ-

133 Cf. Ibid.

134 Ibid., 31.

135 Cf. Ibid., 72.

136 Cf. Ibid.

137 Cf. Ibid., 73.

ences and similarities; and that each person is valuable and unique for God.[138] By becoming aware of the importance of friends, they will realize that trusting others, themselves and God can give support and confidence to life. This can encourage them to see the need to give affection, trust and love to other people.

In the third topic, the pupils will learn how to interact with people of other religions. In their immediate environment, children get to know people with different interpretations of life and religious beliefs. The lesson of this topic will help them become aware of the fact that people often ask about God, call Him by different names and worship Him in various forms.[139] They will also learn especially the basic principles of Islam and become aware of the similarities between Muslims and Christians. They should be made to know how important it is for people of different opinions, world views and religions to treat each other with respect and try to live together in peace and harmony.[140]

The fourth topic raises the issue of suffering and death, before which children react in a very sensitive way.[141] The lesson will inform the pupils how people live with suffering and impermanence, how to deal with their own questions about suffering and death and how to arrive at possible answers.[142] Above all, they will be helped to realize that suffering and death are beyond human comprehension. With selected words of the Psalmist (e.g. Ps. 10:1; 13:2-4; 18:2-7, 29-30; 31:2-4; 142: 2-3), they can be motivated to express their own experiences, fears and hopes.[143] This lesson can also help them realize that the testimony of the life of Jesus, His Death and Resurrection is the fundamental reason for the Christian faith. This can encourage the pupils, even in the most painful situations of life, to trust in God's presence and assistance as well as accept the message of the Resurrection of Jesus.[144]

In the fifth topic, the pupils will learn about the proclamation of the Gospel through the promptings of the Holy Spirit. They have already learned about the life of their local parish but have not yet been informed about the origin and the universal nature of the Church.[145] In the lesson of this topic therefore, they will get to know that the disciples preached the Good News following the injunction of Jesus whose presence they experienced anew through the Holy Spirit

---

138 Cf. Ibid.

139 Cf. Ibid., 75.

140 Cf. Ibid.

141 Cf. Ibid., 77.

142 Cf. Ibid.

143 Cf. Ibid.

144 Cf. Ibid.

145 Cf. Ibid., 79.

at Pentecost. They will also learn about the life of the early Christian communities and how the Gospel message was transmitted. In this way, they should realize that Christians all over the world bear witness to their faith in Jesus Christ in various forms and at the same time recognize their unity with other Christians in the universal Church.[146] The pupils should also understand that the Church is a family which lives and works through her faith in Jesus Christ.

The sixth topic pays attention to the concretization of the Biblical images and symbols. It recognises that the pupils are already familiar with some images and symbols from the Bible. But due to their increasing "critical realism", they often dismiss Biblical stories which are often in metaphorical languages as mere fairy tales.[147] The aim of this topic therefore is to teach the pupils how to recognize different possible meanings from daily realities and understand figurative languages and manifestations. This will help them to understand the language of religious images and symbols in the Bible as well as deepen their awareness of religious language.[148] Particular attention should be paid to Biblical images of trust and hope so that they can understand the images of the kingdom of God and be able to develop their own symbols.

In the seventh and last topic of religious education in the primary school, the pupils are presented with the different denominations of the Christian faith. This is meant to help them realize and recognise the various Christian Churches and communities in their immediate environment and especially gain insight into the expressions of the Protestant faith.[149] The lesson will help them recognise the differences and similarities of the various Christian Churches and find access to the Christian faith in its denominational forms.[150] The co-existence and worship of all Christians in the "Ecumenical Movement" can encourage them to be aware of the various forms of Christian life and faith.

3.7.1.5 Summary

Religious education in the primary school in the state of Bavaria serves as an introduction to the Christian faith. The pupils come together from different family backgrounds and integrate themselves into a common life of a learning environment. The themes mapped out in the curriculum for learning are meant to widen their religious horizon from the idea of God to the life of a community of believers. They are to see themselves as children of one God irrespective of

146 Cf. Ibid., 79.

147 Cf. Ibid., 81.

148 Cf. Ibid.

149 Cf. Ibid., 83.

150 Cf. Ibid.

some religious or denominational differences. The fact of discovering the root of Christianity in the Jewish religion will help them to understand the reason for the existence of many other religions. Thus there is the need for a lesson on a peaceful interaction with people of different religious backgrounds.

3.7.2 Religious Education in the Grammar School

After four years of primary education, the most gifted pupils are admitted into the grammar school for further learning. The grammar school offers them new possibilities and widens their horizon. Among the new discoveries is a new level of religious education which entails a wider scope of learning. Religious education in the grammar school begins with the fifth class and offers the pupils the possibility of a new orientation towards knowing the self, the ability to live and learn with others, the relationship between God and humans, the need for prayers and the different forms of prayer. Furthermore, it exposes them to the use of the Bible and its recognition as a sacred book. It also leads them into the life of Jesus as the Son of God who proclaimed the message of God's unlimited love; this is done with Biblical examples. Lastly it introduces them to the recognition of sacred places and the use of the Church as a house of prayer as well as a place of reverence. The religious education curriculum for the grammar school has been designed to prepare the pupils for the final examination (Abitur) in the 12th class. The articulation of this curriculum from the fifth to the twelfth class will explain in detail the contents and materials of religious education in Bavaria which covers the area of this study.

3.7.2.1 Religious Education in the Fifth Class of the Grammar School

The lessons of religious education in the fifth class build on the previous ones in the primary school and accompany the pupils in their early stages at the grammar school. Starting from their own religious experiences and questions, the lessons will help the pupils to develop core areas of Biblical and ecclesial life, which offer them the religious instructional basis for the following years of their learning.[151] In this fifth class of religious learning, five topics are presented in the curriculum. These are:

1. "A new beginning – living, learning and discovering the faith with one another
2. Human understanding of God – Abraham encounters God

151 Cf. Bayerisches Staatsministerium für Unterricht und Kultus (Hg.),Lehrplan für das Gymnasium in Bayern, München, 2009, Jahrgangsstufe 05, K1.

3. The Bible: experiences of our faith in a book
4. God shows Himself new: Jesus of Nazareth and His message
5. Our Churches: "Local symbols" of universal Christian faith"[152]

The first topic introduces the pupils to new worldviews, challenges, expectations, hopes as well as fears. They begin to experience the presence of God in their school mates and their environment as a fruit of their faith and a sign of spiritual growth. They will be able to identify themselves as distinct persons from particular families. The lesson will help them to discover their abilities, interests and limitations. They will begin to ask questions about the meaning of their names and the relationship with their patron saints.

Under the first topic the pupils learn how to relate to one another – boys and girls – and form study groups. Above all they will learn how to live under a code of conduct as well as maintain a friendly spirit with one another (cf. 1 Cor. 12:4-11; 12-27).[153] They will also learn how to feel God's presence through prayers. They will be taught that God accompanies us in our various life situations as expressed in the basic prayers such as: The Our Father, Ave Maria and some Psalms (Ps. 23; 31:2-6).[154] They will also learn to formulate spontaneous prayers so as to discover religious life in the school.

The second topic introduces God to the pupils using the example of Abraham's encounter with God. At this level they begin to understand that experiences, which are associated with astonishment, fear, joy or insecurity produce moments of deep reflection about the meaning of life and our relationship with God.[155] They begin to realize that people of all times and religions also sought for the answers to the questions of life in their understanding of God and have been influenced by their respective cultures. With Abraham's experience, the picture of God received a new orientation, which has remained the fundamental image for the belief in God in Judaism, Christianity and Islam.[156] Hence the pupils use some of their experiences to ask religious and philosophical questions in order understand the role and position of God in their lives. Some of these experiences include: good luck, sorrow or death and religious tradition (religious feast).[157] They also learn about the age long search for the answers

152 Ibid., K1-K2.

153 Cf. Bayerisches Staatsministerium für Unterricht und Kultus (Hg.),Lehrplan für das Gymnasium in Bayern, München, 2009, Jahrgangsstufe 05, K1.

154 Cf. Ibid.

155 Cf. Ibid.

156 Cf. Ibid.

157 Cf. Ibid., K2.

of the riddles and mysteries of life as well as a personal reflection of God and His various images from the Bible.

The pupils will be guided by a question as: how has God revealed Himself to humans in the past? The answer will be sought from God's relationship with people of various cultures, for example, the European culture. Also God's dealings with the Orientals will be considered; for example the Egyptians, the Babylonians and the Canaanites. Special attention will be given to how Abraham and Sarah experienced God. Through them the God of mysteries opened Himself to humans and has remained a Co-Teacher and a National God (e.g. Gen. 12:1-9; 15; 17), the God who fulfils His promises (e.g. Gen. 28:1-15; 21:1-8) and the God who desires no sacrifice but obedience (e.g. Gen. 22:1-9). Thus, Abraham remains the father of faith for the Jews, the Christians and the Muslims.[158]

The third topic raises the issue of the Bible as a book of faith. Children often look for personalities with whom they can relate in order to gain experience. Hence the Biblical presentation of Jacob and Joseph offers them two people who experienced the presence of God in difficult situations.[159] From this story the pupils should realize that the Bible contains in different language forms, memories of messages of hope and God's help for the people of Israel and the early Christians. They also learn that the Bible does not lose its actuality and that Christians will continue to find help from God for their various life situations. Thus it must be established that the Bible contains stories of God's presence using the example of Jacob and Joseph.

The pupils will be taught the right use of the Bible, beginning with the two major divisions of the Bible into the Old and New Testaments. They will then learn the books of the Old Testament as well as those of the New Testament. They will also be exposed to the daily use of the Bible in Christian worships, images, hymns, advertisements and on the Internet.[160]

The fourth topic introduces the pupils to a new picture of God as expressed in the person of Jesus of Nazareth. Children are known to be excited by strange things and fascinating images.[161] In the life of Jesus they will discover some new behaviour which to a large extent indicates a new orientation in God's dealings with humans. From this background they will discover some new teachings contained in the message of Jesus and its effects on the people of His time. They will also realise that people of the present time are also influenced

158 Cf. Ibid.

159 Cf. Ibid.

160 Cf. Ibid.

161 Cf. Ibid.

by Jesus, and thereby draw their own life orientation from Him. Hence they will learn about the birth of Jesus (Lk. 2:1-20), the Good Samaritan (Lk. 10:25-37), and the Pharisees and the Tax Collectors (Lk. 18: 9-14).[162]

God made new revelations in the person of Jesus Christ who made personal contacts with humans in the proclamation of His Gospel as seen in the eating with tax collectors and sinners (Mt. 9:9-13); the healing of a sick woman (Lk. 13:10-17); and the blessing of children (Lk. 18:15-17). The pupils will learn the need to be active in some youth movements and to be enrolled as altar servers.[163]

In the fifth topic, the Church is presented to the pupils as a house of prayer and a characteristic of the Christian faith. As such they need to visit a Church so as to see its different structures and what exactly makes it different from other buildings. There is also the need to differentiate between Catholic Church buildings and other Churches of the different Christian denominations. The pupils will also be acquainted with the different buildings which can be used as Churches, for example: Chapels, Oratories, Parish Churches, Basilicas and Cathedrals.[164] At the end they will be able to understand the meaning of the word "Catholic" so as to gain a personal conviction of their faith as well as the universal dimension of the Church as the "family of God".

3.7.2.2 Religious Education in the Sixth Class of the Grammar School

In the sixth class of their religious formation in the grammar school, the pupils begin to perceive the religious unity of all mankind. Belief in God exposes them to supernatural help as well as corporal benefits from their fellow human beings.[165] From the example of the early Christians they realize the importance of community life which grows especially from identification with Jesus. Five topics are presented in the curriculum for religious learning in the sixth class. These topics are as follows:

1. "Between the expectations in performance and life experience: finding a personal orientation
2. Children of one world: children of one God
3. Human power under the sustenance of God: Kings of Israel
4. From darkness to light: Jesus gives us hope in sorrow and death

162 Cf. Ibid.

163 Cf. Ibid.

164 Cf. Ibid.

165 Cf. Bayerisches Staatsministerium für Unterricht und Kultus (Hg.),Lehrplan für das Gymnasium in Bayern, München, 2009, Jahrgangsstufe 06, K1.

5. Christian community life: enthusiasm and courage from the beginning – its impulse for today"[166]

In the first topic, the pupils will learn how to grapple with numerous demands and offers from the school, family, peer group and the media. These demands and offers sometimes conflict with one another to the extent that the pupils find themselves in a bizarre situation. The lesson is meant to provide them with moments of reflection over their personal needs, the responsibility of others, the need for personal discipline as well as a balanced use of their leisure.[167] This will help them to discover some points of orientation in their formation. It will also help them to find out the need for a community life and the meaning of certain celebrations such as the feast days in the Church's calendar and Sundays.[168] In this instance, they will be able to set priorities over their activities so as to develop their creative potentials especially in the proper use of computers, mobile phones and other modern means of communication. They will also develop the ability to spend their time in meaningful responsibilities in the class, family, peer group and parish community.

The understanding of globalization does not only mean economic co-operation but also an increased awareness of oneness among peoples of various continents.[169] This is meant to be the principal guide of the second topic in which the pupils are to see themselves as children of the same world and the same God. In the Christian religious perspective, they are to be taught that children of different parts of the world have the right to free growth and development, formation and life opportunities.[170] Hence the coming together with other children of the world will enrich their personal life experience and open up the possibility of a global awareness that they are children of the same God. This will also bind the children together with some global responsibilities aimed at solidarity in their various life styles. A concrete example here is the "World Youth Day" of the Catholic Church which has united many children of various parts of the world. The children use such opportunities to share experiences and to combat the abuse of children in some economic and military actions.[171] They also discuss the celebration of certain feasts of the Church (for example, Christmas and Easter) in other parts of the world.

166 Bayerisches Staatsministerium für Unterricht und Kultus (Hg.),Lehrplan für das Gymnasium in Bayern, München, 2009, Jahrgangsstufe 06, K1-K2.

167 Cf. Ibid., K1.

168 Cf. Ibid.

169 Cf. Ibid.

170 Cf. Ibid.

171 Cf. Ibid.

In the third topic, the pupils will learn, through Biblical stories, the dangers of absolute power and the liberating power of God.[172] They will be taught the understanding of kingship by the Orientals, where a king is also regarded as a deity.[173] From this background the will realize why Samuel criticised the Israelites for demanding for a king. The lesson will help them to realise that the kings of Israel are under God's allegiance and that God will demand an account of their stewardship from time to time. Thus they will be told the story of God's dealings with His people from the time of the Exodus to the time of the Judges and the introduction of kingship in Israel (cf. 1 Sam. 8). The act of anointing sets the kings of Israel apart from other kings. This will be explained to the pupils in connection with the Spirit of God resting on the kings. They will also be introduced to some of the activities of the kings of Israel such as Saul's success and his rejection by God (cf. 1 Sam. 15:1-26), David and Goliath (cf. 1 Sam. 17:1-54), David and Saul (cf. 1 Sam. 24:1-23), David and Bathsheba (cf. 2 Sam. 11ff), the Wisdom of Solomon (cf. 1 Kgs. 3:2-28), Solomon's sin (cf. 1 Kgs. 11:1-13), Naboth's vineyard (cf. 1 Kgs. 21).[174] This lesson will be concluded with issues of abuse of power especially in connection with today's politics, formation of cliques in the school, humiliation of other pupils and the role of the media in the use of power.

The question of suffering and death as well as the problem of evil has continued to pose great difficulties to mankind. The pupils will grapple with these issues from their personal experience and hope to get the answers from the teachings of Christianity.[175] The fourth topic is therefore meant to introduce the pupils to the actions of Jesus which brought consolation and comfort to people who had given up hope in the midst of their sufferings. Such actions can be seen in these stories: the healing of the sick (cf. Lk. 5:17-26), the raising of a dead man to life (cf. Lk. 7:11-17), the deliverance from demonic possession (cf. Lk. 8:26-39), Jesus' own suffering, Death and Resurrection. These will help the pupils to be re-assured by hope when they are confronted with individual problems.[176] From the experience of others such as the Emmaus disciples, they will learn how belief in Jesus and His Resurrection changes human life.

In the fifth and last topic of the sixth class of the grammar school, the pupils will learn the meaning of Christian community life. From here they will discover the experience of the Apostles at Pentecost (cf. Acts. 2:1-13) and the

172 Cf. Ibid., K2.

173 Cf. Ibid.

174 Cf. Ibid.

175 Cf. Ibid.

176 Cf. Ibid.

need to pray together. Using Peter and Paul as examples, the pupils will understand the need for the development and use of personal talents for the good and growth of the Christian community.[177] They will be told the stories of the missionary journeys of Paul and the difficulties he encountered (cf. Acts. 15:1-35) and how he endured hardships for the sake of the Gospel and the Christian community. These impulses of the early Church are meant to motivate the pupils to accept the Christian faith and to be actively involved in some activities of the Church in their various parishes.

3.7.2.3 Religious Education in the Seventh Class of the Grammar School

The personal development of young people can be enriched through a life long embracement of the Christian the faith. In the seventh class of the grammar school, the pupils begin to be enlightened through the use of Biblical pictures with which they learn the sacraments of the Church as signs of life-giving grace.[178] They also learn some of the historical changes that have taken place in the Church since "The Middle Ages" as well as the Islamic religion. The religious education curriculum lists five topics for the seventh class of the grammar school. These topics, which would be discussed in this section, are as follows:

1. "I am no more a child!' – Questions of the young ages
2. The Gospel of Mark – Stories of a better world
3. From the known to the unknown – Symbols and sacraments
4. Changes in culture – Christian Europe in "The Middle Ages"
5. Islam – Meeting the Muslims of our society"[179]

Many boys and girls experience the physical and spiritual changes of the puberty as signs of insecurity, during which their childhood ideas are radically transformed.[180] The first lesson in the seventh class of the grammar school will widen their horizon so that they can criticise their actual knowledge and begin to explore new things. It will culminate in a complete withdrawal from childhood beliefs and a realization of a sense of responsibility. Through social interaction, they will gain new impulse and begin to consider their roles in the

177 Cf. Ibid.

178 Cf. Bayerisches Staatsministerium für Unterricht und Kultus (Hg.),Lehrplan für das Gymnasium in Bayern, München, 2009, Jahrgangsstufe 07, K1.

179 Ibid., K1-K2.

180 Cf. Ibid., K1.

family, school and in their peer groups.[181] They will be confronted with the problems of their age and at the same time be encouraged to make the best use of their opportunities. In this instance, they will gain a meaningful verification of their personal religious views.

In the second topic, the pupils are introduced to the Gospel of Mark for a better orientation of their world views. Young people are often drawn to negative things which they see around them and in which some of them think their dreams for a better world will find fulfilment.[182] In the Gospel of Mark, they hear about the beginning of a new and healing world in the person of Jesus Christ (cf. Mk. 1:14ff). With this Gospel periscope, they follow the ways of Jesus from Galilee to Jerusalem and experience how He elucidated His promise of the kingdom of God with symbolic acts (cf. Mk. 1:40-45).[183] They will also learn the parables as significant elements in the teachings of Jesus so as to understand the other synoptic writings of Matthew and Luke.

In the third topic, the pupils are informed about the use of sacramentals in the Church. Objects which are so appealing to young people are often regarded as little sacred things. Such objects help them to have particular experiences of life and can also help them to understand the demands of their age as well as offer them a sense of security.[184] The lesson of this topic will help them to discover the symbols and rituals of the Church as meaningful signs of a deep reality. From this background they will begin to identify the symbols and sacraments of the Church as encouraging signs of the healing power of God (cf. Mk. 14:22-25).

Christian beliefs often pose as great challenges to the norms of the society. In the fourth topic, the pupils will learn how Christian teachings influenced some of the cultural beliefs of "The Middle Ages" through the individualised catechumenate under the Roman Empire. This lesson will also afford them the opportunity of learning the Christianisation of the Germans not as a result of an individual decision but as a tribal unanimous agreement.[185] This will help in re-awakening the consciousness of the Christian faith in them. In this instance, they will be able to understand the background of the Christian cultural heritage of the German people.

Many young people are today often confronted with different realities of Islam. This happens especially in the school, around the home, in the media

181 Cf. Ibid.

182 Cf. Ibid.

183 Cf. Ibid.

184 Cf. Ibid., K2.

185 Cf. Ibid.

and through journeys. This is because they are often very inquisitive about new things around them.[186] The fifth topic in the seventh class of the grammar school affords them the opportunity of learning about Islam as one of the world religions. They learn some of the elements of this religion and discover some of its influences in their own culture. They learn from the Christian point of view that despite some differences in religion, a peaceful co-existence with people of other religions is also possible.

3.7.2.4 Religious Education in the Eighth Class of the Grammar School

The creation story opens many life orientations to young people. They understand conflicts as signs that the world needs to be rescued. In an historical flash back, the pupils open themselves to Ecumenism and focus on "today's Church" for enlightenment.[187] From the Christian perspective they ask questions about the current happenings in the society. This forms the background of the religious education curriculum for the eighth class of the grammar school. It is presented in five topics which are:

1. "God's creation – Gift and duty for mankind
2. The fallible world – Conflicts, guilt and reconciliation
3. Desire for salvation – The struggle for eternal life in "The Reformation" era
4. Between nearness and distance – Young people encounter the Church
5. Religiosity and life interpretation – Orientation of the psyche"[188]

Young people are often inclined to understanding the creation stories of the book of Genesis as natural information, which originated from an outmoded interpretation of the origin of the world.[189] This is why it is necessary for them to understand the different views about this phenomenon. The first topic of the eight class of the grammar school begins by presenting the pupils with the opinion of the natural scientists who approach the creation of the world from the point of view of explanation especially in the theory of evolution. In the Biblical texts, the pupils will discover some fundamental statements which define the position of the human person in the world. Man and woman were created as equal partners, who are to see to the ordering of things in the world.

186 Cf. Ibid.

187 Cf. Bayerisches Staatsministerium für Unterricht und Kultus (Hg.),Lehrplan für das Gymnasium in Bayern, München, 2009, Jahrgangsstufe 08, K1.

188 Ibid.,K1-K2.

189 Cf. Ibid., K1.

The second topic presents the issue of the ups and downs of life to the pupils. In the time of their development, the pupils will experience with full awareness the many conflicts of the private and social aspects of life especially in the family, school and the larger society.[190] Some of these conflicts range from frustration, aggression and the feeling of failure. They will also experience the feeling of guilt from personal acts and the doings of others. The lesson will help them to discover the root cause of these conflicts as well as look for a possible solution to them. They will discover in some Biblical passages how some conflicts were overcome especially through the intervention of Jesus in such cases as that of the woman caught in the act of adultery (cf. Lk. 7:36-50).[191] In the same vein, they will also discover how many people were freed from their guilt using the example of the story of the merciful father (cf. Lk. 15:11-32) and some healing acts of Jesus (cf. John 7:53-8:11; Matt. 9:1-8).[192] The Church continues with this act in the sacrament of Reconciliation.

The pupils are to learn in the third topic why the answers to some pressing human questions, such as the problem of salvation and eternal life, were expected to come in the late "Middle Ages".[193] That will help them to understand the reason for the "Reformation" and the origin of the Anglican and Lutheran Churches. The need for this is to respond to the inquisitive nature of young people who are often inclined to search for the answers to the question of "why". The lesson will also offer them the explanation of eternal life and the problems of Luther in seeking for the reformation of the Church. It will also present the relationship existing among the various Churches in the "Ecumenical Movement".

The majority of the pupils receiving religious education are already baptised Christians and therefore members of the Church.[194] Their nearness to the Church however depends on the intensity of their response to the Christian faith. The fourth topic uses Biblical images such as: the wine stock (cf. John 15:1-8) and the Body of Christ (cf. 1 Cor. 12:12-13) to bring to their awareness the fact of their full membership in the Church.[195] It also informs them of some of the services of the Church to the society especially in the social service areas. Such services include the works of Charity and the Missions.

190 Cf. Ibid.

191 Cf. Ibid.

192 Cf. Ibid.

193 Cf. Ibid., K2.

194 Cf. Ibid.

195 Cf. Ibid.

In their quest for orientation, young people sometimes come into contact with some religious, esoteric and psychologically connected issues which often contain some elements of different cultures and theories.[196] In the spiritual dimension, they are often inquisitive about the connection of current trends with the Christian teachings.[197] The fifth and last topic of the eight class of the grammar school will therefore offer them lessons that will help them to find the relationship between "today's life" and the Christian faith.

3.7.2.5 Religious Education in the Ninth Class of the Grammar School

In the Exodus tradition and the Prophets, the pupils will not only encounter the promising power of the faith, they will also get to know more about the Jewish religion. From their background as young minds, they will consider the Church's witness to the Christian faith and interpretation of life so as to be properly oriented towards the choice of life partners through friendship and a corresponding occupation. This forms the framework of the religious education curriculum of the ninth class of the grammar school. It is laid out in the following five topics:

1. "The Exodus, the Decalogue (Torah) and the Prophets: God gives freedom and demands justice
2. Judaism: World religion and the root of Christianity
3. The Church and the "signs of the time": Difficulties, awareness and preservation
4. Between publicity and intimacy: Friendship, love and sexuality
5. School, Studies and occupation: What for?"[198]

In the estimation of young people, freedom often ranks high on their list of ideas. This is also greatly connected to the search for life orientation. In the first topic of the ninth class of the grammar school, the pupils will learn with the help of God's deliverance of the Israelites from the Egyptian slavery (cf. Ex. 15), that freedom is a gift of God.[199] They will also see the "Ten Commandments" (the "Torah" or the "Decalogue") as a guide to this freedom. In this instance, they will understand that freedom is not totally free in the strict sense of the word. The Prophets will be presented to them as people who were

196 Cf. Ibid.

197 Cf. Ibid.

198 Bayerisches Staatsministerium für Unterricht und Kultus (Hg.),Lehrplan für das Gymnasium in Bayern, München, 2009, Jahrgangsstufe 09, K1-K2.

199 Cf. Ibid., K1.

called by God to act as "the eyes of God" in checking excesses of freedom and violations of the commandments. The lesson will therefore help the pupils to discover that the Exodus tradition encourages people of all ages to stand against injustice.[200]

In the second topic, the pupils will be presented with Judaism as both a world religion and the root of Christianity. From the Exodus event, they already know the Old Testament and its story of freedom. In the introduction to the Jewish religion, the teacher will help the pupils to understand its relationship with Christianity especially in the use of the Biblical name of God "Yahweh"[201] (cf. Ex. 3:15), the understanding of the Torah as a life orientation and the celebration of the Passover as a life long feast.[202] The lesson will also afford the pupils the opportunity of studying the experience of the Jews with the Christians especially in the persecution of the Jews in the "Middle Ages" and in the twentieth century as concretely expressed in the "Holocaust" of 1945.

The arguments of the twentieth century in which the continued existence of the Church has been seriously questioned, form the basis of today's social and environmental behaviour.[203] Through the analysis of some pressurising and persecuting situations of the period – the twentieth century – (e.g. the National Socialism of the former East Germany), young people will be brought to the awareness that the Christian faith can contribute towards the eradication of totalitarian acts and the protection of the constitution of the German nation. The third topic of this section will present the pupils with "today's Church" and its battle with the norms of our contemporary society. Thus the serious engagement of the Church with the major themes of the Second Vatican Council (e.g. the Aggiornamento) shows the pupils some of the efforts of the Church towards self renewal. The lesson will also expose the pupils to the involvement of the Church in the Ecumenical Dialogue and world politics.

For many young people, the use of their body and sexuality depends on personal experience, the influence of their peer groups and their families. It is also highly influenced by the ungracious presentation of human sexuality through the media.[204] In the fourth topic of the ninth class of the grammar

200 Cf. Ibid.

201 Because of the close connection between Judaism and Christianity and in recognition of the fact that Christianity originated from Judaism, Christians have resolved to no longer use Yahweh in their prayers and hymns. This is also out of respect for the Jewish religious beliefs which hold this Name with utmost sacredness.

202 Cf. Bayerisches Staatsministerium für Unterricht und Kultus (Hg.),Lehrplan für das Gymnasium in Bayern, München, 2009, Jahrgangsstufe 09, K1.

203 Cf. Ibid., K2.

204 Cf. Ibid.

school, the pupils will learn that the Church's presentation of the human person encompasses a comprehensive sexuality which is in harmony with respect for the self, the partner and the life of children (including the unborn). The lesson will help them to accept and handle sexual impulse with full understanding and maturity. It will also lead to the right choice of partners in friendship and the practice of true love in line with Biblical definition and description of love (cf. 1 Cor. 13). They will as well be acquainted with current sexual issues like HIV/ AIDS and the use of contraceptives.

In the fifth and last topic of this section, the pupils are gradually introduced to an occupational life. This is because they are drawing very close towards graduation from the secondary school. At this level they will reflect on some of the expectations from further trainings and occupational capabilities. From the Christian background they will realise that training and occupation are also connected with responsibilities based on performances. The lesson will therefore help them to make rightful choice of life careers. With their knowledge of Christian ethics, they will be expected to work consciously so as to earn truthfully in line with the "Golden Rule" (cf. Mt. 7:12).[205]

3.7.2.6 Religious Education in the Tenth Class of the Grammar School

Young people are fond of thinking and asking questions about the end of life as well as trying to grasp the Christian responsibility for the protection of human dignity.[206] In their orientation towards Jesus Christ as a model, they realise a steady measure of behaviour and hope in life. They discover the power of the inner self and are drawn towards reflections on life after death. Due to the current issue of inter-religious dialogue, they are especially inquisitive about the religiosity of the Far-East.[207] In this instance, they want to discover what differentiates Christianity from the religions of the Far-East especially in relation to such issues as life after death. The religious education curriculum for the tenth class of the grammar school provides opportunity for the pupils to gain deeper insight into these issues and to make personal decisions on some other vital issues of life. It contains five topics namely:

1. "Rightful conscience: Taking up the responsibility of life
2. Living on the border line: Death and the expectations of the hereafter
3. Jesus Christ: The cornerstone of our faith

205 Cf. Ibid.

206 Cf. Bayerisches Staatsministerium für Unterricht und Kultus (Hg.),Lehrplan für das Gymnasium in Bayern, München, 2009, Jahrgangsstufe 10, K1.

207 Cf. Ibid.

4. Finding the inner centre: Meaningful experience and Christian action
5. Christianity in a pluralism of religions and cultures: Hinduism and Buddhism"[208]

Young people are often amazed at the wonder of modern discoveries especially in the area of bio-technology.[209] This creates a feeling of hope in them and at the same time arouses fear and worry especially when they cannot cope with modern challenges. The first topic of the tenth class of the grammar school is meant to prepare the pupils gradually to reflect on the wonders of creation and to use their conscience to apportion themselves some sort of responsibility in life. The lesson will introduce them to the duty of Christians to promote human dignity and protect life.[210] It will be made clear to them that every human person is made in the image of God and according to His likeness and therefore has a natural right to life and human dignity (cf. Gen. 1:27).[211] Some issues of modern medicine and human genetics especially as regards the propagation and protection of life as well as respect for human dignity are therefore committed to the judgement of individual consciences. The pupils will also be introduced to the social activities that are meant to render services to life such as "Caritas" and the "Social Services of Catholic Women".[212]

As a result of reflections on personal experience, some young people ask themselves questions about aging, dying, death and life hereafter. In the lesson of the second topic, the main thrust will be to provide possible answers to these questions from the background of many religious cultures. The Christian tradition which is rooted in belief in the Resurrection shows solidarity with the dying and sees death not as the end of life but the beginning of a new and everlasting one (cf. Mk. 16:1-8; 1 Cor. 15:3-8; 51-57).[213] Islam and Judaism teach that death is a relief from the circle of re-incarnation. Hinduism and Buddhism hold the belief that death is the absolute end of life.[214] Against these backgrounds, Christianity provides the opportunity for the dying to be assisted and helped through prayers and the sacraments (Viaticum) but condemns euthanasia, suicide and the death sentence.

208 Ibid., K1-K2.

209 Cf. Ibid., K1.

210 Cf. Ibid.

211 Cf. Ibid.

212 Cf. Ibid.

213 Cf. Ibid.

214 Cf. Ibid.

The third topic presents the Christian faith as built centrally on Jesus Christ. The pupils will gain a deeper expression of their faith with the help of the many images of Jesus as described in the Gospels (e.g. as a child born in Bethlehem and as a wonder worker). They will learn about the historical Jesus and discover from the New Testament that His person is strongly attached to the belief in His Resurrection (cf. 1 Cor. 15:14).[215] In the Sermon on the Mount, which serves as a provocative concretion of the Christian message, they will gain a deeper impulse in the development of their religious life.

In the fourth topic, the pupils are introduced to the many impulses of the media and leisure which they have to apply meditatively to their various life situations. The introduction of some meditative forms, especially the Taizé spirituality, is meant to offer the pupils an enriching possibility for the discovery and development of the inner self.[216] Many Christians of different times and ages such as, Benedict of Nursia and Ignatius Loyola have ventured to change the world with the "power of silence".[217] Young people can also use this method in order to open themselves to God and by so doing help in giving "their world" a better shape (e.g. through music and literary works).

The fifth and last topic of the tenth class of the grammar school presents Christianity as a religion in the midst of many other religions especially Hinduism and Buddhism. Some Christian young people often show interest in other religions which have been publicised through global relationships and the works of the media. In this instance, the traditions of the Far-East have offered the "global community" some unusual religious movements (such as Yoga), which have gained entry into other cultures and religions. Through an encounter with Hinduism and Buddhism, the pupils will access the peculiarity of the Eastern and Western religious arts; discover the specialty of Christianity so as to see the root of the inter-religious dialogue.

3.7.2.7 Religious Education in the Eleventh Class of the Grammar School

The eleventh class begins the upper level of the grammar school in Germany. At this stage in which the pupils are in the transition age to maturity, they begin to seek their personal life orientation and a comprehensive meaning of the reality of life in the context of their society and European culture.[218] In this eleventh class, the pupils are placed at a higher level of reflection in the Chris-

215 Cf. Ibid., K2.

216 Cf. Ibid.

217 Cf. Ibid.

218 Cf. Bayerisches Staatsministerium für Unterricht und Kultus (Hg.),Lehrplan für das Gymnasium in Bayern, München, 2009, Jahrgangsstufen 11/12, K1.

tian faith. In this way they will assimilate some of the elements of the basic religious educational programmes of the lower school years and other levels of learning. The eleventh class handles questions about God in line with their meaning for human beings and the society.[219] The pupils are helped to understand the religious phenomena and the current questions about God as well as reflect on their personal religious convictions. Four topics are enlisted in the curriculum for this level of learning namely:

1. "Between diversity and choice: Religion in the open society
2. Ways to God: The Bible as a testimony of Divine experience
3. Responsible faith in God: Inquiries, rejection and approximations
4. The human person in the horizon of belief in God: Christian image of the human person"[220]

The first topic introduces the pupils to the understanding and practice of religion in the open society. How to live and act autonomously in the contemporary religiously diverse society can be a problem for a person. The lesson of this topic offers young people the opportunity of developing a reasonable life orientation, the ability to contribute meaningfully in some religious discussions and the willingness to tolerate others.[221] On the basis of individual perceptions, the pupils will approach the influence of religion both at the level of personal understanding and at the level of culture and the society, in order to develop some aspects of a basic understanding of religion. Thus the lesson will enable them to judge religion from the external view as a significant factor for the survival of the society as well as to develop their own religious positions.

In their approach to the complex phenomenon of Divine experience, the pupils will be primarily concerned in the second topic with the basic interpretation of the Scriptures of Christianity and discern the importance of a multidimensional understanding of the text. Using specific examples, the lesson of this topic will enable them to realize that the process of protecting the Biblical text – the historical critical method – and the interpretative developmental steps from the perspective of faith are of equal importance for the Biblical exegesis.[222] In studying the differences of another religion, they will grasp the specifics of the Christian understanding of revelation: the Bible contains the

219 Cf. Ibid.

220 Ibid., K1-K3.

221 Cf. Ibid., K1.

222 Cf. Ibid., K2.

word of God in human words. Finally, the pupils will apply the Holy Scriptures in the broader context of human experience of God.

The third topic is aimed at helping the pupils to develop a strong personal faith in God. In our secularised society, faith in God is not self-evident but must be constantly re-established. The lesson will afford the pupils the opportunity of asking questions about the Christian image of God or whatever they accept as an object of belief. They will also be free to accept or reject God as part of their life plan.[223] However the lesson is designed to help them to show their openness to religious experiences and issues. Towards the development of a personal responsible faith in God, the pupils will learn some past attempts to understand the nature of God from the intellectual point of view (such as Thomas Aquinas, Immanuel Kant and Hans Küng) as well as some philosophical justifications of atheism (such as the opinions of Feuerbach, Nietzsche and Sartre).[224] In this instance, they will grasp the opportunity as well as the ambivalence of an argument directed by reason. They will also understand that faith and knowledge do not contradict each other and at the same time become aware of the limits of human knowledge of God.

The fourth and last topic of this section will introduce the pupils to the question of the Christian understanding of the human person which is closely connected to the question of God.[225] Based on the self-fulfilling understanding of today's society, the pupils will recognise from the lesson, the fundamental aspects of human existence and interpret them from the perspective of modernity, as well as a non-Christian religion. By so doing, they will engage in a comparative analysis which is based on the development of a broad and lasting relevance of the Biblical-Christian image of the human person.

3.7.2.8 Religious Education in the Twelfth Class of the Grammar School

The twelfth class of the grammar school handles questions of the human organisation of the world in the view of the Christian challenges of the present and the future.[226] At this level of learning, the pupils will think of the fundamental image of God and the human person as important tasks and will be helped to understand the possibilities of ethical conduct. In the assessment of some current decision-making areas, they will be empowered to participate in ethical discourse to justify Christian positions.[227] Based on the present situa-

223 Cf. Ibid.

224 Cf. Ibid.

225 Cf. Ibid., K3.

226 Cf. Ibid.

227 Cf. Ibid.

tion, attention will be focused on the dimensions of the future and the Christian eschatological hope. On the basis of the Creed, which is familiar to the learners from previous years, they will develop in repetitive ways, the core messages of Christianity which are rooted in the diverse Christian tradition.

Through the development of their personal religious approaches, the pupils will gain a deepened insight of the relevance of their learning and cultivate an on-going improvement of their religious competence. Thus, they will acquire profound religious prerequisites for lifelong learning. The collaboration with other disciplines opens opportunities for a deliberate change of perspectives and helps to improve the co-operation of the Catholic religious teaching with the Protestant religious teaching. The curriculum for this level of learning contains four topics which are:

1. "Ethical competence from the Christian perspective: Orientation in the pluralism of values
2. Ethical competence from the Christian perspective: Current challenges
3. Dimension of the future: Organisational task for the present
4. Layout of an overview: The Christian (profession of) faith"[228]

In the first topic, the pupils are presented with a large number of images of God and of the human person starting with the field of ethics to a pluralism of values.[229] They will consider the justifiability of values and norms; learn the Christian and other approaches of ethical arguments, so as to reflect on the importance of conscious decision-making. In this way, they will experience help, especially from the lesson on responsible ethics and the summary of the Decalogue (cf. Mk. 12:28-34), which will help them to shape their lives as mature and responsible Christians.[230] This is concretised on the basis of the aspects of life which require individual decision-making, so that instructional links can be made with the lesson of the second topic of the twelfth class.

The second topic deals with issues of global challenges and ethical positions which have a great influence on the individual especially in his or her private life and socio-political engagement. Some of these issues run contrary to the Christian teaching (e.g. marriage, family and partnership) and therefore make the individual face some difficulties in matters of personal decision.[231] In religious education, the pupils are aided in handling this situation responsibly

228 Ibid., K3-K5.

229 Cf. Ibid., K3.

230 Cf. Ibid., K4.

231 Cf. Ibid.

with the help of the ethical discourse. Through the selection of proper information; the processing and presentation of topics, the pupils are offered the opportunity to develop their personal initiatives and widen their capability skills.

The third topic deals with some of the problems which may pre-occupy the pupils at the closing stage of their secondary education. These problems are related to the question of their future in the midst of hopes, fears, uncertainties and social developments.[232] In dealing with secular ideas about the future, the lesson will help the pupils to recognize their limited explanatory power and ambivalent impact on human life. With some eschatological and apocalyptic images (e.g. Mt. 13:31-33; 44-46), they will learn the different patterns of Biblical interpretation of the future so as to develop their life relevance meaningfully.[233]

The fourth and last topic of the twelfth class concludes the lessons of religious education in the upper class of the secondary school. At this level, attention is focused on the in-depth synopsis of the various thematic aspects of religious education and how to secure the core structures of belief.[234] The graduates are now in the position to describe the outlines of the Christian creed so that they recognise on the one hand, the belief in its profile, and on the other hand, understand it as being capable of offering meaning to life. The tripartite structure of the creed (I believe in one God, the father …; and in Jesus Christ …; and in the Holy Spirit) shows itself in its relation to the lessons of the eleventh and twelfth classes as well as those of the preceding years.[235] Hence, the twelfth class provides the pupils the opportunity of revising the contents of their religious learning and at the same time gaining deeper spiritual emphases. It will also offer them the opportunity of a broader studying of the different structural forms of the creed, so that the pupils can understand the potentials of the multi-dimensional expressions of belief, which can in a life-like manner offer them the Christian orientation not only in its human interpretation, but also in its reality as Trinitarian.

3.7.2.9 Summary

The grammar school is regarded as the school for gifted children. Religious education is meant to offer them both religious experience and life orientation. The experience of Abraham introduces the children to an encounter with God as the One who manifests Himself to human beings. He transmits the

232 Cf. Ibid.

233 Cf. Ibid., K5.

234 Cf. Ibid.

235 Cf. Ibid.

task of looking after His people to kings beginning with Saul. Jesus presents a new image of the Divine as the harbinger of hope even in difficult situations. Christianity which traces its root to Judaism is practiced through symbols and sacraments. Because of the pluralistic nature of our contemporary society, the children are also brought to the awareness of other religions such as Islam, Hinduism and Buddhism.

3.7.3 Religious Education in the Intermediate Secondary School

In the intermediate secondary school, the pupils continue to advance in their religious learning with a new scope, a renewed zeal and goal. The curriculum has a six-year programme for this level of academic pursuit from the fifth class to the tenth. The contents of these programmes will now be presented in this section.

3.7.3.1 Religious Education in the Fifth Class of the Intermediate Secondary School

The fifth class of the intermediate secondary school initiates the transition from the primary school to the secondary school and therefore introduces the pupils to a new level of academic life. The pupils require a new orientation in order to adjust to the new class and acclimatize into the new learning environment. The lessons for this level of academic pursuit are therefore meant to serve as an orientation course for the pupils. They are divided into six topics which are:

1. "Beginning together: I am not alone
2. The local Church: Life in the parish and the diocese
3. A book like no other: The Bible
4. Joy and fear, worries and hopes: Coming together in prayer
5. Ways of faith: Abraham and Sarah
6. Opening up with curiosity: Encounter with foreign cultures and religions"[236]

In the first topic, the pupils are to identify themselves as members of the same class. The lesson is to help them find their various positions in the new class and school. They will get to know one another more through the sharing of their prior life experiences. Above all they will realize that they are accepted and cherished by God as His dearly beloved children. This will strengthen their

236 Katholisches Schulkommissariat in Bayern, Lehrplan für Katholische Religionslehre an den bayerischen Realschulen, München, 2001, 68-72.

self-esteem and make them willing to respect and pay attention to one another, to agree on the rules of co-existence and put them into practice.[237]

The second topic introduces the pupils to life in a typical parish. The pupils come from different parishes and therefore have different forms of relationship with the Church. They will therefore need to explore one of the Churches near the school in order to gain insight into the vibrant nature of the Christian life of faith. They will also understand the Church in its functional and artistic form as a visible sign of unity for the community and as a sacred place. The lesson will further help them to discover the variety of the community activities of the parish, so that their interest can be awakened to participate in these activities. Above all, they will realize that each parish is part of a Diocese, which performs larger ecclesiastical functions and also makes even bigger offers for the promotion of community life and awareness of faith.[238]

In the third topic, the pupils will be introduced to the Bible as the word of God to humans and as a diverse collection of texts. They will learn when, where and how the Bible originated so as to acquire an important basis for its better understanding and at the same time appreciate the Old and New Testaments. In order to benefit from the Bible, they will have to learn the proper use of it.[239]

The fourth topic is a lesson on prayer. The religious silence of many people of our time manifests itself in the area of prayer. The pupils will therefore learn how to commit their joys and fears, worries and hopes to prayer. They will be encouraged to form prayer groups so as to find trustworthy partners in whom they can confide. In this way, they will learn the meaning of prayer and the various forms of prayer such as: meditative and ejaculatory. They will also be helped to understand prayer as reaching out to God in search of strength, support and guidance.[240]

The lesson of the fifth topic traces the root of three world religions (Judaism, Islam and Christianity) to the faith of Abraham. With the help of selected Biblical stories (e.g. Gen. 12:1-9; 13:14-18), the pupils will learn the need for strong faith in God. Following the example of Abraham and Sarah who trusted in God's protection despite their fears, questions and doubts, the pupils can be encouraged to keep their faith in God in order to obtain answers to their ultimate questions.[241]

237 Cf. Ibid., 68.

238 Cf. Ibid.

239 Cf. Ibid., 69.

240 Cf. Ibid., 70.

241 Cf. Ibid., 71.

The sixth and last topic in the fifth class of the intermediate secondary school is concerned with the encounter with people of different cultures and religions. This encounter has been made possible especially by the use of new communication technologies such as the Internet and telephones. The increase in international tourism and global economic integration has also contributed to this encounter with people of various cultural and religious backgrounds. With the help of specific examples, the lesson will deepen the attention of the pupils to the difficulties and opportunities that may arise from co-existence with such people especially in the area of religion. The pupils will therefore explore and illustrate the traces of foreign cultures and religions in their regions.[242]

3.7.3.2 Religious Education in the Sixth Class of the Intermediate Secondary School

In the sixth class, the pupils find themselves in their usual familiar learning environment. This makes it possible for them not only to consolidate as members of one class, but also see themselves as forming part of the school community. The religious education curriculum offers the pupils at this level, lessons that would help them to purposefully develop their talents and interests not only as those forming part of the lively school activities, but also as members of a Christian life of faith. These lessons are divided into six topics which are:

1. "Everything has its own time: Time for oneself and others
2. Chosen by God: King David
3. Jesus of Nazareth: Who was He really?
4. Connected to the roots: The life and faith of the Jews
5. People celebrate: Feasts and customs in the Church's year
6. Renewal in sight and understanding"[243]

The first topic is on time management. In the life of many contemporary people, leisure takes a very prominent position. The lesson of this topic will help the pupils to realize the need to organize and utilize their time properly. From their experience of friendship, they are already aware that more time is allotted to precious things. Because of the important role the media plays in the use of leisure, they need to acquire clear points for a conscious and sensible use of the media and leisure. The lesson will also help them to meditatively

242 Cf. Katholisches Schulkommissariat in Bayern, Lehrplan für Katholische Religionslehre an den bayerischen Realschulen, München, 2001, 72.

243 Ibid., 80-85.

contemplate on some Biblical statements on time as a gift and task of God (e.g. Eccl. 3:1-8; Mt. 25:14-30; Gal. 6:9-10; Eph. 5:16). This will encourage the pupils towards a responsible use of their time and opportunities.[244]

The second topic traces the origin of kingship to God. It presents David to the pupils as the prototype and model of a human king chosen by God. From the perspective of faith, the lesson will give the pupils the feeling that David was only successful because God was with him. They will be made to recognise the characteristics of the actions of God who does great things for those who, – even with guilt and failure – trust in His leadership. The pupils will be encouraged to reflect on their experiences, hopes and uncertainties and thereby become aware that God wants to manifest His power in every person.[245]

The third topic is a lesson on the person of Jesus Christ. With the help of their ideas, questions and relationships with Jesus, the pupils will learn about Him through reading and hearing of stories from selected passages in the Gospel (e.g. Lk. 2:41-52; Mk. 2:23-3:6), about Jesus of Nazareth who grew up into Jewish piety in the land of Palestine and proclaimed His message from the background of His contemporary daily life. The lesson will help them to explore some areas of the real life world of Jesus so that they can understand the Biblical narratives more vividly and realistically as well as gain a clearer awareness that Jesus lived and worked in a specific time with His contemporaries. The testimonies of the life of Jesus will help the pupils understand the importance of these events as a source of Christian hope (cf. Lk. 24:13-53).[246]

In the fourth topic of the sixth class of the intermediate secondary school, the pupils will learn the connection between Judaism and Christianity as religions from the same root. In the course of their previous school years, they would have already heard many Old Testament stories and basic information about the land of the Bible. Now in the sixth class, they will realize why the teachings of both religions are based on the same sacred writings. The focus will be less on the teaching than on the practice of piety in Jewish religious life. Together with the insight gained in Jesus Christ, the lesson will help the pupils to be ready for respect, reconciliation and peaceful co-existence with others, especially with the Jews.[247]

The fifth topic introduces the pupils to the celebrations of the Church in the liturgical year. Many adults as well as children look forward to festivals and celebrations as an interruption of everyday life and as highlights of the

---

244 Cf. Katholisches Schulkommissariat in Bayern, Lehrplan für Katholische Religionslehre an den bayerischen Realschulen, München, 2001, 80.

245 Cf. Ibid., 81.

246 Cf. Ibid., 82.

247 Cf. Ibid., 83.

year. The lesson will therefore let the pupils see the need for celebrations of various types such as: school parties and birthdays. Above all the pupils will be helped to understand that the Sunday Eucharistic celebration is a "small Easter feast" during which the faithful gather for the fulfilment of the Lord's injunction (cf. 1 Cor. 11: 17ff). By sharing their festival experiences, the pupils will realize that a successful celebration requires the organization and co-operation of all participants. The lesson will also give them an overview of the rhythm and meaning of the liturgical year so that they will become attentive to the fact that the central mysteries of the Christian faith enrich life and are also reasons for celebration. The pupils will also gain the insight that a Christian community needs specific meeting places and forms of celebration in order to be lively.[248]

In the sixth and last topic for the sixth class of the intermediate secondary school, the Holy Spirit will be introduced to the pupils as the "renewing force" in the practice of the Christian faith. In contemporary society, the Church and young people are often estranged from each other. Using the Pentecost event as a story of the origin of the Church (cf. Acts. 2:1-13; 2:14-36), the lesson is aimed at awakening the interest of the pupils for a life of faith. They will also be introduced to the life and work of the first Christian communities so that they can develop the impetus for a renewal of an understanding of the work of the Holy Spirit in the present day life of the Church. Using the example of the Apostle Paul, who was transformed from a persecutor to a preacher (cf. Acts. 9:1-22; Gal. 1:10-17), the pupils will discover the amazing dynamics that faith in Jesus Christ can release in a person.[249]

3.7.3.3 Religious Education in the Seventh Class of the Intermediate Secondary School

In the seventh class of the intermediate secondary school, the pupils, now in the age of puberty, begin to feel their importance as members of the society. The religious education curriculum of this level of learning presents them with Biblical personalities who can serve as models for their life orientation. They are also introduced to conflict management. The lessons for this level of academic pursuit are laid out in six topics which are:

1. "Speakers in the name of God: Prophetesses and prophets
2. Expression of a deeper reality: Symbols and sacraments

248 Cf. Katholisches Schulkommissariat in Bayern, Lehrplan für Katholische Religionslehre an den bayerischen Realschulen, München, 2001, 84.

249 Cf. Ibid., 85.

3. Learning how to deal with conflicts: Christian guidance
4. Longing for a new world: Jesus' message of the kingdom of God
5. Meeting people of different beliefs
6. Seeking for the origin: The beginnings of Christianity in our land"[250]

The first topic introduces the pupils to the prophets. It presents the prophetic tradition as an essential part of the three great Abrahamic religions – Judaism, Christianity and Islam. The pupils will get to know the prophets as people, who feel that they are called by God for a special mission (cf. Am. 7:12-17; Jer. 1:4-10; Is. 6:1-13; 1 Kgs. 19:19-21). Through their courageous and passionate commitment to their call, they convince other people of the need to follow a pattern of life which is in conformity with the belief in a just, redeeming and liberating God. The lesson will also present the prophets to the pupils as those who see things from the perspective of faith in God and undertake salutary and ominous situations. They are committed to the repentance of the people in spite of bitter experiences and thus counteract the threats to human life at different times. The lesson will help the pupils feel that such commitment is a request for them also to spend part of their lives in service to others. The example of some modern prophets can encourage them to take up the call of God and to act in their own context in a "prophetic" way.[251]

The second topic is a lesson on religious symbols and sacraments as external signs of deeper realities. Some daily objects and gestures acquire a special place in a pupil's personal or communal life. Such experiences foster the awareness and understanding in the pupils for symbols and the symbolic actions in the Church. The lesson will help them recognize that symbols and symbolic gestures can express more than words, especially when it has to do with the action of God in the celebration of the sacraments.[252]

The third topic handles crisis management from the Christian perspective. In the family, at school and among friends, young people often experience conflicts which sometimes clarify relationships and promote positive developments, but in some extreme cases lead to violent clashes. In this connection, the pupils will learn how to perceive specific signs and backgrounds, weigh the motivating factors behind them and devise a fair means of resolving conflicts. They will also learn the teachings of Jesus which promote understanding and

250 Katholisches Schulkommissariat in Bayern, Lehrplan für Katholische Religionslehre an den bayerischen Realschulen, München, 2001, 92-97.

251 Cf. Ibid., 92.

252 Cf. Ibid., 93.

strengthen the willingness to open conversation, moral courage, non-violence and reconciliation.[253]

The fourth topic presents the kingdom of God to the pupils as realised in the person of Jesus Christ. Jesus builds His message of this Kingdom in word and deed. With this message, He opens up the future of mankind, raises the question of life habits and demands a change in lifestyle. Based on the knowledge that the Gospels are testimonies of faith, the pupils will learn that Jesus sets people free from their shackles and fulfils their desires. In this way, the pupils can open up to the Spirit of Jesus who encourages them to think about their personal behaviour and help in building a more humane and more hopeful world. The lives of exemplary personalities (like St. Francis of Assisi and Don Bosco of Turin) who opened up to the Spirit of Jesus can also serve as motivating factors for the pupils to embrace the life of the Spirit.[254]

In the fifth topic, the pupils are meant to learn how to co-exist with people of different religious beliefs, especially the Muslims. Today, Muslims are living in many German towns and all (major) cities. Thus, the mutual willingness and ability to hold conversations with one another is an important educational and upbringing goal for both Christian and Muslim young people. This lesson provides very important information for pupils to perceive how Muslims live their faith. The pupils will therefore need to ask about the origin, founding figure and core beliefs that are accessible, especially in festivals, prayer rituals and precepts of this world religion. This is necessary so that the pupils will find it easier to practice respect and tolerance when they realize how the Islamic culture has enriched European Western life and science in the course of history.[255]

The sixth and last topic for religious education in the seventh class of the intermediate secondary school is a historical course on the origin of Christianity in the State of Bavaria. It must be recognised that life and traditions in the State of Bavaria are characteristically Christian oriented. In this lesson, the pupils will study the foundations and growth of the Christian faith and thereby gain an insight into the important stages of the Christianization of the State of Bavaria. This will help them recognise the importance of Emperor Constantine, who at a time during the "Great Persecution" brought freedom to Christianity. In dealing with the evangelization of the State of Bavaria, the pupils will become conscious of the cultural creative power of the people and

253 Cf. Katholisches Schulkommissariat in Bayern, Lehrplan für Katholische Religionslehre an den bayerischen Realschulen, München, 2001, 94.

254 Cf. Ibid., 95.

255 Cf. Ibid., 96.

the importance of monasticism in the past and present as well as get to know the patron saints of the Bavarian Dioceses.[256]

3.7.3.4 Religious Education in the Eighth Class of the Intermediate Secondary School

In the eighth class of the intermediate secondary school, the pupils strive for independence as well as search for personal values. In an effort to distinguish themselves in their uniqueness, they may tend to make comparisons among themselves which can have some negative tendencies such as jealousy and irreligiousness. The religious education curriculum for this level of academic pursuit therefore offers them lessons that can set them on the proper goals of life. These lessons are divided into six topics which are:

1. "On the way to the self and others: Sexuality as a language of love
2. In search for orientation: Biblical teachings
3. Learning other religions: Hinduism and Buddhism
4. Ways to the self and the fundamentals of life: Prayer and meditation
5. Catholic, Orthodox, Protestant: "… that all be one!" (cf. Jn 17:21)
6. Entrusted to our care: The world as God's creation"[257]

In the first lesson, the pupils are given directives in their search for individual realization. This is because the search for the self, recognition, security and love shows itself in many young people in the desire for reliable relationships. They will derive examples from their experience of friendship and the art of falling in love in order to gain a positive relationship with their own sexuality. Using some Biblical expressions (e.g. Gen. 1:26-27; 2:18, 21-25; Rut 1-3), they will learn the Christian view of sexuality as God-given and a good human attribute which promotes the development of human dignity.[258]

The second lesson presents the Biblical teachings as means for the pupils to gain a proper life orientation. In the Ten Commandments, God is seen as a "lover of life" who gives us guidelines that can help us to succeed in our lives. These commandments point the way of living a decent life in a relationship with God. Based on their search for direction, the pupils will learn to understand and appreciate Biblical teachings as the fulfilment of love for God and the world around them. The Sermon on the Mount (cf. Mt. 5-7) can also help

256 Cf. Katholisches Schulkommissariat in Bayern, Lehrplan für Katholische Religionslehre an den bayerischen Realschulen, München, 2001, 97.

257 Ibid., 104-109.

258 Cf. Ibid., 104.

them to realize that the behaviour to which Jesus calls us is only possible if we allow ourselves to be taken up by the liberating love of God. By being open to this knowledge, the pupils can finally be ready to shape their lives according to Biblical teachings.[259]

Lesson three of the eighth class of the intermediate secondary school deals with the religions of the Far-East. These religions (Hinduism and Buddhism) move through migration and are reinforced in our view through the world-wide media coverage. In this lesson, the pupils will learn how people in one of the oldest religious traditions of the world look for answers to the major questions of life and salvation. They will thereby learn both the character and values of other religious beliefs as well as pay attention to their strangeness. The commitment of the adherents of these religions (who are living with us in the State of Bavaria) in observing the teachings of these religions and their contribution to coping with life can increase the awareness of the pupils and raise their willingness to deal seriously with the contents and practices of other religions.[260]

The fourth topic is a lesson on prayer and meditation. In the search of personal orientation, many people including young people find some forms of meditation very helpful. In this lesson, the pupils will practice and think about silent exercises and other forms of meditation and prayer in order to gain from this background clarity about the meaning and importance of prayer and meditation in the world of today. In this way, they deepen their understanding of the "Our Father" as the hallmark for Christian prayer.[261]

The fifth topic gives the pupils the ecumenical significance of the Christian faith. The pupils will learn the European cultural background which is very much influenced by Christianity in its many denominations. This will help them distinguish between religion and creed. Using the example of the Reformation, it will become clear to the pupils how the separation between the Protestants and the Catholics took place. The Biblical prayer of Jesus for the unity of Christians (cf. Jn. 17) can awaken the willingness to seek common ground, to estimate the direction of the Christian diversity and to open up to the concerns of the ecumenical movement.[262]

The sixth and the last topic is a lesson on the world as God's creation entrusted to human care. The pupils experience the world as both fascinating and

259 Cf. Katholisches Schulkommissariat in Bayern, Lehrplan für Katholische Religionslehre an den bayerischen Realschulen, München, 2001, 105.

260 Cf. Ibid., 106.

261 Cf. Ibid., 107.

262 Cf. Katholisches Schulkommissariat in Bayern, Lehrplan für Katholische Religionslehre an den bayerischen Realschulen, München, 2001, 108.

disturbing. Such an experience can arouse their interest to deal with the question of the origin, meaning and future of our world. Using selected Biblical texts, they will be helped to understand that human beings, according to Biblical belief, are created in the image and according to the likeness of God and are set over all other creatures. The lesson will give them an insight into the attitudes, values and activities of "exemplary images of God" so as to discover that God provides for His creation through responsible human agents. Thus, they will be encouraged to make their personal contributions towards the care of God's creation.[263]

3.7.3.5 Religious Education in the Ninth Class of the Intermediate Secondary School

In the ninth class, the pupils begin to prepare their minds towards a befitting life career. They begin to grapple with questions about the meaning of life and individual life planning. The religious education curriculum for this level of learning offers them lessons that are meant to serve as guidance in the choice of professions. These lessons are divided into six topics which are:

1. "Longing for meaning and support: Variety of religious offers
2. People ask about God: God's ideas of religions
3. Personal decision: Conscience and responsibility
4. Dead – what then? – Hope beyond death
5. Impetus to new experiences: Learning with the Bible
6. Young people are asking: The Church between aspiration and reality"[264]

The first topic is a lesson on the need for the pupils to find meaning in life even in the midst of suffering. It is an indubitable fact that people strive for a life worth living. The pupils will learn in this lesson about the different forms of expression of both the desire for a fulfilled life and the fear of failing in life. The question of meaning finds its inevitable escalation in the confrontation with the observations and expressions of suffering and misery in this world. The Christian message of the Cross can encourage the pupils to believe that God can rescue all people from suffering and difficulties.[265]

The second topic handles imminent questions about God. The questions of whether God exists and how He can be imagined have occupied humanity since time immemorial and they set the limits of human understanding and

263 Cf. Ibid.

264 Ibid., 116-121.

265 Cf. Katholisches Schulkommissariat in Bayern, Lehrplan für Katholische Religionslehre an den bayerischen Realschulen, München, 2001, 116.

explanation. The pupils learn the precepts of God at different ages, in different beliefs and religions. In this lesson, they will discover how the respective images of God influence both the people and world views as well as lifestyles. They will engage in an in-depth discussion on the Christian belief in God and the actions of God in the world. This will help them to examine and further develop their own attitudes towards God.[266]

The third topic treats the conscience as a guide in personal decision-making. The lesson of this topic will help the pupils to discover the voice of their consciences and the need to listen to them in a serious manner. It is only when they trace "the mystery of conscience as the most secret core, where they are alone with God"[267] that the pupils will understand the opinion of the Church that "loyalty to one's conscience is a binding commitment."[268] This is why the pupils should be aware of their own conscience experiences. The lesson will also help them to consider different motives of their own behaviour so as to recognize that people sometimes need help in decision-making in order to act responsibly. Finally the living example of some Christians who remained faithful to their consciences even in moments of conflicts (e.g. Johann Maier) can promote the willingness to form the conscience according to Christian standards and the ability to understand this as a lifelong task.[269]

The fourth topic is a lesson on death and the life hereafter. The belief in the Biblical Resurrection narratives forms the foundation, the characteristic and the distinctive nature of Christianity. The lesson presents the pupils first of all with the experience of the living with death so that they can know how differently people react to it. They will have the opportunity to ask their questions, which they associate with death and the dying, and be able to attempt possible answers. In the encounter with mourners, they will recognize that the painful loss lessens with the thought of the visions of life beyond death. They will also get to know some transition pictures (obituaries) and how they are handled in different religions, but above all, in Christianity. They will also get to know how other religions bear witness to the belief in the resurrection of the dead and learn to appreciate the significance of these witnesses for the life of the world.[270]

---

266 Cf. Ibid., 117.

267 McNicholl A. (Trans.), Gaudium et Spes, 16, in: Flannery A. (Gen. Ed.), Vatican Council II, More Post-Conciliar Documents, Mumbai, 2007, 806.

268 Ibid.

269 Cf. Katholisches Schulkommissariat in Bayern, Lehrplan für Katholische Religionslehre an den bayerischen Realschulen, München, 2001, 118.

270 Cf. Katholisches Schulkommissariat in Bayern, Lehrplan für Katholische Religionslehre an den bayerischen Realschulen, München, 2001, 119.

The fifth topic is on the use of the Bible. People receive help from the Bible in various ways. Some use it to clarify their experiences, discover new standards of orientation and ways out of deprivation or depression, strengthen their faith, find consolation and draw hope. The pupils will first learn the two major divisions of the Bible into Old and New Testaments and understand the Bible as a collection of the "Word of God". With the help of selected Biblical texts, which are meaningful to the teacher, the pupils will learn different ways of accessing the Bible. They will note that expressions, thoughts and interpretations of some Biblical personalities are still significant today. They will thereby gain new insights which will eventually awaken new interest in Biblically testified experiences and realizations. In this way, the willingness to read the Bible will grow and its knowledge can inspire and encourage a life of faith.[271]

The sixth and last topic deals with the anti-ecclesial actions of some young people. Indifferentism and criticism against the Church, but also a positive community experience of young people are starting points for a proper discussion of the Church, understood as a community of believers. The lesson of this topic will give them the opportunity of comparing their ideals or personal images about the Church and what the Church actually is. By examining some statements about the Church, they will be able to weigh their pros and cons so as to ascertain the justifiability of some antagonistic movements against the Church. An encounter with some ecclesial personalities (such as Francis of Assisi, Edith Stein, Mother Theresa of Calcutta and Rupert Mayer) and an insight into the many social and charitable activities in the Church (such as Missio and Caritas) can arouse the interest of the pupils for the task of the Church and encourage them to engage in it.[272]

3.7.3.6 Religious Education in the Tenth Class of the Intermediate Secondary School

The tenth year of learning in the intermediate secondary school requires that the pupils give an account of their previous school years and draw up a balance sheet about their experiences. This account of their previous school years is realized in the final examination which takes place at this level of learning. This examination requires their personal commitment and at the same time offers them the opportunity to participate in building the present and the future. The religious education curriculum at this level of academic pursuit gives them lessons which help to prepare them to deal with crises in their lives, in the family

271 Cf. Ibid., 120.

272 Cf. Katholisches Schulkommissariat in Bayern, Lehrplan für Katholische Religionslehre an den bayerischen Realschulen, München, 2001, 121.

and among friends as well as how to cope with these situations. These lessons are divided into five topics which are:

1. "Say who you are – Discovering Jesus new
2. On the road to partnership: Marriage and family from a Christian perspective
3. Are we allowed to do everything we can? – Chances and dangers of a dignified life
4. Experiencing guilt: Gaining freedom through forgiveness and reconciliation
5. How will everything end? – Peaceful and future hope of Christians"[273]

The first topic serves as a revision lesson on the person of Jesus. The need for this is that the guidance of the pupils in their religious development requires that they should be opened up again and again to new approaches to Jesus. The lesson will therefore give them renewed opportunities to deal with various testimonies about Jesus and thereby discover how meaningful the stories of relationship with Jesus can be. Above all, an experiential learning with images of Jesus from the art world can also help them to perceive Jesus as a model and inspiration for the people who are committed to building a more humane and just world.[274]

The second topic is a lesson on Christian marriage and the establishment of Christian families. All serious challenges to human relationships require the acceptance of and the respect for others in their uniqueness and differences. The lesson will afford the pupils the opportunity of dealing with the conditions of a successful relationship and the importance of Church marriage so as to comprehend the essence of the sacrament of Matrimony. They will also learn that this sacrament can, as a sign of God's nearness, give a new quality to partnership and a reliable basis to a united family life.[275]

In the third topic, the pupils will learn the morality of certain human acts aimed at manipulating life. As a result of the steadily growing possibilities that influence human life, it is necessary to enable the pupils to search for the standards and limits of human life as well as a more differentiated judgement training and responsible opinion about life. The lesson will give them the opportunity of dealing with the basic standards of orientation, especially that of human dignity, so as to be aware that Christians cannot shy away from

273 Ibid., 128-132.

274 Cf. Ibid., 128.

275 Cf. Katholisches Schulkommissariat in Bayern, Lehrplan für Katholische Religionslehre an den bayerischen Realschulen, München, 2001, 129.

their responsibility of protecting creation and life in general. They will also be helped to become aware that a person must be guided in his or her actions not only in individual interest, but also in the interest of technical feasibility and economic benefit of all.[276]

The fourth topic is a lesson on guilt, sin, forgiveness and reconciliation. Even when people perceive and experience the phenomenon of guilt very differently, the various forms and mechanisms of apology will confirm the deep longing for freedom from sin and guilt. The lesson will help the pupils deal with stories about guilt in order to discover how guilt, as a multi-dimensional phenomenon, can be a burden in life. It will further help them to recognize how people deal with guilt and how questionable such handling can sometimes be. In this way, the pupils will be ready to perceive their feelings of guilt differently as well as judge their reactions more critically. With the help of Biblical narratives (e.g. Gen. 3:2; 2 Sam. 12:1-9; Mt. 25:42-45), they will learn how guilt can lead to or become sin, the various ways to which God directs the people in order for them to be free from sin and how to open up to a newness of life.[277]

The fifth and last topic of the tenth class of the intermediate secondary school concludes the lessons of religious education at this level of learning. It handles the social issue of justice and peace in the world. The fact that world peace is constantly threatened does not remove it from being the dream-wish of all humanity. In this lesson, the pupils will be helped to be aware that the Church is entrusted with the eschatological promises of God for the weak, for the reconciliation, justice, peace and the integrity of creation and at the same time remains a sign of hope for humanity. In this way, they can be ready to deal with new attempts at a solution to the problem of a humanly dignified co-existence in the (one) world.[278]

3.7.3.7 Summary

The intermediate secondary school has the task of preparing students for the acquisition of various careers. In religious education, the students are to gain in-depth knowledge of God that can help them to see themselves as an integral part of the people of God gathered together as a Christian community. Using the Bible as a guide, they are to see in the faith of Abraham and Sarah how human beings can react to God's revelation of Himself. They will also learn how to relate to people of other religions especially the Muslims, Hindus and Bud-

276 Cf. Ibid., 130.

277 Cf. Ibid., 131.

278 Cf. Katholisches Schulkommissariat in Bayern, Lehrplan für Katholische Religionslehre an den bayerischen Realschulen, München, 2001, 132.

dhists. Faith in God is presented as a personal decision that can be practiced in accordance with one's conscience. The Christian faith offers opportunities of a happy conjugal life, freedom from guilt through reconciliation and hope of eternal life with God after death.

3.7.4 Religious Education in the General Secondary School

The teaching of religion in the general secondary school has the task of opening the religious dimensions of some unclear realities to the pupils and enabling them to identify and deepen their life perspectives and interpretations of these realities from the point of view of the Christian faith.[279] In religious education, the living conditions and environment of the pupils are taken seriously and the question of the whence, the whither and the why of life unfolds in their manner of reasoning and expression. The objectives and contents of religious education at this level of academic pursuit unfold in three areas of learning. These areas are realized in the Christian faith, the Biblical message and the life of the Church as the inspiration for personal development, interpretation of life and the ability to dialogue effectively with other religions.[280] These objectives and contents will enable the pupils to express the faith in the context of life and to understand life in the light of faith. The religious education curriculum for the general secondary school contains a six-year programme of materials for learning from the fifth class to the tenth class. One unique factor about the general secondary school is the possibility of changing over to the "Mittlere-Reife-Zug" in the seventh class of learning. The pupils who decide to complete their secondary education in the regular system will conclude their religious education courses in the ninth year while those who change to the "Mittlere-Reife-Zug" will continue until the tenth year. The materials for their learning will now be discussed in the subsequent parts of this section.

3.7.4.1 Religious Education in the Fifth Class of the General Secondary School

The entrance into the general secondary school is the beginning of a new phase of life for the pupils. The school and school buildings are often new, and frequently the school location is also new. The class consists of pupils from different places and families. The religious education curriculum is designed to offer the pupils lessons that can help them to deal with their new environment, the new people around them and the requirements of their new status. These

279 Cf. Katholisches Schulkommissariat in Bayern, Lehrplan für Katholische Religionslehre an den bayerischen Hauptschulen, München, 2004, 19.

280 Cf. Ibid.

lessons will also enable them to find their position in the class and to merge their personal interests with the needs of the class. The lessons are divided into six topics which are:

1. "Living together – Being there for one another
2. Faith and trust – God's way with Abraham
3. Having time for oneself and others – Having time for God
4. Tracing the ways of Jesus – The life and mission of Jesus
5. The local Church – A community and its history
6. People in need – Encounter can bring change"[281]

The first topic introduces the pupils to the practice of love of neighbour and love of nature. They are already connected to their contemporaries and other people around them in various ways. The lesson of this topic will help them to be conscious of the people and surroundings that are important in their lives so that they will realize that every living creature needs attention and mindfulness. They will also be helped to be aware that a successful co-existence – at both big and small levels – depends on mutual commitments. Christian life and the impulse of faith can encourage the pupils to participate in a community life, practice respect for all living things and see mutual understanding and support as important basic attitudes of co-habitation.[282]

The second topic presents the pupils with Abraham as the father of faith. In the Bible, the stories of Abraham and Sarah speak of God as the One who turns to humans and humans as the ones who out of trust follow the ways of God. With selected Biblical narratives, the lesson will help the pupils to recognise and perceive the ways of a genuine faith and how people, even in the ups and downs of their lives, adhere to the promptings of God and live under His dictates. They will therefore be helped to be attentive to the various forms of belief in order to discover ways and manners in which they can live out and express their faith in God.[283]

The third topic is meant to introduce the pupils to the need for personal reflection and recollection. They will get to know that taking breaks for rest and contemplation, going to isolated areas in order to interact and celebrate with one another and disrupt the normal everyday activity can sometimes be good and rewarding. In the practice of the basic attitudes of prayer, the pupils will learn to express what motivates them and thereby experience a sense of

281 Katholisches Schulkommissariat in Bayern, Lehrplan für Katholische Religionslehre an den bayerischen Hauptschulen, München, 2004, 21.

282 Cf. Ibid., 26.

283 Cf. Ibid.

acceptance and security. The lesson will help them to develop their own forms of prayer and be aware that the entire life can be converted to a life of contemplation. The experience that prayer connects people with one another can help them to appreciate important feasts and celebrations of the liturgical year as the highlights of the community of faith.[284] This is concretized in the theme of the visit of Pope Benedict XVI to Regensburg in September 2006: "He who believes is never alone" (wer glaubt, ist nie allein).

The fourth topic is a lesson on the person of Jesus Christ. The pupils already have different ideas and references about Him (from their previous religious learning in the primary school). The lesson will give them the knowledge about the home life of Jesus and His lifestyle so as to illustrate how He grew up and lived in Jewish piety. They will get to know how people, through an encounter with Jesus experienced acceptance, redemption and salvation; followed Him or rejected Him. They should however be more concerned with the witnesses of the consistent appearances of Jesus until His Crucifixion and Resurrection. By so doing, they will understand the meaning of the Death and Resurrection of Jesus Christ as the focal point of the New Testament preaching and thereby open themselves to the Christian feast of Easter.[285]

The fifth lesson introduces the pupils to life in a typical parish. Many of the pupils come in contact with the parish only when the occasion demands. The lesson is meant to help them to know the services and forms of organization in the parish and to become aware of how people believe with one another and are there for one another so that the interest in the community can be awakened and strengthened in them. They will also perceive the Church building, in its artistic and functional form, as the centre of the community. An insight into the history of the community will help them be aware of what the faith meant to their forefathers and how they preserved and transmitted it. The pupils will also be helped to recognise the essence of important feasts of the local Church and see the parish as part of a diocese.[286]

In the sixth topic, the pupils will learn the mystery of suffering. Pictures and news of emergency situations in the world pass daily into our lives through the media and lead to very different reactions. Even in our immediate environment, we often meet people in need. The lesson will therefore help the pupils to recognise with corresponding examples, the needs of children and adults far and near as well as become aware of the causes of their sufferings. In Biblical stories (e.g. Mt. 25: 31-40; Lk. 6: 6-11), they will get to know the love of Jesus

284 Cf. Katholisches Schulkommissariat in Bayern, Lehrplan für Katholische Religionslehre an den bayerischen Hauptschulen, München, 2004, 27.

285 Cf. Ibid., 28.

286 Cf. Ibid.

for suffering people. The example of Jesus can encourage the pupils to actively participate in some help-oriented projects and actions such as the Star Singers, Misereo and Missio.[287]

3.7.4.2 Religious Education in the Sixth Class of the General Secondary School

In the sixth class, the pupils have already become accustomed to the system of teaching, learning and life of the secondary school. The structures that govern the co-existence and co-operation of the class have been formed. Attention is no longer focused only on the organisation of the class but also on the establishment of a life of togetherness in the entire school community. From this background, the lessons offered the pupils in religious education are meant to guide them in discovering the meaning of life not only from within but also from without. These lessons are divided into six topics which are:

1. "People are asking for God – In search for answers
2. The emergence of Christian communities – From Jerusalem to the world
3. Leisure – Between interests and boredom
4. Liberation and salvation – Basic experiences of faith
5. Dealing with expectations – Finding guidance for actions
6. Expressions of deeper experience of reality – Symbols and sacraments"[288]

The first topic is a lesson on the nature of God. Young people are often concerned with questions of whether God exists, whether and how His existence can be imagined. The lesson will therefore give the pupils the opportunity of dealing with children's, adolescents' and adults' visions of God. Using the example of Biblical stories (e.g. Gen. 18:1-10; Ex. 3:1-15; 1 Kgs. 19:1-13; Is. 46:1-4), they will be able to discover how God reveals Himself and how people describe their experience of God. This will help them to open up to learn how Jesus brings people close to God and to be aware that Christians believe in the triune God (cf. Mt. 28:19ff).[289]

The second topic handles the Christian faith from its history as an apostolic community. Many young people are finding it increasingly difficult to hear and accept the appeal of the Christian faith. Using the example of the coura-

287 Cf. Katholisches Schulkommissariat in Bayern, Lehrplan für Katholische Religionslehre an den bayerischen Hauptschulen, München, 2004, 29.

288 Ibid., 21.

289 Cf. Katholisches Schulkommissariat in Bayern, Lehrplan für Katholische Religionslehre an den bayerischen Hauptschulen, München, 2004, 32.

geous departure of the disciples of Jesus who followed new ways and forms of life (cf. Mt. 28:1-8; Acts. 2:1-42), the pupils can be aroused to have interest in the life of the Christian faith. In this way, they will also learn how the first Christian communities lived and also fought against conflicts (cf. Acts. 2:43-47; 4:32-37). This will also help them to get the sense of cohesion and charisma that characterised the then "young" Church. Using a range of (living) witnesses (e.g. the story of the life and works of St. Corbinian[290]), they can discover what an amazing power faith can release.[291]

The third topic deals with the use of leisure especially in connection with the media. The need for this lesson is as a result of the fact that the pupils, most often, experience their leisure primarily as "freedom" which does not need to be disrupted in order to pursue their interests and inclinations or try something new. The lesson will help them first and foremost to realize that time is precious. Based on the important role the media play in the use of leisure, the pupils should be helped to be aware that the media often represent a pre-conceived view of reality. In this way, they can be moved to a more conscious and meaningful use of the media. A (possible) meeting with individuals and groups of the (Church) youth apostolate can help to identify their interests, abilities and talents in order to meaningfully use their time, also in the Christian sense, with and for one another.[292]

The fourth topic is a lesson on the Christian hope for salvation following the faith in the Exodus event. Just like people always remember their dramatic experiences, so too does Israel remember the basic events of its history of faith. Among them is the key liberation from Egyptian slavery (cf. Ex. 13:17-14:31). This lesson will help the pupils to deal with the Exodus narratives so as to become aware of the outline of the traditional history of the Israelites. With the help of further Biblical evidences (e.g. Ps. 78:1-29; Is. 51:9-12), the pupils will become attentive to basic faith experiences and learn to understand the Bible as diverse collection of texts. Concrete examples of (living) faith (e.g. personal life experience) can also encourage them to relate the existential Christian hope for redemption and salvation to the Exodus narratives.[293]

290 St. Corbinian was the first Bishop of the diocese of Freising. As a result of the Bavarian concordance, the diocese of Freising and the diocese of Munich were merged together in 1817 and elevated to the status of an archdiocese. St. Corbinian was adopted as the patron saint of the archdiocese. His feast day is the 2oth of November.

291 Cf. Katholisches Schulkommissariat in Bayern, Lehrplan für Katholische Religionslehre an den bayerischen Hauptschulen, München, 2004, 32.

292 Cf. Ibid., 33.

293 Cf. Katholisches Schulkommissariat in Bayern, Lehrplan für Katholische Religionslehre an den bayerischen Hauptschulen, München, 2004, 33.

In the fifth topic, the pupils will learn the right use of the conscience. Young people increasingly want to be self-responsible and therefore begin to question the essence of some usual patterns of behaviour as well as their values. Using concrete examples, the pupils will recognise that standards or norms are not only narrow but can also be very helpful. The lesson will help them to learn to weigh which rules contribute to a successful life and, in this context, appreciate Biblical guidance as life-enhancing teachings. Various texts and articles can be used to clarify that the conscience is the innermost point of rest/unrest and an advocate of life. In this way, the pupils can develop a positive feeling of the power of the conscience.[294]

The sixth and last topic of this section is a lesson on the Christian symbols and sacraments as outward signs of inward grace. Regular signs of life (e.g. water, light) can be given special status and, often, can be preserved as precious. This can also be attributed to learning. This lesson will help the pupils to become aware of the multifaceted possible meanings of the ordinary things they see around them. Through texts, songs and images, they will realize that symbols allow for an in-depth view of the world. They should therefore learn to understand Christian symbols and rituals as expressions of decisive life and faith and at the same time become sensitive to the sacraments as effective and encouraging signs of God's nearness to humans.[295]

3.7.4.3 Religious Education in the Seventh Class of the General Secondary School

The seventh class of the general secondary school is a unique class in the sense that some of the pupils, in collaboration with their parents and guardians, will change from the regular secondary school system to the so called "Mittlere-Reife-Zug".[296] This system is aimed at offering the pupils the chances of securing better certificates and more opportunities in the labour market. Those who continue in the regular secondary school system will be mobilized to pursue a life career that can guarantee their success in life. The religious education curriculum will offer them, at this level of their academic pursuit, lessons that can help them to be strengthened in their self-esteem and self-confidence. These lessons are divided into six topics which are:

1. "Source of courage – Jesus' message of the kingdom of God
2. Yielding or asserting – Resolving conflict fairly

294 Cf. Ibid., 34.

295 Cf. Ibid., 35.

296 Cf. Ibid., 37.

3. Muslims in our midst – Understanding one another better
4. Starting anew – Ways out of guilt and fear
5. Who am I, how do I want to be? – In search for the self
6. One God and Lord – Different denominations"[297]

The first topic is a lesson on the Gospel message of Jesus Christ as the source of courage for all Christians. In this lesson, the pupils will get to know that the Gospels, with their message of the kingdom of God, belong to the basic contents of Christianity. They will be helped to recognize the Gospels as testimonies of a faith-based community. In this way, they will become aware that the message of the kingdom of God is the central theme in the life and ministry of Jesus. They can therefore see the promise of God for salvation in the words and actions of Jesus and open up to His Spirit Who inspires them to help in building a more humane and just world. The pupils will further get to know more testimonies of the New Testament and people who live by the power of the Gospel so as to be aware of the importance of the Bible for the faith of the individual and the Church.[298]

The second topic deals with conflict. On the basis of daily struggles, the pupils will in this lesson identify the causes of tension, be aware of conflicts in their own behaviour and consider very carefully the consequences of some of their behavioural patterns. They should therefore know the value of conflict management and open up for the responsible ways of handling conflicts. It will be made clear to them in this lesson that there are essential elements of a humanly dignified way of handling quarrels from the Christian perspective which challenge them to recognize the meaning of non-violence, dialogue, moral courage and reconciliation. These elements also challenge them to incorporate these virtues into their lives.[299]

The third topic is a special lesson on how to relate to Muslims. In school and everyday life, the pupils often encounter people of the Islamic faith. A closer look into some Muslim lifestyles, feasts and customs may arouse interest in their religion. In this lesson, the pupils will learn the basics of Islamic doctrine and thereby perceive how Islam shapes the daily lives of its adherents. They will take note of some similarities and differences between Christianity and Islam. In this way, they will examine their own religious beliefs, seek

297 Katholisches Schulkommissariat in Bayern, Lehrplan für Katholische Religionslehre an den bayerischen Hauptschulen, München, 2004, 21.

298 Cf. Ibid., 38.

299 Cf. Ibid.

means of breaking down prejudices and develop the possibilities for a tolerable and peaceful co-existence.[300]

The fourth topic handles the issue of guilt, sin and a possible way out through reconciliation. The pupils will be helped to understand that there are ups and downs in life. If only success, perfection and strength count, then self-esteem will be questioned through failure, guilt and fear. The pupils will learn that failure is only an invitation to try again and not a cause of despair. Concrete examples of how people deal with guilt, fear and sin can therefore help them to perceive their own behaviour with more consciousness and a better understanding of the meaning of sin. The way Jesus handled guilty people should make it clear to the pupils that God accepts every human being unconditionally and through His approach to humans, makes repentance and forgiveness, reconciliation and new beginnings possible. This can encourage the pupils to accept themselves, seek means of starting afresh and be ready for forgiveness and reconciliation.[301]

The lesson of the fifth topic has a psychological significance. It is meant to help the pupils discover who they are and be able to situate themselves properly in the society. In the contemporary society, it has become increasingly necessary for young people in the puberty stage of life to give their lives personal direction. This is why they need to emulate some holy men and women, whose lives can help them to consciously perceive their own ideas and wishes of life. In this lesson, they will be given some insights into the developmental stages of the puberty so that they can understand themselves and others better. They will also be helped to realize that everyone has strengths and weaknesses and that no one is perfect. They will therefore learn the basic Christian attitudes and virtues as means of supporting life. The Biblical message of God as One, Who loves people can assist them to find their own ways of life.[302]

The sixth and last topic of this section is a lesson on Christian unity. The pupils will be helped to recognize the significant Christian denominations in their immediate environment and discover some of their similarities and differences. These differences, especially, will be understandable when the pupils gain insight into the historical reasons that gave rise to the emergence of the various Christian denominations. They will learn the basic similarities of the Christian belief and be aware of the concern of the Ecumenical Movement.

---

300 Cf. Katholisches Schulkommissariat in Bayern, Lehrplan für Katholische Religionslehre an den bayerischen Hauptschulen, München, 2004, 39.

301 Cf. Ibid., 40.

302 Cf. Ibid.

The brotherhood of Christians can fortify the pupils to engage in various forms of Christian fellowship.[303]

3.7.4.4 Religious Education in the Eighth Class of the General Secondary School

The central theme in the eighth class of the general secondary school is the choice of career.[304] This why the lessons the pupils receive at this level of their academic learning are geared towards preparing them for their encounter with the labour market. In the religious education curriculum, they are offered a series of lessons that can help them to organize themselves in the society so as to live and work neatly, reliably and responsibly. Above all, they will be trained to recognize their opportunities and make use of them.[305] These lessons are divided into six topics which are:

1. "Longing for life – In search for meaning
2. What the Church represents – Giving support to life
3. Going together – Friendship and love
4. "Hear O Israel, the Lord our God is one" – The Jewish religion
5. Creation is entrusted to us – Safeguarding and organizing the world
6. In search of a personal way – What supports and directs life"[306]

The first topic is a lesson on the search for the meaning of life. The pupils will be made to understand that young people are often longing for a life that is worthwhile. The lesson will help them to learn different expressions of the desire to know the meaning of life and be aware that this longing is not a completely individual matter but an open affair which constantly challenges personal creativity. Using concrete examples, they will get to know the fate of some people who have fallen into addiction due to the wrong approach in the search for the meaning of life. The pupils will therefore be encouraged to look for ways which can help them to express their lives in freedom. They can thereby discover what promotes their happiness and transform this into their daily lives.[307]

303 Cf. Katholisches Schulkommissariat in Bayern, Lehrplan für Katholische Religionslehre an den bayerischen Hauptschulen, München, 2004, 41.

304 Cf. Ibid., 43.

305 Cf. Ibid.

306 Ibid., 22.

307 Cf. Katholisches Schulkommissariat in Bayern, Lehrplan für Katholische Religionslehre an den bayerischen Hauptschulen, München, 2004, 44.

The second topic introduces the Church to the pupils as an institution which gives support to life. The need for this is based on the fact that many young people are uninformed about the services and functions of the Church. The pupils will therefore be helped to be aware of the work of the Church in their immediate environment. In this way, they will learn to understand the Church as a community of faith, whose duty it is, to cater to other people – the poor, the needy and the oppressed. An insight into some Church activities and projects for justice and peace in the world can help them to identify some aspects of a responsible lifestyle and to develop an interest in the Church.[308]

The third topic is a lesson on the establishment of a lasting human relationship. Questions about friendship, love and sexuality occupy the minds of many young people to a high degree. In this lesson, the pupils will be helped to become conscious of the different settings in these areas of life and to learn how to question their personal ideas about social life. They will be encouraged to deal with their own individuality and questions of human sexuality so as to understand that sexuality is a precious gift which deserves to be respected and appreciated. They will also learn the Biblical statements about the relationship between man and woman and be aware that affection, tenderness and sexuality are forms of an intimate relationship and processes of a lifelong love. In this way, they will be helped to understand the Biblical-Christian view of love as a measure of life and also be sensitive to the transforming power of love.[309]

The fourth topic presents the pupils with the Jewish religion. They will be helped to understand that Christianity is rooted in Judaism. The lesson will allow them to be attentive to the religion of the Jews in their culture and will help them know the basics of Judaism. In this way, they can perceive the wealth of faith contained in this religion and discover how Judaism strongly shapes Christianity. The often tragic history of the Jews in Europe and the story of how Christians feel guilty due to some of their actions against the Jews should serve as warnings towards any form of anti-Semitism. Thus, the pupils should be encouraged to strive for the dignity of every person and for understanding and reconciliation.[310]

The fifth topic is a lesson on the love of nature. The pupils often experience the magnificence of nature and at the same time the depressing fact of ecological degradation. This experience can arouse their interest in dealing with the questions of the meaning, origin and destiny of our ecological world. They will therefore learn the basic statements of the Biblical creation texts and be able

308 Cf. Ibid.

309 Cf. Ibid., 45.

310 Cf. Ibid., 46.

to interpret the world as God's creation. They will also learn the Biblical message of the human person as a being created in the image and according to the likeness of God. Furthermore, they will become aware that the entire creation was subjected to the responsible care of the human person. Thus, they would be encouraged to behave in an environmentally conscious manner and develop a caring and respectful attitude towards all creatures.[311]

The sixth and last topic of the eighth class of the general secondary school is concerned with the human conscience. It is becoming increasingly difficult today to come to terms with the ever faster changing world of career, technology and science as well as to cope with life and some life ideas. With regard to independent living, the pupils will learn how to deal with the values and attitudes of people and know the importance of the conscience for every person. They will thereby familiarize themselves with the Christian understanding of conscience. They will also get to know people who found a lasting and sustainable foundation in a vital relationship with other people and with God. They will further discover that some people feel addressed by God in different ways and also express this in various forms in their lives. In this way, they can be encouraged to open themselves up anew to God and people.[312]

3.7.4.5 Religious Education in the Ninth Class of the General Secondary School

In the ninth year of their general secondary education, the pupils feel more than ever that they are responsible for their lives.[313] They develop new forms of motivation which promote one's progress in a goal-oriented manner. In religious education, they are offered lessons which will help them to differentiate between their own points of view and those of others; separate the desirable from the achievable and stand against some attempts which have manipulative effects.[314] These lessons are divided into five topics which are:

1. "'Human dignity is inalienable' – Respect and help for other people
2. Jesus Christ – An impetus and a challenge
3. The Church in history – The struggle for the realization of the Gospel
4. Things have their limits – Not giving up hope

311 Cf. Katholisches Schulkommissariat in Bayern, Lehrplan für Katholische Religionslehre an den bayerischen Hauptschulen, München, 2004, 47.

312 Cf. Ibid.

313 Cf. Katholisches Schulkommissariat in Bayern, Lehrplan für Katholische Religionslehre an den bayerischen Hauptschulen, München, 2004, 49.

314 Cf. Ibid.

5. "It is not good that the man should be alone" – Partnership, marriage and family"[315]

The first topic makes it clear to the pupils that the respect for human dignity belongs to the basic foundations of the society. The pupils will learn the various stages of human development so as to discover the need to value human dignity and hold humanity in a high esteem. They will be made to take note of the Biblical message that everyone is accepted and loved by God. The realization that the commitment to human dignity and the right to life belong to the basic mission of Christians should strengthen the willingness of the pupils to be oriented towards the guidelines for the protection of human life.[316]

The second topic presents the pupils with the person of Jesus Christ. In today's religious diversity, the figure of Jesus is viewed from different angles. Even the pupils may have, in the course of their school days, developed their own attitudes and beliefs. They will therefore deal with the many images of Jesus and the testimonies of the Bible in order to be aware of the deep humanity of Jesus which comforts, challenges or even induces pity. They will be helped to discover that people experience God's love in their encounter with Jesus Christ and also gain access to the statement of faith concerning Him as the Son of God. This can encourage them to rethink their own relationship with Jesus and give His words and deeds a chance in their lives.[317]

The third topic deals with the Church. The pupils will learn that the Church, just like any other large group in society, also experiences encouragement and criticism. To get a balanced picture of the Church therefore, the pupils need to be aware that a number of settings, requests and decisions regarding the Church require a historical perspective. They will learn the examples of the important periods of Church history in the general historical context; deal with the changing relationship between the Church and the society and also explore the question of the mission of the Church. An insight into the struggle for the realization of the Gospel should make the pupils aware that the joint action of all Christians designates the real Church.[318]

The fourth topic is a lesson on limitations and hope. It is becoming increasingly difficult, in a performance and progress oriented world, to live with limits and to accept one's limitations. The pupils will learn in this lesson that the experiences of imperfection, finitude and powerlessness belong to human

315 Ibid., 22.

316 Cf. Ibid., 50.

317 Cf. Katholisches Schulkommissariat in Bayern, Lehrplan für Katholische Religionslehre an den bayerischen Hauptschulen, München, 2004, 50.

318 Cf. Ibid., 51.

life. They will also learn the different ways of dealing with extreme experiences especially how people live with suffering, impermanence and death. They will bring their questions and possible answers about dying and death into full expression and also be attentive to the Christian belief in the hereafter. The Biblical-Christian message of the resurrection will also be taken into consideration so that the pupils can discover the hope of the resurrection as the central power of faith in people's lives. By opening themselves up to the faith of the resurrection, it may be clear to them that God carries every person in suffering and death and also promises eternal life.[319]

The fifth and last topic of this section introduces the pupils to the sacrament of marriage and life in the family. The need for security and love presses itself on many young people in search of a reliable relationship. In this lesson, the pupils will be helped to become conscious of their attitudes towards friendship and partnership and also become aware of the many expressions of love. Above all, they should be helped to recognize that a sexual relationship without tender loving care and personal responsibility for the dignity of the other partner and the self is not justified. They will therefore learn the requirements and standards for a happy partnership. They will further learn the importance of the sacrament of Matrimony for Catholics and be helped to understand the ecclesial teachings on marriage. In this way, they will become aware of basic Christian family life and the value of marriage and family.[320]

3.7.4.6 Religious Education in the Tenth Class of the General Secondary School

With the tenth class of the general secondary school, most pupils complete their full-time schooling. At the end is the final certificate examination. Their graduation is often attached to an open choice of career. While in school, they prepare themselves for their forth-coming career life through such areas as: social engagement, help for the younger pupils, undertaking responsibilities in school committees and projects.[321] The religious education curriculum offers them lessons that serve as revision in preparation for their final examination. These lessons are divided into five topics which are:

1. "The human person and power- Between temptation and responsibility
2. Faith – Is it overtaken?

319 Cf. Ibid., 52.

320 Cf. Katholisches Schulkommissariat in Bayern, Lehrplan für Katholische Religionslehre an den bayerischen Hauptschulen, München, 2004, 52.

321 Cf. Ibid., 77.

3. Living as a Christian – Diverse forms of expression
4. Meeting foreign cultures and people – Hinduism and Buddhism
5. My way of life – My ideas of life"[322]

The first topic raises the issue of power and its uses. In human interaction, the importance and influence of power is often felt. The pupils will learn in this lesson the different forms of expression of power, recognize its ambiguity and develop basic rules for its responsible uses. They will also reflect on some Biblical texts which deal with the issue of power. Using concrete examples, they will examine the extent to which power is used at the expense or benefit of other people and the world around them. Christian standards can help them to understand some social issues and develop responsible attitudes towards the use of power.[323]

The second topic treats once more the issue of faith. In the world of today, many people seem to be of the opinion that knowledge and belief are two incompatible opposites. But the lesson is meant to counteract this erroneous position. The pupils will be helped to be aware that knowledge and belief can serve as complementary approaches in their relation to the definition of the reality. They will therefore deal with different perceptions and attitudes of faith in God in order to recognize some questionable ideas and forms of faith. This can help them to develop a workable understanding of faith and to open up to the question of the significance of faith for their lives.[324]

In the third topic, the pupils are again meant to review what it means to live a Christian life. Christianity found and still finds its expression in a variety of ways. Young people who are looking for an authentic life and self-realization can find excitement and orientation for their own life practices through an encounter with various expressions of the Christian life. They will thereby recognize some basic elements of Christian spirituality and open up themselves for self-discovery as a means of experiencing God.[325]

The fourth topic handles once more the presence of foreign religions, cultures and people in Germany, but this time in a different direction. The pupils will be introduced to Hinduism and Buddhism as two world religions that have also influenced many people including the Bavarians. The teachings, symbols and rituals of these religions show themselves in many ways in the entire European culture. The pupils will get to know these strange but often seemingly

322 Ibid., 22

323 Cf. Ibid., 78.

324 Cf. Katholisches Schulkommissariat in Bayern, Lehrplan für Katholische Religionslehre an den bayerischen Hauptschulen, München, 2004, 78.

325 Cf. Ibid., 79.

impressive ideas and ways of life in order to be aware of how Hinduism and Buddhism explain the mysteries and problems of life and also try to solve them. The basic statements of faith of these religions are to be identified and analysed in relation to Christianity. In this way, the willingness to meet people of other faiths with tolerance and respect can grow in young people.[326]

The fifth and last topic of the tenth class concludes the religious education lessons in the general secondary school. In this lesson, the pupils are to be given a sense of confidence in their new phase of life. This is because after the tenth class, the pupils are in connection with various future prospects. The lesson will therefore help them to have a flash back into their previous lives in order to discover and also reflect on some important steps of their lives. The interpretation of life through faith in God can give them the necessary impulse, confidently to go into the future with determination and hope.[327]

3.7.4.7 Summary

The general secondary school is the school of artisans. Those who attend this school are bound to graduate as professional craftsmen or women in the vocational school. In religious education, they gain the idea of God from the Biblically recorded encounter between God and humans, especially from the story of Abraham. From this story, they develop the sense of having time for God in prayer. Jesus is presented to them as a man of prayer whose mission is the salvation of mankind. Apart from gaining knowledge of the Christian religion and its different denominations, they are also informed about other religions such as: Judaism, Islam, Hinduism and Buddhism. Both Christianity and Islam trace their roots to Judaism, following their common paternity in Abraham. The students therefore learn the need for a peaceful co-existence with people of different religions as a means of preserving God's work of creation.

3.7.5 Religious Education in the Vocational School

In the vocational school, religious education is concerned with a variety of goals and values in the contemporary society from different attitudes of the pupils towards religion; and from the point of view of the Catholic faith, giving answers to some pressing questions of life.[328] The pupils are groomed to find some measures for success in life. Religious education entrusts them with

326 Cf. Ibid., 80.

327 Cf. Ibid.

328 Cf. Katholisches Schulkommissariat in Bayern, Lehrplan für die Berufsschule und Berufsfachschule, München, 1997, 6.

some traditions of faith and makes them to be aware of some personal ideals. It introduces them to the concepts of the Christian life and helps provision for them to come to terms with such concepts. Furthermore, religious education in the vocational school enables the pupils to make personal decisions in dealing with the choice of denomination and religion, philosophies and ideologies, and also helps them to show understanding and tolerance with regard to the decision and religion of others.[329] A course in religion also motivates the pupils to live a religious life and to perform responsible roles in the Church and in the society. The religious education curriculum offers the pupils a four-year programme of learning from the tenth class to the thirteenth class. Because the vocational school is a post-secondary institution, a detailed explanation of its religious education curriculum will not be given in this work. Its programmes of learning can only be summarised as follows:

Tenth Class of the Vocational School

1. "Who am I?
2. Work and leisure
3. Responsible partnership
4. Aggression – violence – non-violence
5. Mysterious powers – the one God
6. Joy of living and consumption"[330]

Eleventh Class of the Vocational School

1. "Christianity in everyday life
2. Unavailability of life
3. Responsibility – guilt – reconciliation
4. Religious currents
5. Opportunities to meet God
6. Death – and what next?"[331]

Twelfth and Thirteenth Classes of the Vocational School

1. "The question of the meaning of life
2. Questions for the Church
3. Human rights and social justice

329 Cf. Ibid.

330 Ibid., 10.

331 Katholisches Schulkommissariat in Bayern, Lehrplan für die Berufsschule und Berufsfachschule, München, 1997, 36.

4. Contribution to peace
5. Marriage and family
6. Faith and science
7. The human person in God's creation"[332]

3.8 Evaluation

The teaching of religion is very well incorporated into the German schools, especially in Bavaria which covers the area of this study. The mutual understanding between the Church and the State is seen in their joint effort in working for the upbringing of children. The Church plays a special role in inculcating religious norms into the children, both within and outside her immediate scope of operation. However, the antagonism against the Church, especially in the modern times, is seen in the refusal of some pupils (often under the influence of their parents) to accept and assimilate the teachings of the Church. This is the case especially in the new (communist) states of the German Federation.

Religious education in the German schools between 1945 and 1974 was mainly based on the catechism. A new wave of religious teaching was introduced into the school system in 1974 after the synod of the German Catholic dioceses. This synod categorised religious education into a number of conceptual analyses which were also accepted by the Protestant or Evangelical Churches.

In Munich and Fresing, religious education is jointly organised by the schools and the parishes within their location, using the curriculum of the State of Bavaria. All the schools in Bavaria use the same curriculum to ensure a uniform system of education, especially in the religious dispensation. Care was also taken to groom the pupils into the didactic of other religions in order to encourage a harmonious and peaceful co-existence with the adherents of these religions.

3.9 Summary

Germany is a religiously pluralistic country. Adherents of the major world religions can be found within its territory. Such religions are: Judaism, Christianity, Islam, Buddhism and Hinduism. Among these religions, Christianity influenced the cultural background of the German people. This can be seen in the many Christian feasts that play fundamental roles in the lives of the people. Such feasts include: Christmas, Easter and Pentecost. In Munich and Freis-

332 Ibid., 64.

ing, Marian feasts are also held in high esteem. The feast of the Assumption is celebrated with great festivities and visits to Marian shrines at pilgrimage centres. This day is also observed as a public holiday in the State of Bavaria. Religious education has undergone many series of historical setbacks due to wars (especially the First and the Second World Wars) and external (communist) influences. Under the current dispensation, the teaching of religion in the schools is directly under the control of State Governments. This is why religious education is regionally organised. The school system is designed to suit the academic disposition of the pupils. The primary school forms the basis of assessment. All children attend the same primary school. After acquiring a primary education, the pupils are sent to different schools for the acquisition of secondary education in accordance with their academic performances. These schools are: the grammar school, the intermediate secondary school and the general secondary school. The vocational school is attended by students who graduated in the general secondary school and is therefore a post-secondary institution. Religious education forms part of the curriculum of both the primary and the secondary schools and it is meant to prepare the pupils for two sacraments of initiation namely: First Holy Communion and Confirmation as well as give them a proper life orientation. First Holy Communion takes place in primary three while Confirmation is administered to the pupils at different classes of the secondary school. The candidates for the two sacraments are often prepared in a joint effort of the school and the parish of its jurisdiction. This combination of school catechesis with parish catechesis plays a very important role in integrating the pupils into the life of the Christian community located in their immediate environment.

4. Religious Education in the Family and in the Church

This chapter deals with the family and the Church as two separate places where religion is taught, outside the school. Chapters two and three have already surveyed the teaching of religion in the Nigerian and German schools respectively, paying particular attention to the schools in the diocese of Ahiara and in the archdiocese of Munich and Freising. In addition to the schools, religious education in the family and the Church within these two resource areas is also based on giving children the basic teachings about Christianity. However, religious education in the family and in the Church differs from the teaching of religion in the schools in the sense that the former is purely denominational and therefore is mainly concerned with the preparation of children for the reception of the sacraments, their integration into the life of the Church and their training for a responsible future life in society. Family catechesis is meant to offer the children parental upbringing so that they might grow into responsible adulthood. This chapter therefore presents the family and the Church as places which "have always served as centres for transmitting knowledge, centres of instruction for both the old and the young".[1] It considers among other things, the contents and goals of religious education in these two places with regard to the roles of the resource people involved (the parents and children; the priest and catechist). This will be undertaken in two steps. The first step will elucidate the typical life of a family so as to find out how the teaching of religion contributes to the upbringing of the children and the unity of the parents. The second step will be an examination of the teaching of religion in the Church within a typical parish setting. It will be focused on what the Church offers the children as a means of contributing to their religious and life orientation. In this work, the terms "religious education in the family and in the Church" will be inter-changeably used with the terms "family catechesis and parish catechesis" respectively.

4.1 Religious Education in the Family

Religious education in the family takes place as a joint effort of both the biological parents and other members of the extended family such as grandparents, uncles and aunts. It was defined by Lombaerts and Osewska as follows:

1 Nwaoru E. O., Youth Upbringing: A Process of Making Adult Christians, in: Nwatu F., Eze A. (Eds.), Bigard Theological Studies, 27, 1, Enugu, 2007, 74.

In the family context "religious education" does not mean only the process of teaching and learning the content of what makes up Christianity. "Religious education" within the family may refer to that process of learning and sharing everyday events in the light of religious understanding, in most cases in the light of Christian understanding.[2]

Parents especially exhibit their worth in a way and manner in which they see to the upbringing of their children by teaching them those norms which generate the process of Christian nurturing. The education of children is one of the obligations which parents receive as part of the properties of marriage.[3] Children come into the family as fruits of marriage and have the right to a proper upbringing. Parents therefore perform this duty as an on-going process in the lives of their children and as a sign of love and acceptance. Their goal is to deepen and support the growth of the faith of their children. They aim at raising their children not only as religious persons, but also as those fully integrated into the social norms of the society. The goals of religious education in the family were summarised by Lombaerts and Osewska as follows:

The organization of religious education in the family is a complicated process, which involves several components: supporting universal human conditions for personal and religious development, creating a general religious climate full of love, respect, peace and justice but also religious symbols and rituals, clarification of various "pre-understandings", exploration of meaning and religious traditions, open communication and interactions between parents and children, accepting religious sensitivity, convictions, and practices among family members, assisting youngsters in the process of discovering and communicating values.[4]

In this section, religious education in the family will be treated with regards to the meaning of the family, the role of parents and the role of children.

4.1.1 Meaning of the Family

Before ever formal education of the child begins in schools, the general education for life begins at home, right there in the family … It continues even later

2 Lombaerts H., Osewska E., Family Catechesis/Religious Education in the 21st Century Europe in: Osewska E., Stala J. (Eds.), Religious Education/Catechesis in the Family: A European Perspective, Warszawa, 2010, 43.

3 Cf. The Code of Canon Law, Number 1055, Paragraph 1.

4 Lombaerts H., Osewska E., Family Catechesis/Religious Education in the 21st Century Europe in: Osewska E., Stala J. (Eds.), Religious Education/Catechesis in the Family: A European Perspective, Warszawa, 2010, 43.

after formal education has started both in the nuclear family as well as in the extended family, the kindred, the village, etc.[5]

The family is seen here as both an important human institution and the first house of formation. It is also recognised as the most important value in life.[6] In the view of Kunstmann:

> *The family enjoys high esteem. It is regarded as a home and place of security but also considered by many as "sacred".*[7]

The sacred character of the family is realised in the fact that the family was instituted by God to guarantee the propagation of the human species. In the traditional African setting, the family is understood to be of two ties – nuclear and extended. The nuclear family is also regarded as the immediate family. It is made up of the father, the mother and the child (children). Every member is accepted and given a position, regardless of any condition of life. This nuclear perspective of the family also reflected in the *Britannica World Language Dictionary* in which it was defined as: "a group of persons consisting of parents and their children".[8] It is a gathering of father, mother and child or children in an enclosed familiarity which encourages cordiality and intimacy.[9] The family is situated within the larger society with which it is in constant relationship. Lombaerts and Osewska defined it as follows:

> *The family is a dynamic organism which is in continuous interaction with its environment, receiving impulses, responding to the endless opportunities to establish solidarities or antagonisms.*[10]

The family serves as the place where the upbringing of the child begins. Nwaoru describes it as follows:

---

5 Nwaoru E. O., Youth Upbringing: A Process of Making Adult Christians, in: Nwatu F., Eze A. (Eds.), Bigard Theological Studies, 27, 1, Enugu, 2007, 74.

6 Cf. Lombaerts H., Osewska E., The Modern Christian Family as a first Setting for Religious and Moral Education?, in: Osewska E., Stala J. (Eds.), Religious Education/Catechesis in the Family: A European Perspective, Warszawa, 2010, 18.

7 Kunstmann J., Religionspädagogik, eine Einführung, 2.Auflage, (trans. Nwandu P.), Basel, 2010, 89.

8 Britannica World Language Dictionary, Vol. 1, New York, 1964, 457.

9 Cf. Bendel H., Biesinger A., Familienkatechese, in: Bitter G., Englert R., Miller G., Nipkow K. E. (Hg.), Neues Handbuch religionspädagogischer Grundbegriffe, 2. Auflage, München, 2009, 310.

10 Lombaerts H., Osewska E., The Modern Christian Family as a first Setting for Religious and Moral Education?, in: Osewska E., Stala J. (Eds.), Religious Education/Catechesis in the Family: A European Perspective, Warszawa, 2010, 12

The family is regarded as the most important social unit in human development and, by implication, the most important agent in youth upbringing.[11]

The social character of the family is realised in the interaction which exists among its members. The father relates to the mother in a matrimonial concept while the children respond to the love of their parents in a reciprocal relationship. Through their parents, children receive their first instructions as well as make their first inter-personal experiences in the family. These experiences and instructions play a fundamental role in their future social and spiritual lives. Some families are also made up of single parents and child or children, foster or adoptive parents and child or children. There are also patchwork families whereby a man and a woman may decide to come together to raise children in partnership which may not necessarily mean that they will live together. This type of relationship does not constitute any matrimonial bond which is an exchange of consent between a man and a woman to live together all their lifelong in a mutual and lasting fidelity.

The extended family consists of other relatives, both by blood and marriage or adoption. Some of these individuals are: grandparents, uncles, aunts, nephews, nieces, cousins, parents-in-law, brothers-in-law, sisters-in-law, etc. Unlike the African situation where family ties are very strong, there exists an individualistic culture in Europe. This is realized in the dependency syndrome whereby Africans look for help and support from members of their extended families. The European culture on the other hand is built on the "do it yourself" syndrome.

The upbringing of a child, both in the nuclear and extended family, within the African context is a joint effort. It takes only the biological union of the parents for a child to be born but a combined effort of other members of the family is required for his or her training. This is realised especially in the religious upbringing of the child in which all the members of the family play significant roles. This is the opposite of the European background where the training of the child is solely the responsibility of the biological parents. In this instance, there is no interference from any external body in the duty of the parents towards their child or children. The family therefore remains the place where the future of religion is nurtured, developed, upheld or in some cases destroyed.[12] The future of religion is nurtured and developed through the faith

11 Nwaoru E. O., Youth Upbringing: A Process of Making Adult Christians, in: Nwatu F., Eze A. (Eds.), Bigard Theological Studies, 27, 1, Enugu, 2007, 74.

12 Cf. Lombaerts H., Osewska E., The Modern Christian Family as a first Setting for Religious and Moral Education?, in: Osewska E., Stala J. (Eds.), Religious Education/Catechesis in the Family: A European Perspective, Warszawa, 2010, 12.

of the parents but it fades away if the parents are unbelievers. This educational function of the family is a true ministry through which the Gospel is transmitted and radiated, so that family life itself becomes an itinerary of faith and in some way a Christian initiation and a school of following Christ.[13]

As a place of religious education, the family is also called the domestic Church.[14] Lombaerts and Osewska described this ecclesial function of the family as follows:

> *The family is the natural unit for sharing Christian living. Within the informal style, the natural love, the caring atmosphere and mutual recognition, children assimilate and integrate, as an osmosis, the religious images, stories, emotions, vocabulary and language, rituals, relationships, behaviour related to sacred places, etc. They enter into the religious universe, which parents set for themselves and then intend to live with their children.*[15]

The ecclesial function of the family gives children their basic Christian identity, which may last for the rest of their lives. It will let them recognise themselves as people born and bred from a Christian background which they cherish and may not be ready to lose in the course of time. Hence the slogan: I was born a (Catholic) Christian. This function of the family prepares the children for a healthy encounter with other people in the larger society whether their backgrounds are similar or not.

4.1.2 The Role of Parents in Religious Education in the Family

Parents are known as the first teachers of their children, who not only train them by words but also by example. This is the view of the African Bishops during the second African Synod which is expressed in the post synodal exhortation (Africae Munus) of Benedict XVI:

> *By virtue of their ministry of educating, parents are, through the witness of their lives, the first heralds of the Gospel for their children… they become fully parents, in that they are begetters not only of bodily*

13 Cf. Africae Munus (AM), 2011, 46, http://www.vatican.va/holy_father/benedict_xvi/apost_exhortations/documents/hf_ben-xvi_exh_20111119_africae-munus_en.html, 09.11.2012.

14 Cf. O'Donnell C. (Trans.), Lumen Gentium (LG), Chapter II, The People of God, 11, in: Flannery A., (Gen. Ed.), Vatican Council II, The Conciliar and Post-Conciliar Documents, Mumbai, 2007, 330.

15 Lombaerts H., Osewska E., Family Catechesis/Religious Education in the 21st Century Europe, in: Osewska E., Stala J. (Eds.), Religious Education/Catechesis in the Family: A European Perspective, Warszawa, 2010, 28-29.

life but also of the life that through the Spirit's renewal flows from the Cross and Resurrection of Christ.[16]

This responsibility is given to them in the very act of contracting marriage in which they pledge their readiness to accept children lovingly from God and train them according to the law of Christ and His Church. Nwaoru is also of this opinion when he says:

As the first teachers of their children, parents have the duty to lead them gradually and systematically into the mysteries of faith and, through the process of deepening that faith, associate them with the life of the Church.[17]

Parents therefore act as "catalysts" for their children, who depend so much on them for their enlightenment. The children imitate whatever they see in their parents and follow their "footsteps" since they regard them as their immediate models in every aspect of life. In this sense, religious education in the family falls directly under the guidance of the parents, who by virtue of their position play the most significant role. They perform their duty to their children by inculcating in the family, the different aspects and functions of the life of the entire Church. These aspects and functions are: mission, catechesis, witness, prayer, etc.[18] Hence, religious education in the family under the parents is a Christian education more witnessed to than taught, more occasional than systematic, more on-going and daily than structured into periods.[19] The mission of the parents is to transmit the Gospel to their children, who in turn bear witness to it especially before their peers. The Gospel is therefore transmitted in the family, from which it also extends.[20] From this background, the parents play their role in the religious education of their children through the teaching of Bible readings, prayers and songs. In the European context, they are also involved in the preparation of the children for the First Holy Communion and the sacrament of Confirmation.

Family catechesis involves teaching children the basic norms of the Christian faith. It refers to the development of a relationship with God as a teaching and learning process in terms of communicating and living the word of God

16 AM, 2011, 46, http://www.vatican.va/holy_father/benedict_xvi/apost_exhortations/documents/hf_ben-xvi_exh_20111119_africae-munus_en.html, 09.11.2012.

17 Nwaoru E. O., Youth Upbringing: A Process of Making Adult Christians, in: Nwatu F., Eze A. (Eds.), Bigard Theological Studies, 27, 1, Enugu, 2007, 77.

18 Cf. General Directory for Catechesis, 255.

19 Cf. Ibid.

20 Cf. Ibid.

in a specific forum which involves a guided support of parents for their child or children.[21] In this instance, the family serves as a faith sharing environment and therefore a dimension of parish catechesis. Parents embark on family catechesis by creating a "good environment for learning" for their children. They need to establish a home in which the Christian faith can be communicated and transmitted among its members. Such a home should nurture love, trust, respect, forgiveness and joy. Under such an atmosphere, children can meaningfully participate in any discussion about God and religious life. This view was portrayed by Lombaerts and Osewska as follows:

> *Often catechesis in the family has been associated, in the first place, with what parents offer their children: the "Christian home" they intend to set up, the deepening of faith with other parents, deepening their experiences, doubts or questions.*[22]

The first task of Christian parents is to teach their children the basic Christian signs and prayers such as: The Sign of the Cross, the Our Father, the Hail Mary, and Grace before and after meals. Children learn these prayers with such enthusiasm that they celebrate their success by often reciting these prayers as a sign of mastery. They make the Sign of the Cross before elderly people in order to show the correct movement of the hands from the forehead to the chest and then to the left and right shoulders. Grace before and after meals is highly rated in a typical African Christian family setting. This is realized in the fact that children often report their siblings who failed to pray before eating to their parents as offenders who should be punished. During the missionary era in Nigeria, Catholic parents forbade their children from eating in Protestant homes in order to avoid eating without praying or praying without making the Sign of the Cross.

The teaching of catechism is another means through which parents play their role as the first catechists of their children. By so doing, they teach their children important Church doctrines and also help in preparing them for the sacramental life. This is the hallmark of religious education in the family. It involves a discussion on the Christian faith.[23] The work of parents is not com-

21 Cf. Bendel H., Biesinger A., Familienkatechese, in: Bitter G., Englert R., Miller G., Nipkow K. E. (Hg.), Neues Handbuch religionspädagogischer Grundbegriffe, 2. Auflage, München, 2009, 310.

22 Lombaerts H., Osewska E., Family Catechesis/Religious Education in the 21st Century Europe in: Osewska E., Stala J. (Eds.), Religious Education/Catechesis in the Family: A European Perspective, Warszawa, 2010, 36.

23 Cf. Jakobs M., Neue Wege der Katechese, München, 2010, 75.

plete if their children have not been admitted to the sacraments which are the means of celebrating the Christian mysteries.

4.1.3 The Role of Children in Religious Education in the Family

Children are considered important in the family. Their presence gives joy and happiness to the parents who see in them their ability to share in the procreative work of God. These were the views of Kunstmann who also recognised some of the challenges of religious upbringing under liberalization in which attention is focused more on appeal and not on command.[24] The presence of children most often influences the marital relationship of their parents in the sense that they are placed at the centre of every family action. This makes it difficult sometimes for them to experience the authority of their parents. Their role in religious education is always characterised by questions which sometimes are very difficult for the parents to answer. Some of these questions range from those of the nature of God to where God lives and what He looks like, life and death, heaven and what happens after death.[25] The ability of the parents to provide answers to some of their questions depends to a large extent on the religious background and upbringing of the parents. Parents who grew up in poor religious homes and environments will be "at sea" in providing answers to the religious questions of their children. This is especially the case of some parents whose religious practices were suppressed or who at a later age dropped their faith for various reasons. Such a situation was identified by Schweitzer and Biesinger as some of the challenges of religious education in the family in the post-modern times. According to them:

> *A portion of today's adults have at a certain time of their age experienced the discontinuation of their religious practices. Their unanswered religious questions of childhood will remain with them as well as the children's faith, from which they may have perhaps distanced themselves in adolescence. When these adults become parents and their children ask them some questions about God, they often lack the appropriate answers to the questions of their children. Can parents who themselves do not know what they believe actually educate their children religiously?*[26]

24 Cf. Kunstmann J., Religionspädagogik, eine Einführung, 2.Auflage, Basel, 2010, 89.

25 Cf. Schweitzer F., Biesinger A., Religiöse Erziehung in evangelisch-katholischen Familien, Freiburg, 2009, 12.

26 Ibid., 9.

The above-quoted question calls for adequate attention. How can parents who are not religious give their children a religious upbringing? Following the Latin adage: "nemo dat quod non habet" (no one gives what he or she does not have), it can be argued that irreligious parents cannot afford family religious education for their children. But experience has often proved the above claim wrong. This is because some children of atheists have ended up becoming very active Christians and sometimes even priests. On the other hand, many unbelievers are the children of very pious and religious parents. (Hence the slogan: "bad children of good parents"). This does not however deny the fact that a situation whereby the parents are not religious will adversely affect the participation of their children in religious education within the family. They will be yearning for knowledge which the parents are unfortunately unable to supply. This indicates that the religious situation of the parents is of great importance to the children who long to be encouraged to develop their own religious inclination. They especially look to the mother for proper direction. This is the opinion of Lombaerts and Osewska:

> *As regards the more direct impact, children observe both parents in slightly different ways. In connection with the mother, the church attendance, the intrinsic religious attitude and faithfulness to the traditional faith convictions seem to have an impact upon the intrinsic religious attitude of the children. Whereas in relation to the father, it is rather his personal experience of God's presence, and his support of his children's religious behaviour that seems to affect their religious conviction.*[27]

Thus it is the explicit communication about religion that plays an intrinsic role in the involvement of children in religious education in the family. If they see that religious communication is flowing between their parents, they will then appreciate their religious upbringing; otherwise they regard it as irrelevant. This communication is especially realised in communal prayer and the sharing of life experiences. Children like to take part in family prayer so as to prove to their parents that they can recite some of the basic Christian prayers by heart. They long for this opportunity and get confused if it is not forthcoming.

27 Lombaerts H., Osewska E., Family Catechesis/Religious Education in the 21st Century Europe in: Osewska E., Stala J. (Eds.), Religious Education/Catechesis in the Family: A European Perspective, Warszawa, 2010, 34.

4.2 Religious Education in the Church

The Church as a mother is under an obligation … to provide for its children an education by virtue of which their whole lives may be inspired by the spirit of Christ. At the same time it will offer its assistance to all peoples for the promotion of a well-balanced perfection of the human personality, for the good of society in this world and for the development of a world more worthy of man.[28]

The primary assignment of the Church consists in teaching and sanctifying her members for the sake of their salvation. Religious education in the Church is therefore aimed at proclaiming the way of salvation to all people, informing all believers of the life of Christ and helping them with unremitting care that they can come to the fullness of salvation.[29] This exercise is fundamentally carried out through catechesis in which the faithful are formed and imbued into the Body of Christ.

In fulfilling its educational role, the Church, eager to employ all suitable aids, is concerned especially about those which are her very own. Foremost among these is catechetical instruction, which enlightens and strengthens the faith, nourishes life according to the spirit of Christ, leads to intelligent and active participation in the liturgical mystery and gives motivation for apostolic activity.[30]

This catechetical instruction is realized in a communal parish catechesis where the full life of the Church is established and actively carried out.[31] Within the parish set up, catechetical instructions are given by the priest, the deacon, the catechist and the religious education teacher on whom this task is primarily laid. In this section, religious education in the Church will be discussed with regard to the meaning of the parish, the role of the priest and the catechist as well as the catechumens who receive the instructions.

28 Dillon M. (Trans.), Gravissimum Educationis (GE), 3, in: Flannery A., (Gen. Ed.), Vatican Council II, The Conciliar and Post-Conciliar Documents, Mumbai, 2007, 646.

29 Cf. Leimgruber S., Die Erklärung über die christliche Erziehung, Gravissimum educationis, in: Bischof F. X., Leimgruber S. (Hg.), Vierzig Jahre II. Vatikanum, Zur Wirkungsgeschichte der Konzilstexte, 2. Aufl., Würzburg, 2005, 194.

30 Gravissimum Educationis, 4.

31 Cf. Leimgruber S., Die Erklärung über die christliche Erziehung, Gravissimum educationis, in: Bischof F. X., Leimgruber S. (Hg), Vierzig Jahre II. Vatikanum, zur Wirkungsgeschichte der Konzilstexte, 2. Aufl., Würzburg, 2005, 194.

4.2.1 Meaning of the Parish

The parish is the life-stream of the Church as well as the prime mover and pre-eminent place for catechesis.[32] Through it information which contributes to the realization of the Christian message is disseminated. In the *General Directory for Catechesis*, the parish was described as follows:

> *The parish is without doubt, the most important locus in which the Christian community is formed and expressed. This is called to be a fraternal and welcoming family where Christians become aware of being the people of God. In the parish, all human differences melt away and are absorbed into the universality of the Church. The parish is also the usual place in which the faith is born and in which it grows. It constitutes, therefore, a very adequate community space for the realization of the ministry of the word at once as teaching, education and life experience.*[33]

The parish was described by Lombaerts and Osewska as "the local Church where the official membership of the Church is established".[34] Commenting further they said:

> *While the parents already offer a variety of aspects of the Christian tradition, the parish organises the official initiation into the Church and into sacramental life, the Eucharist in particular. The parish offers opportunities for children to discover the social dimension of Church and of the commitments Christians take on inside the community and in society.*[35]

In the parish, the faithful celebrate their unity and love as a means of integrating the children into their fold. They come together and form a community of love united in the Eucharistic table. They pray together, sing together and eat together as a sign of fraternity, communion and agape. In the diocese of Ahiara, parishes exist as small entities entrusted into the care of a priest who sees to the pastoral needs of the faithful. The situation is different in the archdiocese of Munich and Freising, where parishes are merged together to cover

32 Cf. Catechesi Tradendae, 67, http://www.vatican.va/holy_father/john_paul_ii/apost_exhortations/documents/hf_jp-ii_exh_16101979_catechesi-tradendae_en.html, 10.11.2012.

33 General Directory for Catechesis, 257.

34 Lombaerts H., Osewska E., Family Catechesis/Religious Education in the 21st Century Europe in: Osewska E., Stala J. (Eds.), Religious Education/Catechesis in the Family: A European Perspective, Warszawa, 2010, 29.

35 Ibid.

very large areas under the supervision of a chief priest and other designated priests and catechists (male and female) who work in collaboration with him. The pastoral care of young people in a parish setting is aimed at preparing them for the reception of the sacraments, especially the Eucharist and Confirmation. In the two dioceses under investigation (Ahiara and Munich and Freising), this exercise is carried out in different ways. This will be treated in two different sub-sections.

4.2.2 Parish Catechesis in the Diocese of Ahiara and in the Archdiocese of Munich and Freising

Parish catechesis for young people in the diocese of Ahiara and the archdiocese of Munich and Freising begins with catechetical instruction which is aimed at preparing them for the reception of the sacraments, especially the sacraments of initiation. Another area in which parish catechesis is carried out in two dioceses is through the formation of some youth associations as well as some spiritual and social offers which the Church makes to young people in order to win their attention and train them into faithful and committed Christians. These three systems of handling parish catechesis will now be discussed in relation to the promotion of the Christian faith among young people in the two dioceses.

4.2.2.1 Catechetical Instruction

Catechetical instruction in the parishes of the diocese of Ahiara is given with the aid of two catechisms: *Doctrine for Adults* and *Katikizim nke Abuo*. These two catechisms are only different in language. They contain the same teachings and have made a great impact in the lives of the faithful in the diocese of Ahiara. Because of their question and answer forms, they appeal to the taste of the young people to who they are primarily addressed, in line with the universal *Youth Catechism of the Catholic Church, YOUCAT.*[36] Each of the two catechisms contains nineteen chapters in which the Catholic doctrines are summarised. Their contents are:

1. Creation and The Fall
2. Good Spirit and Bad Spirit
3. Jesus Our Saviour
4. The Blessed Virgin Mary
5. The Blessed Trinity

36 YOUCAT is the abbreviated name of the Youth Catechism of the Catholic Church published in April 2010. It contains the official teachings of the Church and is addressed primarily to young people.

6. Grace
7. The Church
8. Baptism and Confirmation
9. Extreme Unction, Holy Orders and Matrimony
10. Penance
11. The Blessed Eucharist
12. The Sacrifice of the Mass
13. Prayer
14. The Laws of God and Sin
15. The Love of God
16. Love of our Neighbour
17. Other Obligations
18. The Last Things
19. If you will be perfect.[37]

These topics are very important in the preparation for the reception of the sacraments especially the sacraments of initiation. Hence their mastery is particularly pivotal for the making of First Holy Communion (Eucharist) and the reception of the sacraments of Confirmation and Reconciliation.

Unlike the situation in the diocese of Ahiara, there is no unifying text for parish catechesis in the archdiocese of Munich and Freising. Each parish works out materials that are considered suitable for a proper education of children and adults in the areas of the Christian faith. This is done in collaboration with the parish priest and catechist using some catechetical books and catechisms considered worthy of giving a corresponding insight into the Christian doctrines. These materials are mainly used for the preparation of candidates for the reception of First Holy Communion, the sacrament of Confirmation and the sacrament of Reconciliation. These three sacraments have a great deal of inter-connectivity and therefore form the focal point of parish catechesis in the two dioceses under investigation. They will now be discussed in relation to their connection to other sacraments.

4.2.2.2 First Holy Communion (the Sacrament of the Eucharist)

The Eucharist is the source and summit of every Christian life.[38] Children are very enthusiastic about participating in this life-giving sacrament. First Holy Communion serves as a sign of growth and integration into the life of the Church. Parish catechesis strives to offer children the full membership of the

37 Unegbu M. O., Doctrine for Adults, Owerri, 2000, 1.

38 Cf. LG 11.

Church by admitting them to Communion and confirming them in the faith. First Holy Communion is also of great importance to the family.[39] Parents encourage and help their children to prepare for it and celebrate it as a family feast.

First Holy Communion has its history in the Church. It was introduced as a special ceremony for children by the decree "Quam Singulari" of Pope Pius X on August 8th 1910.[40] This document of the Church contains teachings based on the participation in the Holy Eucharist with regards to children. It stipulates the time at which children can be admitted to this sacrament and what they are required to know about it in order to qualify for its reception. In the early Christendom, Holy Communion was given to both children and adults alike. This practice continued until the 13th century, when children's Communion was eventually forbidden. Pius X traced this history as follows:

> *The Catholic Church ... took care even from the beginning to bring the little ones to Christ through Eucharistic Communion, which was administered even to nursing infants. This, as was prescribed in almost all ancient Ritual books, was done at Baptism until the thirteenth century, and this custom prevailed in some places even later.*[41]

This practice later died out in the Latin Church, and children were not permitted to approach the Holy Table until they had come to the use of reason and had some knowledge of this august Sacrament. This new practice, already accepted by certain local councils, was solemnly confirmed by the Fourth Council of the Lateran, in 1215, which promulgated its universally celebrated Canon XXI, whereby sacramental Confession and Holy Communion were made obligatory for the faithful after they had attained the use of reason, in these words:

> *All the faithful of both sexes shall, after reaching the years of discretion, make private confession of all their sins to their own priest at least once a year, and shall, according to their capacity, perform the enjoined penance; they shall also devoutly receive the Sacrament of Holy Eucharist at least at Easter time unless on the advice of their own priest, for some reasonable cause, it be deemed well to abstain for a while.*[42]

39 Cf. Jakobs M., Neue Wege der Katechese, München, 2010, 72.

40 Cf. Quam Singulari (QS), 8, http://www.papalencyclicals.net/Pius10/p10quam.htm, 09.11.2012.

41 Quam Singulari (QS), 1, http://www.papalencyclicals.net/Pius10/p10quam.htm, 09.11.2012.

42 Ibid.

Because of the confusion surrounding the interpretation of "the age of reason", Pius X declared in his Encyclical "Quam Singulari" that children are to be admitted to both sacraments at the completion of the age of seven.

The age of discretion, both for Confession and for Holy Communion, is the time when a child begins to reason, that is about the seventh year, more or less. From that time on begins the obligation of fulfilling the precept of both Confession and Communion.[43]

The essence of this is to bring to fulfilment that tremendous love which Jesus has for little children. This love is still realised in the Church due to the position of importance which is given to children. The Church holds her young ones in high esteem and strives to address herself to them in their own language and understanding. Pius X commented on this love of Christ for children which the Church upholds in her teachings:

The pages of the Gospel show clearly how special was that love for children which Christ showed while He was on earth. It was His delight to be in their midst; He was wont to lay His hands on them; He embraced them; and He blessed them. At the same time He was not pleased when they would be driven away by the disciples, whom He rebuked gravely with these words: "Let the little children come to me, and do not hinder them, for of such is the kingdom of God." It is clearly seen how highly He held their innocence and the open simplicity of their souls on that occasion when He called a little child to Him and said to the disciples: "Amen, I say to you, unless you turn and become like little children, you will not enter into the kingdom of heaven....And whoever receives one such little child for my sake, receives me."[44]

The preparation for First Holy Communion in the diocese of Ahiara lasts for a period of about one year but only for two months in the archdiocese of Munich and Freising. The long period of preparation in the diocese of Ahiara is because of the practice of celebrating First Communion during Easter which is regarded as the "birth" of the Church. The children attend catechism classes in order to be properly instructed on the meaning and value of the Eucharist. This instruction will expose them to an in-depth understanding of the Eucharist as the Body and Blood of Christ under the appearances of bread and wine.[45] Their preparation should cover all the topics that make up the parish catechesis

43 Ibid.

44 Ibid.

45 Cf. Unegbu M. O., Doctrine for Adults, Owerri, 2000, 61.

so as to learn and respect the sacredness of this noble sacrament. The children will be helped to appreciate this sacrament as a gift of Christ to His Church. This sacrament unites us with Christ for He says: "He who eats my flesh and drinks my blood lives in me and I in him" (Jn 6:56). The children therefore need to understand the meaning of the "trans-substantiation"[46] (nrughari achicha or mgbanwo achicha) which is the changing of the bread and wine into the Body and Blood of Christ at Mass during the "consecration".[47] The Eucharist as the sacrament of the Body and Blood of Christ indicates the real presence of Christ in His Body and Blood, Soul and Divinity.[48] That is why this sacrament is greatly revered as the source and summit of the Christian life.[49]

The celebration of First Communion in the diocese of Ahiara is often used to inculcate the African spirit of communalism (nriko) into the children. Africans value their sense of togetherness and express this heritage in the act of eating and celebrating together during which they share their joys and sorrows with their kin. This is realized in the African philosophy of "igwe bu ike" or "ujama" which is the expression of the English adage "no one is an island".

The celebration of First Communion in both the diocese of Ahiara and the archdiocese of Munich and Freising often takes place within a festive mood. It records a tremendous success in the sense that it defies the decline of active Church membership.[50] Even those parents, who for various reasons are no longer active in the Church, accompany their children to the Church in order to witness their children's admission to the life of the sacraments. The occasion therefore affords them the opportunity for a renewed encounter with the Church after a period of very few activities in the Church. Also for some parents and relatives, the liturgy of the First Communion of their children is one of the very few possibilities for them to participate in the sacrifice of the

46 The dogmatic teaching of the Church on trans-substantiation is too difficult for the understanding of children at their Fist Holy Communion level. The use of this word here only indicates that the children are instructed on the difference between normal bread and consecrated bread. With the use of the Igbo word "mgbanwo achicha", the children are able to understand the reverence accorded to the consecrated bread.

47 Consecration implies the highest point of the Eucharistic prayer during which the bread and wine are changed into the Body and Blood of Christ through the action of the priest who acts in the person of Christ (in persona Christi).

48 Cf. Unegbu M. O., Doctrine for Adults, Owerri, 2000, 61.

49 Cf. Rodgers J. (Trans.), Sacrosanctum Concilium, 10, in: Flannery A., (Gen. Ed.), Vatican Council II, The Conciliar and Post-Conciliar Documents, Mumbai, 2007, 26; O'Donnell C. (Trans.), Lumen Gentium, Chapter II, The People of God, 10, in: Flannery A., (Gen. Ed.), Vatican Council II, The Conciliar and Post-Conciliar Documents, Mumbai, 2007, 329.

50 Cf. Jakobs M., Neue Wege der Katechese, München, 2010, 72.

Mass.[51] The celebration of the Mass is often done amid very great festivities. The sight of festively dressed or uniformly-clad children is highly uplifting. Most often the occasion affords some children of lapsed parents the opportunity of an encounter with the Church which may not be repeated. In most cases, the children are made to be especially involved in the liturgical celebration through the readings and prayer of the faithful. They also participate in the presentation of the gifts during which they bring the bread and wine to the altar and are received by the priest. The central point of the celebration is the reception of Holy Communion during which the children, (in most cases), before all other communicants, participate for the first time in their lives in the eating of the "heavenly bread".[52] Holy Communion above all assures them of the presence of Christ in them and strengthens them to be more committed to a life of holiness.[53]

First Holy Communion is linked with some religious and social expectations. It indicates an act of initiation into the life of the Church and affords the children more opportunities to become actively involved in the activities of the Church as Mass servers, lectors and choristers. It is therefore a transition from the life of a child to that of responsibility. The Mass of First Communion is not a children's Mass but a celebration of change. The central meaning of First Communion will be lost if the focal point is diverted to one of merely showing off and child's play. All the events of the celebration – symbolic entrance and festive dresses – are meant to indicate the full membership of the children into the life of the Church. They are thus encouraged to enrol into some youth associations such as the Catholic Youth Organisation of Nigeria (CYON) and the scout movement, which are meant to serve as on-going catechetical activities for young people. The fact of being a communicant is meant to have a lasting spiritual effect on the children as well as arouse the interest of many others. Socially, First Holy Communion gives the children a positive status. It designates them as "good" children who are worthy of emulation.

4.2.2.3 The Sacrament of Confirmation

Confirmation belongs to the sacraments of initiation. It constitutes an entity together with Baptism and the Eucharist in the plan of salvation. Confirmation completes the Baptismal grace through the act of anointing with chrism

51 Cf. Ibid., 88.

52 Cf. CCC 1328-1331. The Holy Eucharist is addressed by a number of names in the Church such as: the Blessed Sacrament, Holy Communion, the Lord's Supper, the heavenly food, the bread of life, the Body of Christ, the bread of angels, the Viaticum, and bread from heaven.

53 Cf. Unegbu M. O., Doctrine for Adults, Owerri, 2000, 62.

and imposition of hands.[54] It also completes the rite of Christian initiation and makes the recipient a full member of the Body of Christ.

In the early days of the Church, the three sacraments of initiation were administered as one single operation. Baptism was represented by the immersion in water, Confirmation was realised in the anointing after the immersion while participation in the celebration of the Eucharist and sharing in the Eucharistic food signified full communion with the Church.[55] At this time, Confirmation was not a separate sacrament as we have it in the Church today. With the recognition of Christianity as the state religion under Constantine, the Christian communities increased in number. Rural parishes also increased thereby enlarging the dioceses.[56] At the same time the office of the Church was divided into three: that of the deacon, the priest and the bishop. The rite of anointing after the immersion was reserved for the bishop. But the increase in the number of parishes and rural communities made it difficult for the bishop to be present at all baptismal celebrations. As a result of this, the anointing after the immersion was separated from the baptismal rite and was to be completed by the bishop at a later date.[57] Confirmation thereby became an independent sacrament reserved for the bishop in which the theological content of the sacrament remained the completion of Baptism. With this separation, an attempt was made to compare the action of God in these two stages of initiation. According to an idea which dates back to Peter Lombard, the release of the Spirit in the first instance is for the forgiveness of sin, while the Spirit is released in the second instance for the strengthening of the faithful.[58]

At the beginning of the 1970s, Confirmation was widely regarded as a forgotten sacrament.[59] This is because it had no great significance both in the life of the Christian communities and in the lives of the individual Christians. It was only administered and received along with the visitations of the bishop. This is the view of Höring when he says:

> *Confirmation took place when the bishop came around on one of his visitations and was generally celebrated as a casual school programme*

54 Cf. CCC 1285.

55 Cf. Hofrichter C., Färber E., Vogelmann W., Ich glaube, Handreichung zur Firmvorbereitung, München, 2005, 18.

56 Cf. CCC 1290.

57 Cf. Hofrichter C., Färber E., Vogelmann W., Ich glaube, Handreichung zur Firmvorbereitung, München, 2005, 18.

58 Ibid.

59 Cf. Höring P. C., Konzeptionslinien der Firmkatechese in: Kaupp A., Leimgruber S., Scheidler M. (Hg.), Handbuch der Katechese für Studium und Praxis, Freiburg, 2011, 416.

on a weekday. It did not require much preparation. It took place only after a short rehearsal in the Church.[60]

Confirmation as a sacrament gained an enrichment of content with the rediscovery and understanding of the parish as a "Christian community" and as the structural and contextual centre of Christian life.[61] That is why it has developed into one of the major areas of catechesis and youth apostolate in contemporary times. In accordance with the prolongation of the age of Confirmation from childhood to adolescence, Confirmation has become more of the sacrament of maturity and responsibility.[62] Because of this rapid change in the understanding and perception of the sacrament of Confirmation, the need for an intensive preparation for its reception became necessary so that young people could be integrated into the Church due to a substantive personal faith. This preparation does not take place in the school but exactly in the place where life and faith flow together, where the sacrament is shared and anxiously realized, lived and celebrated: in the Christian community.

The task of preparing young people for the sacrament of Confirmation belongs essentially to the Church as a Christian community. This task however is assumed by all the members of the Christian community as a collective responsibility. In this instance, the priest, the catechist, the parents and other volunteers team up using their distinctive roles to prepare the candidates for their final stage of Christian initiation. This is because the Christian community is an association of people who share life with one another, care for one another, align with the message of the Gospel and celebrate their faith together.[63] The preparation of young people for the sacrament of Confirmation serves as an opportunity for the members of the Christian community to refresh their memories about the importance of Baptism and Confirmation for the life of both the Christian community and the life of the individual members. This preparation will also open some avenues for the young people to learn more about the Christian community in order to understand it and be properly integrated into it. The need for this is the seeming fact that young people and the Christian community have few points of contact. What they experience on weekends and in their leisure is relatively different from the life of a typical Christian community. The preparation will therefore help them to have the desire to grow in the Christian community. This desire will be better realised if they feel the hon-

60 Ibid.

61 Cf. Ibid.

62 Cf. Ibid.

63 Cf. Hofrichter C., Färber E., Vogelmann W., Ich glaube, Handreichung zur Firmvorbereitung, München, 2005, 44.

est effort which people make to live their lives in accordance with their faith as convinced members of the Christian community. This means that young people want to belong to a Christian community in which the members bear witness to their faith through an exemplary life.[64] Above all, they want to be part of a lively community in which the strengthening force of the Holy Spirit is realised as an essential part of this community.

The fact that the Holy Spirit is the force that strengthens the faithful with His gifts as a theological priority is realised especially in the liturgy of Confirmation. In the invitation for the faithful to pray for the outpouring of the Holy Spirit on those to be confirmed, the bishop addresses them with the following words:

> *My dear friends, in Baptism God our Father gave the new birth of eternal life to His chosen sons and daughters. Let us pray to our Father that He will pour out the Holy Spirit to strengthen His sons and daughters with His gifts and anoint them to be more like Christ the Son of God.*[65]

In these words, the mission of the Holy Spirit to those to be confirmed and indeed to the entire faithful is stated with a strong emphasis. The giving of this Spirit is realised however in the imposition of hands on the candidates for Confirmation by the bishop as he invokes the outpouring of the Spirit in these words:

> *All-powerful God, Father of our Lord Jesus Christ, by water and the Holy Spirit you freed your sons and daughters from sin and gave them new life. Send your Holy Spirit upon them to be their helper and guide. Give them the Spirit of wisdom and understanding, the Spirit of right judgement and courage, the Spirit of knowledge and reverence. Fill them with the Spirit of wonder and awe in your presence. We ask this through Christ our Lord.*[66]

In the liturgy of Baptism, the Holy Spirit is also given to the newly baptised in the rite of anointing. In the two acts of receiving the Spirit, it is clear that the Holy Spirit is a vital principle in the life of the Church and the Church expresses the works of the Holy Spirit in many ways. Thus at Confirmation, a person is addressed in a special way with the action of the Holy Spirit so as to be able

64 Cf. Dillon M. (Trans.), Evangelii Nuntiandi (EN), 21, in: Flannery A. (Gen. Ed.), Vatican Council II, More Post-Conciliar Documents, Mumbai, 2007, 744.

65 Pocket Ritual (Rituale Parvum), Bangalore, 2008, 35.

66 CCC 1299.

to confront society and the environment in a more conscious and decisive way. The confirmed become full members of the Church and thereby experience the completion of the integration movement started at Baptism.

The close connection between Baptism and Confirmation shows that the sacrament of Confirmation also means a new aspect of a relationship with Jesus Christ who also received the Spirit through the same act of anointing at His Baptism in the Jordan.[67] In His lifetime, He worked through the power of the Spirit. After His Resurrection, He promised and gave His Spirit to His disciples as a lasting gift to His Church. The Holy Spirit therefore is the way and manner in which Jesus Christ remains close to the people. In this respect, Confirmation is a means of deeper growth in relationship with Jesus Christ. By giving His Spirit to His disciples, Jesus at the same time gave the same Spirit to His Church. The Church therefore possesses the Holy Spirit in its fullness. From the gifts of this same Spirit she builds herself into a fellowship of believers. Every confirmed person is therefore called to this fellowship with other members of the Church.[68] In this way, Confirmation brings the community aspect of the life of the Church to its realisation. The entire confirmed are hence encouraged towards participating in the mission of the Church as well as contributing to the unity of the people of God in the ecumenical movement.

4.2.2.4 The Sacrament of Penance and Reconciliation

The sacrament of Penance and Reconciliation is directly connected to the sacraments of initiation and especially to First Communion (the sacrament of the Eucharist). In the early Church, the rites of initiation did not include the sacrament of Penance and Reconciliation since all sins were washed away in the waters of Baptism. Sacramental confession became necessary because these sacraments (of initiation) would in the course of time be celebrated independently at different times and places. Thus the sacrament of Penance and Reconciliation became part of the First Communion catechesis so that forgiveness of the sins committed after Baptism could be received.[69] Through this sacrament, the life of grace received at Baptism, which due to human frailty has been weakened or even lost by sin, is restored and renewed.[70] This is realised in the action of the priest through the words of absolution and in the acts of the penitent. These words of absolution express the action of God as the Father of

67 Cf. Hofrichter C., Färber E., Vogelmann W., Ich glaube, Handreichung zur Firmvorbereitung, München, 2005, 19.

68 Ibid.

69 Cf. Unegbu M. O., Doctrine for Adults, Owerri, 2000, 56.

70 Cf. CCC 1420-1421.

mercies who reconciles Himself with sinners through the action of His Son and the work of the Holy Spirit realised in the ministry of the Church.[71] The acts of the penitent include the three essential steps which the penitent has to take in order to ensure a fruitful reception of this sacrament. These are: contrition, confession and satisfaction.[72]

The starting point for a penitential catechesis in the post-modern times in connection with the sacraments of initiation and especially with First Communion needs to have a new reflection on the sacrament of Penance and Reconciliation for adults and for the Church as a whole. This is because the sacrament of Penance and Reconciliation needs to be embedded in a positive and life-affirming image of the human person in order to be relevant in the post-modern times. It has to be integrated into the Church as a convincing means of dealing with guilt and also be seen as an individual, community and structural way of dealing with debt as well as the problem of punishment, reparation and revenge.[73] It is only with this understanding that an interface of the penitential catechesis with any other sacrament can be considered in relation to young people preparing for First Communion. Penitential catechesis of children and young people is doomed to fail if the sacrament of Penance and Reconciliation has no apparent relevance to adult believers. Its relevance needs to have a community effect and not only be limited to individual confession. Hence the need for the celebration of joint penitential rites in which the members of the Christian community come together to reconcile with God and with one another through prayers and hearing of the word of God. Such a communal penitential service deepens and unfolds the process of repentance and forgiveness. It makes it clear that repentance is a turning away from evil and turning back towards God (metanoia) which is not only necessary for the individual but also for the community because the community often offends some of its members.[74] The occasion of a communal penitential service offers the possibility of receiving instructions for an in-depth examination of conscience.[75] Within a communal penitential service, the sacrament of Penance and Reconciliation can be celebrated in the perceptible signs of individual confession and absolution. The priest, acting in the name of the Church reconciles the penitent with God and the Church using the power of Christ realised in the "power of the keys" (cf. Mt. 16:19).

71 Cf. CCC 1449.

72 Cf. CCC 1450.

73 Cf. Jakobs M., Neue Wege der Katechese, München, 2010, 91.

74 Cf. CCC 1431.

75 Cf. CCC 1454.

The sacrament of Penance and Reconciliation is introduced in one's life in childhood or early adolescence and often as part of First Communion. From this time onwards, it serves as a connecting point for the sacramental life of individual Christians. This is because it creates the opportunity for a renewed (and worthy) reception of Holy Communion after a breach from an unforeseen and unintended act of sin. In this way, the sacrament of Penance and Reconciliation plays a vital role for a fruitful and (often) valid reception of the other sacraments. The question has often been raised, whether or not this sacrament should be reserved only for adults who are fully capable of sin, and to what extent it makes sense at all to introduce this practice in childhood.[76] But the exclusion of children from this sacrament would mean losing the communal and ecclesial character of the sacrament. The theological and anthropological essence of this sacrament is reconciliation with God and reconciliation among humans. This sacrament needs to be given its central position and upheld as a means of obtaining the mercy of God for the entire Christian community. Children form part of the "Body of Christ" which is wounded by the sins of its members and therefore need to be a part of the reconciliatory act with God.[77] They make atonement for their sins and the sins of others when they approach this sacrament with reverence and piety. A guided preparation for this sacrament will help them to understand the richness of the sacrament. Hence they need to learn the various things forbidden by the Ten Commandments in order to know when they have been exposed to an occasion of sin.[78] They should also (if possible) practice how to go to confession with their teacher (catechist) in the course of their preparation for First Holy Communion. This is the opinion of Lutz, who suggests that children should at least discuss their confessional matter with a trustworthy adult, who will not discuss it any further.[79] This will give them the proper disposition required to make their first and subsequent sacramental confessions.

In the traditional African setting, sin is associated with the feeling of shame while reconciliation is celebrated under the precepts of the community which presents itself as the victim of the sin. The magnitude of the sin is not determined by the individual offender but by the community whose laws and customs have been violated. The community therefore confronts the offender with his or her sins publicly and imposes corresponding punishments which must be

76 Cf. Jakobs M., Neue Wege der Katechese, München, 2010, 92.

77 Cf. CCC 1422.

78 Cf. Unegbu M. O., Doctrine for Adults, Owerri, 2000, 56.

79 Cf. Lutz B., Buße und Beichte für Kinder und Erwachsene positive motivieren, in: Kaupp A., Leimgruber S., Scheidler M. (Hg.), Handbuch der Katechese für Studium und Praxis, Freiburg, 2011, 401.

accomplished for the expiation of the offence. A reconciliation process takes place which culminates in a communion of the offender with the community, the ancestors and God in the act of "nriko" or "oriko".[80] Against this background, the understanding of sin in Christianity is related to the feeling of guilt and not shame. The gravity of the sin is left to the judgement and determination of individual conscience. Reconciliation is sacramentally celebrated whereby the penitent privately or secretly confesses his or her sins and makes reparations in the acts of penance. A communal reconciliation takes place in the celebration of the Eucharist during which the Church as a reconciled community comes together to eat of the same bread and drink from the same cup with the offender (cf. 1 Cor. 11:26). This freedom of judgement has led some people (including some youth) to hide their enslavement to particular sins and at the same time parade themselves as good Christians under pseudo spirituality.

Children also experience the act of forgiveness and reconciliation in the family from the quarrels of their parents, brothers and sisters, relatives and other members of the extended family. From this idea, they realize that quarrels and misunderstandings are not meant to result to a total break up of relationships. However irreparable damage is done in the growth of children of broken families. Cases of unresolved misunderstandings which later resulted in divorce bring about unbalanced parental care in the lives of the affected children. This is why it is necessary for children to experience reconciliation in their families so as to appreciate the value of the sacrament of Reconciliation in the larger Christian community. A better forum for children and young people to experience reconciliation is in the midst of their peers. This is why they are encouraged to form study groups and youth associations or join the already existing ones in their locality so that they can realize the usefulness of their youthful age in the Christian faith.[81] These youth associations which provide them the opportunity of interaction among their peers will be discussed in the next section.

4.2.3 Youth Associations in the Diocese of Ahiara and in the Archdiocese of Munich and Freising

The Church as a universal institution has a mission to the youth. This mission is exercised and carried out in different ways through the various means of evangelization that are available in the Church. Very prominent among these means of evangelization is the formation of some youth associations which provide a corresponding atmosphere for the youth to express themselves as

80 Cf. Unegbu M. O., Doctrine for Adults, Owerri, 2000, 25.

81 Cf. Youcat, 9.

"bona fide" members of the "family of God". These associations vary in relation to the two areas of this study, namely: the diocese of Ahiara and the archdiocese of Munich and Freising. As a result of this, the youth associations in these two places will be tabulated and discussed differently.

4.2.3.1 Youth Associations in the Diocese of Ahaira

In union with the universal Church, the diocese of Ahiara makes some serious efforts to lead the youth in the ways of the faith. These efforts are meant to win the attention of young people as a means of propagating the Christian (Catholic) teachings. Such efforts are seen in the existence of some youth associations in the diocese. The pastoral care of the youth is carried out through these associations. Some of these associations are: the Altar Servers, the Catholic Youth Organization of Nigeria (CYON), the Mary League Girls, the Boy Scouts and Girl Guides, and the Man of Order and Discipline (MOD).

4.2.3.1.1 The Altar Servers

The altar servers are Catholic boys and girls who are especially responsible for various services at the altar. They serve at Mass and other liturgical celebrations such as Eucharistic adorations, benediction, the celebration of the sacraments and funerals. Besides these functions, they also prepare the altar for various liturgical activities and tidy it up. Through their services at the altar, they grow in the knowledge of the teachings of the Church. The altar servers learn some of the prayers and songs used at the various liturgical exercises. They also learn the priest's vestments and the meaning of the liturgical colours. Membership to this group is open to all Catholic boys and girls who have made their First Holy Communion. However, the age at which these boys and girls can serve at the altar differs from parish to parish because in some parishes there are some altar servers who have not yet made their First Holy Communion.[82] The altar servers also carry out some leisure activities such as sports and excursions.

4.2.3.1.2 The Catholic Youth Organization of Nigeria (CYON)

The Catholic Youth Organization of Nigeria (CYON) was formed in 1985 by the Catholic Bishops' Conference of Nigeria (CBCN) to co-ordinate the affairs of the youth at the parish, deanery and diocesan levels.[83] It is an association of

82 Cf. http://histclo.com/act/rel/altar.html, 13.02.2012.

83 Cf. http://cyonanniversary.blogspot.com/p/history.html, 16.02.2012.

all Catholic youth (male and female) within the age bracket of 15 to 25 years.[84] As a national body, it incorporates all other existing youth organizations in the schools, higher institutions of learning and parishes such as: the Mary League Girls, the Catholic Boys, and the Nigeria Federation of Catholic Students etc.[85]

The CYON affirms the place of the youth in the life of the Church and promotes youth involvement in the work of evangelization. It outlines, promotes, directs and evolves a network of support for youth initiatives as groups or individuals for the development of the Church and the society.[86] Attention is primarily given to human development, youth empowerment and catechesis. Its motto is: "Let your light shine."[87]

The CYON is an example of a grass root organization which can be effectively utilized in the spiritual and social development of Nigeria. Under this organization, the youth come together in their respective parishes to plan and execute their Christian functions within a specific parish situation. The aims and objectives of the organization are:

1. The spiritual development of the youth through personal prayers, Bible reading and regular participation in the sacraments
2. The promotion of Catholic identity and the teachings of the Church
3. Loyalty to and recognition of the constituted authority of the Catholic Church in her mission of evangelization
4. The implementation of the decisions and policies of the Catholic Bishops' Conference of Nigeria especially in matters concerning the youth
5. To promote and encourage prayers for vocations
6. To promote and encourage prayers for good Christian families
7. To promote and encourage youth formation through lectures, symposia, seminars and retreats
8. To organize cultural, social, outdoor, and sports activities for the youths[88]

4.2.3.1.3 The Mary League Girls

The Mary League Girls Association is an organisation of unmarried girls who devote themselves to Mary through their services in the Church.[89] The association has existed in all the parishes of the diocese of Ahiara from its inception. The Mary League Association came about through St. Catherine Laboure after

84 Ibid.

85 Ibid.

86 Ibid.

87 http://saintcypriancathchurch.org/cyon.html, 16.02.2012.

88 Cf. Ibid.

89 Cf. http://ourlady.bulletinstudio.com/parish-groups/mary-league-girls-association/, 06.03.2012.

her apparition of the Blessed Virgin on the nights of 18th & 19th July 1830 in the chapel the Daughters of Charity of St. Vincent De Paul, Rue du Bac, Paris France.[90] Its aims and objectives are: personal sanctification and works of the apostolate, a life of purity and the life of a true Christian through prayers and service to the Church.[91] The Mary League Girls devote themselves to some spiritual activities such as:

1. Eucharistic celebration on every first Friday of the month
2. Dressing the altar with the altar servers
3. Weekly meetings and prayers
4. Washing and pressing of altar clothes
5. Teaching of catechism
6. Cleaning the Church environment
7. Cleaning the parish house and offices
8. Corporal works of mercy
9. Outdoor activities[92]

They also organise solemn Eucharistic celebrations and hold special gatherings on some feasts of the Blessed Virgin Mary such as the Assumption (15th August), Birthday of Mary (8th September) and Immaculate Conception of Mary (8th December).[93] Membership in the association is open to all unmarried girls after First Holy Communion.

4.2.3.1.4 Young Catholic Students of Nigeria (YCS)

The association of Young Catholic Students of Nigeria is comprised of young Catholics who strongly believe in the importance of the relationship between God and human beings. The association fosters the need for Catholic students to be given the opportunity to deepen the knowledge of their religion according to the teachings of Christianity. This involves an incorporation of the Christian beliefs into their daily lives in the classroom, on the playgrounds and in their homes. This association therefore serves as a movement that co-ordinates the affairs of young Catholic students by providing a forum that promotes their common interaction and a manifestation of their faith.[94] The association has the following aims and objectives:

90 Ibid.

91 Cf. Ibid.

92 Cf. Ibid.

93 Cf. Ibid.

94 Cf. http://www.ycsnigeria.org/?u=page&page_id=2, 05.05.2012.

1. To bring Christ to the students and the students to Christ
2. To help students live their Christian faith
3. To infuse into its members a sense of responsibility and leadership
4. To provide an opportunity for a systematic study and discussion on matters of religion and on the practical living of Christianity
5. To provide a forum for discussion on social problems with a view to alleviating them
6. To form a link between Christian students at National and International levels
7. To work with other lay apostolate organizations
8. To work in collaboration with other youth movements
9. To participate actively in the work of evangelization
10. To critically address issues of National importance
11. To organize excursions for its members[95]

4.2.3.1.5 The Boy Scouts and the Girl Guides

Scouting is a worldwide youth movement with the aim of supporting young people in their physical, mental and spiritual development, so that they may play constructive roles in the society. The movement was founded for boys in 1907 by Robert Baden Powell.[96] Later in 1910 a new movement with the name "Girl Guides" was founded for girls. These two movements were introduced in Nigeria in 1915 with the coming of the British colonial administrators.[97] The two movements developed as voluntary and non-Governmental organisations for young people. In the Catholic diocese of Ahiara, these movements have been adopted as the strong arms of the youth pastoral. Membership is open to all boys and girls from school age to 25 years. Scouting is taught with informal educational methods which lay emphasis on practical activities in the outdoors. The scouting programme also emphasizes citizenship training and community service projects. These include such things as literacy campaigns, road safety projects, service at national and community events and providing help in case of disaster by working in co-operation with other voluntary organisations. Other aims of the scout movement are learning by doing and the building of self-confidence. Outdoor activities provide the scouts with an opportunity to have contact with the natural environment. Such outdoor experiences build

95 Cf. http://www.ycsnigeria.org/?u=page&page_id=8, 05.05.2012.

96 Cf. http://www.nigeriascouts.org/index.php?option=com_content&view=article&id=25&Itemid=28, 13.02.2012.

97 Cf. Ibid.

up self-reliance and readiness for action which characterise the motto of the movement: “Be prepared”.

4.2.3.1.6 Man of Order and Discipline (MOD)

The Man of Order and Discipline (MOD) was formed in Nigeria in 1980. It is a youth movement in the Catholic Church whose major aim is to check indiscipline and disordered behaviour in the Church.[98] It has many similarities with the scout movement and has spread to all the dioceses in Nigeria. It has also gained the recognition of the Catholic Bishops’ Conference of Nigeria. Membership in this movement is open to all Catholic youths.[99] Its motto is: “Faith in charity and good conscience”.[100] Other aims and objectives of the movement are:

1. The promotion of unity among members through out door programmes
2. To provide a forum for the youth to put into practice some of the virtues and disciplinary norms which they learnt in and out of school and other youth associations
3. To maintain moral discipline among the youth, especially students
4. To promote sacramental life among the youth
5. To generate, encourage and maintain a spirit of prayer among members
6. To bear witness to the Christian message
7. To maintain order and discipline during religious processions such as on Palm Sunday and The Feast of Christ the King
8. To maintain order and discipline during some diocesan and parish programmes such as Ordinations and harvest/bazaars[101]

4.2.3.1.7 The Block Rosary Crusade

The block rosary crusade is an old association in the Catholic Church. In the diocese of Ahiara, it refers to the gathering of people, especially young ones, living in the same block or kindred for the purpose of saying the rosary. It is usually a daily gathering in which children are taught home manners and how to pray. Adults are sometimes invited to give children moral instructions. It also offers children the opportunity of learning the catechism and the rudiments of the Catholic faith. Although this practice is fading away as a result of

98 Cf. http://modwarridmc.com/index.php, 16.02.2012.

99 Cf. http://modwarridmc.com/membership.php, 16.02.2012.

100 Ibid.

101 Cf. http://modwarridmc.com/aim.php, 16.02.2012.

urbanization, it is still realized as one of the easiest means of gathering young people for the purpose of Catholic religious education. There are usually many block rosary units in a particular village or parish. These units hold a monthly congress at the parish level, where they hold singing or a quiz competition. On some feasts of Our Lady, (such as the Assumption or Immaculate Conception), the adults in each block or kindred organize celebrations for the block rosary children as a means of encouraging their practice of the Catholic faith. The celebrations involve eating and drinking as well as dancing.

4.2.3.1.8 The Age Grade

Among the Igbo people of Nigeria, age grades cut across descent lines to bring people of about the same age into life-long bonds with one another while at the same time separating them from much older or younger people.[102] The age grade system is used by the Church in the diocese of Ahiara to facilitate the activities of the youth at the parish and village levels. In some villages, the age grades form the central governing body, which is comprised of representatives from the various age groups. This central governing body acts as a system of checks and balances on the lifestyle of the village people as well as seeing to the maintenance of peace and order in the entire village. Young people are assigned the task of forming vigilante groups, whose duty it is, to see to the protection of the lives and property of the people. These vigilante groups sometimes organize social and leisure programmes for their members, which involve outdoor activities. They gather in the evenings for prayers and reflections before going to their duty posts and meet again at dawn for thanksgiving before departing for their various homes.

4.2.4 Youth Activities in the Diocese of Ahiara

Apart from the above-mentioned youth associations, the Church in the diocese of Ahiara also organises some spiritual and social activities through which the youth are offered some pastoral assistance. Some of these activities are: the monthly youth convention, the annual youth week, sports programmes and computer training.

4.2.4.1 Monthly Youth Convention

Every third Saturday of the month is set aside for youth convention in the diocese of Ahiara. The youth begin with the Eucharistic celebration and spend

102 Cf. Imoagene O., Know Your Country Series, Handbooks of Nigeria's Major Culture Areas Vol. 3, The Ibo of East Central Nigeria, Ibadan, 1993, 29.

the rest of the day with other programmes such as personal reflections, workshops and spiritual talks. During the workshop, the participants are divided into discussion groups. The topics for the discussions are chosen from some of the problems of the youth and each group is expected to present possible solutions to the problems. Such discussions are sometimes centred on faith and the sharing of experience. The convention is sometimes concluded with the Eucharistic procession and benediction.

4.2.4.2 Annual Youth Week

Once a year, the Catholic Secretariat of Nigeria (CSN) organizes a week of various pastoral activities for the youth as a means of enlightening them spiritually. This is aimed at ensuring that similar activities are carried out nationwide among the Catholic youth. This exercise is widely observed in the diocese of Ahiara. Within this week, the youth engage in various activities and practices such as symposia, lectures, picnics, excursions and film shows. They use the opportunity to ask questions in order to understand some of the fundamental teachings of the Church. The youth find this programme very helpful for their spiritual growth.

4.2.4.3 Sports

Sports are a very worthwhile means of gathering the youth as well as a good means of providing pastoral care for them. The Catholic diocese of Ahiara organises some sports events as a means of pastoral care of the youth and ensuring the physical and corporal well-being of young people following the adage: "a healthy mind lives in a healthy body" (mens sana in corpore sano). Such sports events are football, volleyball, basketball, tennis and athletics.

4.2.4.4 Computer Training

The youth of the diocese of Ahiara are offered the opportunity of gaining computer literacy as a means of helping them to come to terms with the demands of the society. As a result of the rapid development in technology, computer literacy has become a great necessity in post-modern times. The youth therefore need to be well trained in the use of the electronic media for the proclamation of the Good News of salvation. Although the use of the electronic media can be negatively directed, the Church in the diocese of Ahiara makes some efforts to focus the attention of the youth on the use of the electronic media as a means of enhancing spiritual growth.

4.2.5 Youth Associations in the Archdiocese of Munich and Freising

The youth associations in the archdiocese of Munich and Freising are co-ordinated by the arch-diocesan youth office known as "Erzbischöfliches Jugendamt" (EJA). This office takes on this responsibility on behalf of the Arch-Bishop as a means of promoting the youth apostolate in the archdiocese. The office designs the Church's youth ministry in the archdiocese as well as supports the youth pastoral in the parishes and among the Catholic youth organizations. Under the management of this office are such youth associations as: the Catholic Youth Society (Katholische Junge Gemeinde – KJG), the Altar Servers (Die Ministrantinnen und Ministranten), the Federation of German Catholic Youth (Bund der Deutschen Katholiken Jugend – BDKJ), the Catholic Rural Youth Movement (Katholische Landjugendbewegung – KLJB), the Kolping Youth (Die Kolpingjugend).

4.2.5.1 The Federation of German Catholic Youths (Bund der Deutschen Katholischen Jugend – BDKJ)

The Federation of German Catholic Youth is an umbrella organization for the other Catholic youth organizations. Nationwide in 27 dioceses, it represents the interests of about 450,000 children, adolescents and young adults.[103] In the archdiocese of Munich and Freising, seven member associations are organized under the Federation of German Catholic Youth.[104] These seven associations are:

1. Christian Youth Workers (Christliche ArbeiterInnenjugend – CAJ)
2. German Boy Scouts of St. George (Deutsche Pfadfinderschaft St. Georg – PDSG)
3. Catholic Youth Society (Katholische junge Gemeinde – kjg)
4. Catholic Rural Youth Movement (Katholische Landjugendbewegung – KLJB)
5. Catholic Students and Young Christian Life Societies (Katholische Studierende Jugend and Gemeinschaften Christlichen Lebens – KSJ & GCL)
6. Kolping Youth (Kolpingjugend – KJ)
7. Female Scout Union of St. George (Pfadfinderinnenschaft St. Georg – PSG)

103 Cf. BDKJ, Wer wir sind, http://www.eja-muenchen.de/bdkj.html, 12.03.2012.

104 Cf. Ibid.

The Federation represents the leading organizations in the fields of youth policy and youth apostolate in the entire archdiocese and thus has about 60,000 teenagers and young adults as its members.[105] In matters concerning Catholic youth organizations, volunteer work, the spirit of volunteerism and democracy are very important. Young people get involved in this project for its own sake and are supported by full-time employees. The arch-diocesan BDKJ is led by four full-time elected chairmen.[106] At regular meetings, important decisions on programmes, positions and persons are taken. The work of the Federation of German Catholic Youth extends from sub-urban areas, cities and deaneries to the arch-diocesan level. The work of the member associations on the other hand begins where that of the BDKJ stops, that is, in the parishes, schools and the rural areas where young people are close to one another. The BDKJ offers training opportunities to about 70 young men and women annually during which they are expected to help others through their work while at the same time achieving personal growth.[107]

The Federation of German Catholic Youth has existed under its present dispensation since 1947 (after having been banned in 1938 by the National Socialistic regime) both at the national level and in the archdiocese of Munich and Freising.[108] Since then, it has been providing opportunities for young people to express their opinions both in the Church and in the society. This defines the major objective of the Federation which is self-discovery and the self-realization of young people. Other aims are:

1. To support young people in the search for meaning and to help them to discover their personality
2. To encourage the spirit of willingness among young people to take up responsibilities in their immediate environments and to motivate them to act in solidarity – today in the youth group and tomorrow in the various sectors of the society
3. To introduce young people to Jesus Christ
4. To protect and create optimal conditions, so that Church youth ministry can function – from training to grants
5. To provide opportunities for the Church to be experienced
6. To organize the annual youth Corbinian's pilgrimage to Freising, where thousands of young Christians meet to celebrate their lives and faith

---

105 Cf. Ibid.

106 Cf. Ibid.

107 Cf. Ibid.

108 Cf. BDKJ, Was wir wollen, http://www.eja-muenchen.de/bdkj.html, 12.03.2012.

7. To create a youth forum, as part of the annual youth pilgrimage, where young people come together with the Arch-Bishop and other Church leaders and express their minds on some current topics[109]

4.2.5.2 The Christian Youth Workers Association (Christliche ArbeiterInnenjugend – CAJ)

The Christian Youth Workers Association was founded in 1925 by the priest, Joseph Cardijn in Brussels.[110] The concern of Cardijn was to awaken the consciousness of young workers to their dignity through campaigns and seminars. He thus succeeded in helping young people to recognize their responsibilities towards themselves and the society. His efforts initiated the slogan of the association, "See, Judge, Act." Within 40 years, the Christian Youth Workers Association spread to over 100 countries.[111] It was established in Germany in 1947.[112] The aims and objectives of the association are:

1. To support young workers in exploring and developing their creativity and skills
2. To encourage young workers, based on their individual living conditions and interest, to engage in collaborative actions so as to effect some changes in their places of work, at school, among friends, in the Church and society[113]

The target groups of the association are secondary school students, professional students, job seekers, trainees and young workers. The motto of the association is "Every young worker is worth more than all the gold of the earth."[114]

109 Cf. Ibid.

110 Cf. CAJ, Geschichte, http://www.eja-muenchen.de/bdkj/die-organe-in-der-erzdiözese/mitgliedsverbaende/caj.html, 12.03.2012.

111 Cf. Ibid.

112 Cf. Ibid.

113 Cf. CAJ, Selbstverständnis und Ziele, http://www.eja-muenchen.de/bdkj/die-organe-in-der-erzdiözese/mitgliedsverbaende/caj.html, 12.03.2012.

114 Cf. CAJ, Zielgruppe, http://www.eja-muenchen.de/bdkj/die-organe-in-der-erzdiözese/mitgliedsverbaende/caj.html, 12.03.2012.

4.2.5.3 The German Boy Scouts of St. George (Deutsche Pfadfinder St. Georg – DPSG)

The German Boy Scouts of St. George are the union of Catholic boys' physical training units in Germany. The union is divided into five diocesan associations and within these associations there are 140 districts and 1388 units.[115]

The publication of the book *Scouting for Boys* in 1908 by Lord Robert Baden-Powell led to the foundation of the worldwide scout movement.[116] The German Boy Scouts of St. George were founded on 7th October 1929.[117] They were later banned by the National Socialistic Regime but were re-organized after the Second World War. Since 1971, girls and young women adults can also be members.[118] The target groups of the scout union are children of school age, adolescents, young adults and adult leaders. The association is aimed at inculcating into young men and women the ability to be independent, especially in learning the rudiments of wearing the scout uniform which is made up of hat, scarf, knot, shorts and long stockings.[119] Other aims of the scout union are:

1. Commitment against xenophobia and violence
2. Supporting the integration of the disabled
3. Environmental protection
4. Encouraging partnership and solidarity through international meetings
5. Going out from the rudimentary life of television and video to the experience of the outdoor life
6. Spending the leisure in the company of friends, peers and colleagues[120]

4.2.5.4 The Catholic Youth Society (Katholische junge Gemeinde – KJG)

The Catholic Youth Society is a large democratic organization of children and youth in the Catholic Church. It was founded in 1896 under the name "Catholic Young Men's Association" in Dusseldorf.[121] Its feminine counterpart was founded in 1915 with the name "Young Catholic Women's Association" also in

115 Cf. DPSG, Struktur, http://www.eja-muenchen.de/bdkj/die-organe-in-der-erzdiözese/mitgliedsverbaende/dpsg.html, 12.03.2012.

116 Cf. DPSG, Geschichte, http://www.eja-muenchen.de/bdkj/die-organe-in-der-erzdiözese/mitgliedsverbaende/dpsg.html, 12.03.2012.

117 Cf. Ibid.

118 Cf. Ibid.

119 Cf. DPSG, Selbstverständnis und Ziele, http://www.eja-muenchen.de/bdkj/die-organe-in-der-erzdiözese/mitgliedsverbaende/dpsg.html, 12.03.2012.

120 Cf. Ibid.

121 Cf. http://www.kjg-muenchen.de/seite/index.php?id=42, 21.03.2012.

Dusseldorf.[122] The two organizations were dissolved in 1939 under the regime of the National Socialistic Party. The male part of the association regrouped in 1952 under the name "Catholic Young Men's Group" (katholische Jungemännergemeinschaft - KJG).[123] Its female counterpart re-surfaced in 1954 with the new name "Catholic Women's Youth Group" (katholische Frauenjugend Gemeinschaft – KFG).[124] These two societies were merged in 1970 in Altenberg and adopted the common name "Catholic Youth Society".[125] Under this society, over 8,000 children, adolescents and young adults are currently organized into 24 diocesan associations in Germany.[126] Participation in the activities of this society is open to everyone who is committed to its principles and objectives, regardless of sex or creed. The arch-diocesan association of Munich and Freising has an approximate membership of 850 people at the present time.[127] The association engages in team work as a means of connecting and uniting young people. Parties, games and sports are part of the activities and actions of the association. The Catholic Youth Society understands itself as "Church" in the world of children and adolescents.[128] It sets out to give young Christians the opportunity to live their faith with the "signs of the time". In addition, it is committed to ensuring that children, adolescents and young people are involved in the decision-making processes of the Church. That is the beginning of its democratic ventures. The issues, interests and needs of children and adolescents are the key points of its goals. It is therefore the intention of the Catholic Youth Society that children and young people should co-discuss and co-decide in matters concerning them. This is why the association makes some efforts to help its members by representing their common interest in the Church and society.

4.2.5.5 The Altar Servers (Die Ministrantinnen und Ministranten)

The Altar Servers Association exists in the Archdiocese of Munich and Freising under the Catholic Youth Society. Its motto is "Faith, Spirit and Good Humour".[129] The Catholic Youth Society as a youth organization for openness,

122 Cf. Ibid.

123 Cf. Ibid.

124 Cf. Ibid.

125 Cf. Ibid.

126 Cf. Ibid.

127 Cf. Ibid.

128 Cf. Ibid.

129 Cf. http://www.kjg-muenchen.de/seite/index.php?id=183, 21.03.2012.

tolerance and democracy offers the Altar Servers Association the necessary support to realize its goals. These goals are:

1. To uphold the opportunities for exchange and learning as well as the development of adolescent spirituality
2. To establish a relationship between the ministry at the altar and everyday life
3. To train senior altar servers and group leaders and support them in their places of assignment
4. The organization and encouragement of youth spirituality
5. To counsel and help altar servers in the youth ministry of the archdiocese
6. To help the altar servers to experience the faith of the Christian community through some leisure activities
7. To accompany and encourage young people in their ways of faith as well as help them to make the faith fruitful in their lives[130]

4.2.5.6 The Catholic Rural Youth Movement (Katholische Landjugendbewegung – KLJB)

"The Catholic Rural Youth Movement is one of the biggest Catholic youth movements in Germany with about 70,000 members".[131] It was formed in 1947 by Dr. Emmeran Scharl.[132] Through his commitment, young people across the rural areas were assembled from their various villages to organize both their ecclesial and community lives. The Catholic Rural Youth Movement understands itself as a responsible and democratic movement aimed at shaping the lives of young people in the Church and society. Following the principle, "See, Judge, Act", the Catholic Rural Youth Movement supports young people in securing their positions and in representing the public.[133] In this movement, young people assume some responsibilities in the society and learn about their own abilities in joint operations. The movement is very rural so that the value of rural life can remain viable and lovable. The target groups of the movement are adolescents and young adults in the countryside from about 12 years old.[134]

130 Cf. ibid.

131 http://kljb.org/internationale-vorstellung/english/, 06.03.2012.

132 Cf. http://www.eja-muenchen.de/bdkj/die-organe-in-der-erzdiözese/mitgliedsverbaende/kljb.html, 12.03.2012.

133 Cf. ibid.

134 Cf. ibid.

4.2.5.7 The Catholic Students and Young Christian Life Societies (Katholische studierende Jugend und Gemeinschaften Christlichen Lebens – KSJ und GCL)

The Catholic Students and Young Christian Life Societies are two different youth movements that came together in 1974 to form one entity.[135] They existed independently as "Catholic Students Association" and "Young Christian Life Association". The Catholic Students Association was founded in 1919 as "The Federation of New German Youth Society", comprised only of boys.[136] In 1923, its female part was founded as "Federation of Heliand Girls' Circle".[137] Following the insurgence of the National Socialistic regime, the two associations ceased to exist during the Second World War. They were however re-organized after the war in 1948. In 1971 they were merged together under the name "Catholic Students Association."[138]

The Young Christian Life Society was founded in 1564 as a Marian congregation by Jean Leunis.[139] The association also suffered the same fate as the Catholic Students Association under the regime of the National Socialistic Party. It was however re-organized in 1948 after the war.[140] In 1969, it was given its current name and was merged with the Catholic Students Association in 1974.[141]

The two associations have the following aims and objectives:

1. To encourage young people to participate actively in school and other educational projects such as tutorial work, training projects and the running of school cafes
2. To motivate young people to be involved in political, social and religious issues
3. To organize common recreational events and trips as a counterpoint to the hectic school programmes and steadily increasing work load
4. To educate young people so that they can seek, find and follow the youthful forms of spirituality of St. Ignatius of Loyola[142]

---

135 Cf. http://www.eja-muenchen.de/bdkj/die-organe-in-der-erzdiözese/mitgliedsverbaende/ksj-gcl.html, 12.03.2012.

136 Cf. Ibid.

137 Cf. Ibid.

138 Cf. Ibid.

139 Cf. Ibid.

140 Cf. Ibid.

141 Cf. Ibid.

142 Cf. Ibid.

To achieve these aims and objectives, the two associations have children of secondary school age, adolescents and young adults as their target groups.[143]

4.2.5.8 The Kolping Youth (Kolping Jugend – KJ)

The name of the organization comes from the founder, Adolph Kolping (1813-1865).[144] He was a cobbler and later a priest. The Kolping youth association is a large organization of young people up to 30 years old.[145] It has about 2,000 members in the archdiocese of Munich and Freising.[146] The members are made up of children, adolescents and young adults. The society is represented in over 50 countries.[147] In Germany, there are about 2,800 Kolping families. The members take responsibility for young Christians, their fellow human beings and their environment. They organize camping and courses in the outdoors, during which they look after the spirituality of their members in order to promote a common life of faith. Other aims and objectives of the society are:

1. To search for the answers to the questions that concern young people
2. To create awareness of the need for relationships in faith, life, politics and ecology
3. To plan for a common future[148]

4.2.5.9 The Female Scout Union of St. George (Pfadfinderinnenschaft St. Georg – PSG)

The Female Scout Union of St. George was founded in 1947 in Munich as the Association of Catholic Girl Scouts Movement and it assumed the tradition of the Federation of Catholic Girl Scouts which was banned in 1935 by the National Socialistic regime.[149] Its membership is open to all girls of school age, adolescents and young women. The aims and objectives of the movement are:

1. To create the opportunity for girls to learn how to value their activities and capabilities

---

143 Cf. Ibid.

144 Cf. http://www.eja-muenchen.de/bdkj/die-organe-in-der-erzdiözese/mitgliedsverbaende/kolpingjugend.html, 12.03.2012.

145 Cf. http://www.kolping-muenchen.de/jugend/kolpingjugend.html, 21.03.2012.

146 Cf. http://www.eja-muenchen.de/bdkj/die-organe-in-der-erzdiözese/mitgliedsverbaende/kolpingjugend.html, 12.03.2012.

147 Cf. Ibid.

148 Cf. Ibid.

149 Cf. http://www.eja-muenchen.de/bdkj/die-organe-in-der-erzdiözese/mitgliedsverbaende/psg.html, 12.03.2012.

2. To help girls to find and develop their identity, regardless of the prevailing gender tussles[150]

4.2.5.10 Youth Action (Junge Aktion – JA)

Youth Action is the youth wing of the Ackermann community and a member of the East-West action of the Federation of German Catholic Youth (BDKJ). It is an organization of children and young people between the ages of ten and twenty-six.[151] The activities of the association are to contribute to a "Europe of citizens".[152] As a youth organization, it is aimed at promoting the growth and development of young people on their way to responsible lives in the state and society. The members participate actively in the integration of Europe. The focus of their work is based on the history of the organization. The organization was founded in 1950 by teenagers expelled from Bohemia, Moravia and Silesia, in a meeting with the Central and Eastern European neighbours.[153] The organization has four principles which are:

1. Christian life
2. Human rights
3. Meeting with their Central and Eastern European neighbours
4. Europe of citizens[154]

4.3 Evaluation

The Church in the diocese of Ahiara and in the archdiocese of Munich and Freising recognises three basic places of religious education namely: the family, the school and the parish. These three places play an inter-connected role in the education and upbringing of children. In these places, different people are involved. The parents co-ordinate the religious upbringing of their children in the family, the teachers guide the religious knowledge of their pupils at school while the priest and the catechist oversee the religious instructions of children in the parish set-up.

The success of family catechesis depends greatly on the parents, who are said to be its primary resource people. Children by their nature are very docile. They can easily adapt to the stimuli of their immediate environment. This ap-

150 Cf. Ibid.

151 Cf. http://www.junge-aktion.de/, 21.03.2012.

152 Cf. ibid.

153 Cf. ibid.

154 Cf. ibid.

plies also to their religious development. Children of religious parents have often turned out to be religious, although there are also non-religious children of religious parents. The failure of family catechesis is often attributed to the laxity of the parents. Families who attend Church activities as a common programme have often produced children who later became very active in Church affairs. This is the case with some families in which the children are brought up under loving parental care. In such families, the children participate in family prayers and attend catechism classes at the proper time. The parents in turn relate to them in a loving and caring manner so that they may have a sense of belonging and acceptance by their parents. Before their peers, they try also to have good behaviour in order to promote the good image and reputation of their parents and families. This is one of the goals of the Christian upbringing of children.

Parish catechesis is especially aimed at preparing and leading the children to the reception of the sacraments as well as equipping them for a responsible life. Principal among the sacraments are the sacraments of initiation – Baptism, Confirmation and Holy Eucharist. The sacrament of Penance and Reconciliation is also very important since it accompanies the preparation and reception of First Holy Communion. This became the case after the separation of Baptism and Confirmation in the course of the Church's history. Parish catechesis at this level provides the fundamentals of faith formation but has proved insufficient to take care of young people after the reception of the sacrament of Confirmation. This lack of youth catechesis that can guarantee an on-going evangelisation before marriage is the basic concern of youth apostolate. Following a qualitative research especially within the areas of investigation, it can be comfortably asserted that there is no substantial Catholic religious educational programme yet designed for this demography. This means that this essential period of life is yet to receive adequate attention from a pastoral perspective. Some dioceses, and in most cases, some parishes have in the course of history organised programmes for the youth in the form of retreats, seminars and workshops. Sometimes these programmes have also included sports activities and excursions. But a programme which is meant to guarantee the pastoral care of the youth with on-going formation has not yet been designed.

In the diocese of Ahiara and in the archdiocese of Munich and Freising, youth pastoral is exercised through the existing youth associations in the two dioceses. But the extent to which these associations have appealed to the attention of the youth is yet to be guaranteed. Although these youth organizations have a substantial number of young people as their members, the integration of the religious aims and objectives of these associations into the daily Christian lives of young people is yet to be seen.

The preparation for First Holy Communion and Confirmation and their celebration in the archdiocese of Munich and Freising are in some cases seen as family tradition. Children often say that they participate in the reception of First Holy Communion and the celebration of Confirmation because all the members of their family before them did the same. The sanctifying aspect of these sacraments is in this case not the underlying reason for their reception but the fear of breaking the traditional family chains. Often some of them join in celebrating these sacraments because they are means of receiving gifts from friends and family members. A young girl once said that she enrolled for the sacrament of Confirmation because her granny made some monetary promises to her if she allowed herself to be confirmed in the Church. The emphasis is no longer on grace but on material enrichment. Another reason for the reception of these sacraments for some children is social influence. Some of them participate because all their friends and the members of their peer groups are also taking part. It is therefore a means of solidifying their membership in a particular peer group and not a source of strengthening their faith in the Church.

The sacrament of Penance and Reconciliation is losing its grip on the faithful in these post-modern times. This is seen in the reluctance of some people to embrace the richness of this sacrament through individual confession and reconciliation. Children's confessions before First Holy Communion have also been used as a criticism against the Church in the sense that it is a means of inculcating the idea of sin into children. Some people claim that the Church trains children at an early age in a practice which as a rule they do not experience from their parents.[155]

4.4 Summary

The youth apostolate is very active in the diocese of Ahiara and in the archdiocese of Munich and Freising. This can be seen in both family and parish catechesis. The parents play a major role in the preparation of their children for the reception of the sacraments of Holy Eucharist and Confirmation. For the reception of Confirmation in the archdiocese of Munich and Freising, the candidates are divided into groups. Each group is led by one of the parents of the candidates. They carry out common exercises like joint lessons, civil activities and excursions. Much work remains to be done for young people after the reception of Confirmation. So far, the Church has succeeded in forming youth associations as a way of keeping young people close to the faith but has not yet designed a catechesis that can accompany their maturity into adulthood.

155 Cf. Jakobs M., Neue Wege der Katechese, München, 2010, 91-92.

Youth associations abound in the two dioceses, to which young people are free to enrol as members. Almost all the Catholic youth in these two dioceses are members of various youth associations. Young people in the archdiocese of Munich and Freising have a greater variety of associations than their counterparts in the diocese of Ahiara. They engage in the activities of these associations mainly on the social level. This is because these associations have not yet developed enough programmes that can guarantee an on-going formation and instruction of young people in the doctrines of the Church. These associations are meant to encourage the development of lay spirituality especially among young people. However, the fact that they belong to these associations is also an indication that they have not lost their faith in the Church. The only difference is that they manifest their faith in their own way. These associations offer them the opportunity of communality with their peers as a means of expressing their identity with the Christian faith.

In the diocese of Ahiara, it can be seen that religious education in the family, in the school and in the Church is not fortified with African elements. This is because both the work of evangelization and colonialism in Nigeria did not favour African culture and identity. This can be very clearly seen in the mentality of many Africans in the post-modern times and especially in their Christian praxis. Liturgical activities are more Roman than African just as their daily lives are more Western oriented. This is however an unfortunate situation for African culture. It was expected that the Christianization of Africa would have taken African culture, mentality and values into consideration. But unfortunately the reverse is completely the case. This is why the pastoral care of the youth in the diocese of Ahiara and indeed in many other parts of Africa is seen more from the perspective of Western and Roman culture than African.

5. Challenging the Situation

In the previous chapters, an attempt had been made to present the components of the religious education formation of children from the beginning of primary education to the end of secondary education in the diocese of Ahiara and in the archdiocese of Munich and Freising. This includes the teaching of religion in the school, in the family and in the Church. Attention had also been given to some extra and post-curricula activities which form parts of the youthful programmes of the youth organizations existing in the diocese of Ahiara and the archdiocese of Munich and Freising through which young people exhibit their characteristics. In this chapter, the aim is to analyse the religious perspectives of children in these two places in order to find out their differences and similarities as well as to discover the impact of these perspectives on the religious and spiritual development of these children later in life. It will consider the important religious educational elements which the two dioceses can learn from each other in order to improve the level of religious awareness of their young ones. Another important goal of this chapter is to explore the extent to which religious education has helped in the promotion of youth apostolate in the two dioceses. This will be done in the form of offering important suggestions that will hopefully help young people integrate their religious knowledge into a practical reality in their lives. Such suggestions will help in enlivening the seemingly passive religiosity of young people so that they can find meaning in the spiritual activities of the Church as well as see the need to participate actively in them. It will take note of some social and environmental phenomena affecting the religious assimilation of young people as a means of eradicating the notion of religious indifference ascribed to some of them. Such suggestions will also help young people in recognising religion as an important aspect of their lives.

5.1 Social Phenomena Affecting Religious Education

Heraclitus identified change as the only permanent reality since according to him "all things are in a state of flux".[1] Change, therefore, is a constant occurrence. It brings about new ideas, realities and modes of perception. Kunstmann identified the presence of change in the world situation, especially in relation to the Church as follows:

1 Cf. Schwachulla, W. (Red.), Der Brockhaus in einem Band, Leipzig, 1998, 378.

During The Middle Ages, unprecedented authority resided with the Church. At this time, the Church almost single-handedly defined every change as sedition and heresy. In the post-modern time, the situation is completely the opposite.[2]

This situation is realized because there are currently visible signs of great changes in worldviews and attitudes of life. Since the Enlightenment and the complete mechanization of the world in the 20th century, humanity has largely been living with the consciousness and confidence of a maximum personal freedom in which regulations and regimentations are often seen as mere inconveniences.[3] That is why Kunstmann maintains that flexibility, dynamism, vitality and the acquisition of purchasing power have become the conditions of life.[4] The essence of life is therefore no longer one of care and service but rather one of self-realization and the elevation of the ego. The "aesthetic decade" of the 1980s according to Timm ushered in new waves of perceiving a reality which is no longer based on the established truths but on possibilities, options and personal concerns.[5] The implications of these changes especially for the Church should hardly be underestimated. With this situation, old securities have been replaced with new threats. These threats are seen in some of the social phenomena affecting religious education and the pastoral care of young people. Such threats can be categorised under religious pluralism, secularism and the media.

5.1.1 The Influence of Religious Pluralism on Religious Education

In the first chapter of this work, religious pluralism was identified as the underlying social reason for the study of religion (cf. 1.1.4.3). The word pluralism indicates multiplicity. Religious pluralism therefore describes a situation whereby many religions co-exist in a particular heterogeneous society. Heterogeneity denotes the coming together of people of different cultural, religious and linguistic backgrounds in the same environment. This coming together is principally the fruit of the migration of people from one place to another. In post-modern times, freedom has greatly encouraged pluralism. With the opening of the borders of many nationalities under globalization, there is a massive

2 Kunstmann J., Religionspädagogik, Eine Einführung, 2. Auflage, Tübingen, 2010, 249.

3 Cf. Ibid.

4 Cf. Ibid.

5 Cf. Timm H., Das ästhetische Jahrzehnt. Zur Postmodernisierung der Religion, Gütersloh, 1990, 11, 17-18, quoted by: Kunstmann J., Religionspädagogik, Eine Einführung, 2. Auflage, Tübingen, 2010, 249.

free movement of people from one place to another. This is also coupled with the fundamental right of freedom of worship in many countries. This has escalated religious pluralism because people have an inalienable right to practice their religion in any place of their residence. This is in line with the definition of pluralism by Kunstmann when he says:

> *Pluralism is the result of the enforced differentiation processes which are caused by the modern principle of free expression.*[6]

Pluralism has its "pros and cons". It provides opportunities for the exchange of ideas in various fields of life as well as generating conflicts among people due to differences in ideologies and beliefs. Pluralism denotes a situation in which people of diverse backgrounds live together in the same neighbourhood, go to work daily using the same transportation systems, work together in offices and factories, find recreation in the same facilities, send their children to same schools but worship under different roofs.[7] This idea of worshiping in different places points to religious pluralism. The fact of many religions in a particular conglomeration indicates that many religious groups are involved in religious education in which case they have to devise means of learning and living with one another.

In the diocese of Ahiara, about 500,000 people live and interact together. Of this number, about 385,000 are Catholics, 114,700 are Protestants and only about 300 are Traditionalists.[8] Although there is no presence of other religions such as Islam, Buddhism, Hinduism and Judaism, the fact of religious pluralism in this environment however cannot be completely ignored. Due to the difference in denominations, reference can be made to a "denominational pluralism" as a result of which religious education in the schools is devoid of confessional or denominational teachings. The curriculum allows only the teaching of Biblical stories and national issues that may have religious connotations. The religious education teacher is not free to teach from the background of his or her religious beliefs but from an ecumenical point of view in which the Bible stands as the point of intersection. The word ecumenism was used by the Second Vatican Council to denote the concern of the Catholic Church for the unity of Christians, irrespective of their various denominational inclinations. It involves a dialogue among all Christians. Such dialogue according to the Af-

6 Kunstmann J., Religionspädagogik, Eine Einführung, 2. Auflage, Tübingen, 2010, 253.

7 Cf. Thompson N. R., The Challenge of Religious Pluralism, in: Thompson H. N. (Ed.), Religious Pluralism and Religious Education, Birmingham, 1988, 12.

8 Cf. Chikwe V., Catholic Diocese of Ahiara Mbaise, Diary and Calendar of Pastoral Events, Nguru, 2009, 7.

rican Bishops seeks to direct the journey towards Christian unity.[9] In religious education, ecumenical learning indicates that members of the different Christian Churches can learn from one another in relation to life, faith and religion.[10] It involves a co-operation of all Christians in the propagation of the Christian teachings. This stems from the fact that Christianity originated from one source, which is belief in Christ and his teachings. Ecumenical learning further means all cognitive and action-oriented processes, which contribute to mutual awareness and promote respect among the members of the different Christian denominations.[11] Children need to be made aware of the differences in the practice of Christianity. This is one of the goals of ecumenical learning. These differences need to be harmonized so that a point of unity can be established. Ecumenical learning therefore strives to disabuse the idea of difference in the minds of children and young people so that denominational boundaries can be neglected in human interaction. This explains why the majority of children and young people in the diocese of Ahiara no longer cling to denominational identity as it was during the missionary era, when denominational differences were strictly observed. Hence, the major Christian feasts such as Christmas, Esther and Pentecost are now celebrated together among all Christians irrespective of denominational variances. This decline in denominational identity is as a result of a growing interest in the central religious questions of life such as the questions on meaning, future, God, justice and peace.[12] Many people have transcended the stage of denominational inclination as a result of their awareness of the unity of humanity. Thus, ecumenical learning has contributed to the achievement of sustainable unity and other set goals in the diocese of Ahiara. Such goals are: the use of Christian denominational identity to create an open ecumenical dialogue; competent perception of denominational cultures, which create the awareness of values in other denominations; strengthening the unity of Christians and respecting their differences; learning from each other and one another as a means of establishing sustainable human development. Although denominational differences among the various Christian Churches abide, they are not used to the detriment of social, ethical, cultural and religious interaction among the people.

The situation in the archdiocese of Munich and Freising is quite different. The major world religions are represented in this demography. Hence, next door neighbours are sometimes people of different religious persuasions. This

9 Cf. AM, 89.

10 Cf. Leimgruber S., Ökumenisches Lernen, in: Hilger G., Leimgruber S., Ziebertz H. G., Religionsdidaktik, Ein Leitfaden für Studium, Ausbildung und Beruf, München, 2010, 453.

11 Cf. Ibid., 457.

12 Cf. Ibid., 458.

raises some difficulties in the teaching of religion especially in the schools which are attended by children of different religious convictions. What should form the basis of such teaching? And what should be its goal and objective? In chapter one of this work, one of the aims of religious education was identified as that of fostering an overall human development (cf. 1.3.2). This entails ethical learning. In ethical learning according to Ziebertz, pupils deal with values and norms.[13] The contents of ethical learning are moral values which have personal, religious and social connotations. Hence it is concerned with the ability to perform practical values and to develop a discourse of discernment which enables one to make responsible decisions regarding the questions: What must I do?; What should we do?; What is to apply?; What is desirable and durable for me and others?[14] The treatment of these questions has a permanent place in religious education and social ethics. In a pluralistic religious society, the teaching of religion should therefore be focused on relating one religion to another and the knowledge that allows the assessment of values within the horizon of established moral principles. It should also create room for dialogue, and more than dialogue, to the discussion of issues and problems which separate human beings and respect the traditions of the affected religions.[15] In this situation, reference is to be made to an "ecumenism of religions", which is concerned with the harmony of all religions.[16] This is why religious education should not be limited to the school but should also be handled by other institutions such as the family and the Church so that it can be centred on the perspective of uniting the world and its different peoples under the heading of "global learning".[17] The result here will be a dual requirement for socio-ethical learning in religious education whereby students will develop a competence of socio-ethical or moral judgement and learn the assessment of values in the light of religion. This gives rise to a balanced education because students will have the ability to judge moral values on the basis of both social and religious principles and thereby achieve sustainable human development.

13 Cf. Ziebertz H. G., Ethisches Lernen, in: Hilger G., Leimgruber S., Ziebertz H. G., Religionsdidaktik, Ein Leitfaden für Studium, Ausbildung und Beruf, München, 2010, 434.

14 Cf. Ibid.

15 Cf. Thompson N. R., The Challenge of Religious Pluralism, in: Thompson H. N. (Ed.), Religious Pluralism and Religious Education, Birmingham, 1988, 21.

16 Cf. Leimgruber S., Ökumenisches Lernen, in: Hilger G., Leimgruber S., Ziebertz H. G., Religionsdidaktik, Ein Leitfaden für Studium, Ausbildung und Beruf, München, 2010, 460.

17 Cf. Bahr M., Leimgruber S., Verantwortung für die Eine Welt, in: Hilger G., Leimgruber S., Ziebertz H. G., Religionsdidaktik, Ein Leitfaden für Studium, Ausbildung und Beruf, München, 2010, 472.

5.1.2 The Influence of Secularism on Religious Education

Secularism is the term used to denote the marginalization of religion by the modernization processes of industrialization, urbanization and mass education.[18] Its aim is the suppression or total elimination of religious values, beliefs and practices.[19] McMohan defined it as follows:

> *Secularism is a form of humanism that limits true value to those temporal qualities that contribute to man's natural perfection, both individual and social, to the actual exclusion of the supernatural.*[20]

Secularism was developed in the mid 19th century as a distinct philosophy by George Holyoake and Charles Bradlaugh.[21] This philosophy postulated:

- Principles of natural independence of all revelation and supernatural orientation;
- Absolute freedom of opinion on all matters, including morality;
- Natural improvement in this life;
- Absolute separation of Church and State.[22]

The influence of secularism is felt more in the developed countries than in the developing ones. It brought a sharp difference between the pre-modern and modern worlds in which the influence and value of religion in the former has been greatly devalued. In the pre-modern age, religion constituted the essence of almost all human enterprises and therefore encouraged an encounter with God in many spheres of human endeavour including politics. All these have changed in the modern times. This was the view of Taylor in the following statements:

> *The difference would then consist in this, that whereas the political organization of all pre-modern societies was in some way connected to, based on, guaranteed by some faith in, or adherence to God, or some notion of the ultimate reality, the modern Western state is free from this connection. Churches are now separated from political structures ...*

18 Cf. Kuru T. K., Secularism and State Policies Toward Religion, The United States, France and Turkey, Cambridge, 2009, 1.

19 Cf. Ibid., 2.

20 McMohan T. F., Secularism, in: Carson T. & Cerrito J. (Eds.), New Catholic Encyclopedia, Second Edition, Vol. 12, Detroit, 2003, 863.

21 Cf. Ibid., 865.

22 Ibid.

Religion or its absence is largely a private matter. The political society is seen as that of believers (of all stripes) and non-believers alike.[23]

Under secularism, political engagements are sometimes devoid of religious as well as moral values and promote the principle of "might is right" syndrome. Here, the winner takes it all and there is no recourse to the judgement of the conscience because one can fully engage in politics without ever encountering God.[24] Moreover, the public spaces have been allegedly emptied of God, or any reference to the transcendental reality. Thus secularism in the present post-modern society consists in the falling off of religious belief and practice, in people turning away from God, and no longer going to Church.[25] Hence, in the post-modern era, faith, even for the staunchest believer, has become a human possibility among others as against the background of the pre-modern society, in which it was virtually impossible not to believe in God.[26] The case study of this work shows that secularism plays a more influential role in religious education within the schools in the archdiocese of Munich and Freising than in the diocese of Ahiara. In the former demography, religion is experiencing a bitter resistance due to the secularized nature of our contemporary world.[27] This is especially realized in the case of some students' refusal to study religion at the attainment of 14 years, and choose ethics or philosophy as a replacement in the name of modernism. Such students regard religion as an old-fashioned phenomenon which has lost its essence.[28] They accept any process of the physical, moral, social and mental development of the human person that is devoid of religious principles. For such people, participation in religious activities and adherence to religious beliefs do not belong to the present technological age. In this situation, there is an increase in spiritual and ideological disintegration in the name of intellectual freedom as well as a deterioration of behaviour, morals and deeds in the name of individual freedom.[29] In the contemporary society, books and newspapers appear whose sole aim is to weaken or destroy the influ-

23 Taylor C., A Secular Age, Harvard, 2007, 1.

24 Cf. Ibid.

25 Cf. Ibid.

26 Cf. Ibid.

27 Cf. Rellstab T., Anstoß erregend, in: Heinemann C. (Hg.), Gottes Wort im Kirchenjahr 2006, 3. Band, Würzburg, 2006, 124.

28 Cf. Kunstmann J., Religionspädagogik, Eine Einführung, 2. Auflage, Tübingen, 2010, 256.

29 Cf. Clarke P. B., Islam, Development and African Identity: The Case of West Africa, in: Petersen K. H. (Ed.), Religion, Development and African Identity, Uppsala, 1987, 126.

ence of any religion on the masses. As a result, young people are religiously lost and the educated are in a state of doubt and confusion.[30]

Although the situation in the schools within the diocese of Ahiara is not the same as that of Munich and Freising, the reluctance of some students to attend religious education lessons and the low rate of candidates who enrol in this subject at the "Senior Secondary Certificate Examination " (SSCE) level are things of great concern. This is expressed by the Ministry of Education as one of the challenges facing religious education in Nigeria.[31] Some students use the time for religious education lesson for their private studies or even recreation. They turn away from the lesson because it is sometimes too boring and non-captivating. They are no longer motivated to be hearing only stories from the Bible which do not tickle their fancy but create boredom and induce them to sleep. Because of secular influence, they prefer lessons on human relationships which can enhance friendship and interaction such as sex education and social ethics.

5.1.3 The Influence of the Media on Religious Education

The media are means of mass communication through which many people receive the same information within the same range of time and space. They are divided into the electronic media and the print media. The electronic media include television, radio, telephone and computer while the print media are newspapers, books and magazines. As information carriers, the media are very significant in shaping the lives of contemporary individuals, especially the lives of young people. Listed under the electronic media are the multimedia through which multiple data can be stored at a higher density and transmitted without much burden. These include both software and hardware gadgets such as flash drives, hard drives, MP3 players and blu-ray discs. The electronic media especially present a dramatic change for religion. Indeed they show the presence of religion, but in a more complex and more difficult way than it is seen in everyday life. Some religious programmes such as a worship series or Sunday Church services are unadulterated broadcasts which portray the real teaching of a particular religion. Other religious programmes such as films, movies and drama are filled with religious symbols, structures and myths only to win the attention of the public, without any religious overtone. This is why the religion of the media according to Kunstmann is no longer the Christian re-

30 Cf. Ibid.

31 Cf. Federal Ministry of Education, Senior Secondary School Curriculum, Christian Religious Studies for SS 1 – 3, Abuja, 2010, v.

ligion.[32] Even when such programmes are presented with Christian references and allusions, they are in a different context and usually have very different intentions which sometimes occur ironically or even as satire.[33] In this instance the religious analogical levels of such programmes are without reference to God and are built on simple schemes which are hardly fair to the complexity, the nature and the richness of the transmitted religion. Thus the religion of the media presents itself as being independent of the established religion. A typical example of such is the "Liquid Church" which has won the sympathy of many young people on Facebook. However, this does not necessarily mean that the established religions could not use the media for their transmission. The use of the media in religious education will be treated in another section of this chapter.

In the archdiocese of Munich and Freising for instance, young people spend an average of four hours daily watching television and/or using the computer.[34] This includes the time they spend on playing video games, watching television programmes, using computer games, communicating in chat rooms and writing emails. The media have so shaped their lives that they are always busy with mobile telephones, with which they write text messages (SMS), browse the Internet and listen to music. Other gadgets like MP3 players have become steady companions which some of them use even while in the school. In this way, the media affects the teaching, learning and practice of religion in the lives of young people.

A similar situation is also applicable to the young people in the diocese of Ahiara. Although their intake and use of the media are not at the same level as their counterparts in the archdiocese of Munich and Freising, their lives are also greatly influenced by the use of electronic media. A good percentage of them spend an average of two to three hours daily watching television and/or using the computer. This time is mainly spent on television programmes especially sports and on the Internet. Some even engage themselves with browsing and chatting all night long. Mobile telephones also play significant roles in their lives in the sense that they write many text messages (SMS) and make numerous "midnight calls" because such calls are usually free of charge. Because of the lack of adequate sleep during the night, some are very weak during the day and can no longer concentrate on their school activities. The media in this sense play a negative role in the teaching and learning of religious education.

32 Cf. Kunstmann J., Religionspädagogik, Eine Einführung, 2. Auflage, Tübingen, 2010, 269.

33 Cf., Ibid.

34 Cf., Ibid., 268.

5.2 Environmental Phenomena Affecting Religious Education

The environment plays a substantial role in the religious training and upbringing of the child. This is why people of a particular district sometimes behave and reason alike. This trend is sometimes likened to the fact that they have peculiar slogans and means of expressing particular situations. The religious education and upbringing of a child can therefore not be separated from his or her immediate environment. In this section, attention will be focused on the agents of those environments where the child lives and learns. Thus, the aim of this section is to survey the extent to which such agents like the parents, the religious education teacher and the peer groups influence the religious assimilation of the child in the two resource areas of this work – the diocese of Ahiara and the archdiocese of Munich and Freising.

5.2.1 The Influence of Parents on Religious Education

In chapter four of this work, it was argued whether non-believing parents can have believing children and vice versa (cf. 4.1.3). For an adequate handling of this issue, especially with regard to the resource areas, some analyses have to be drawn. In the diocese of Ahiara as well as in many places in Africa, beliefs and principles are strongly built on an orally handed-over tradition. This is why most African values are not literally documented. Africans cling strongly to the religious traditions and practices of their fore-fathers and ancestors. These fore-fathers and ancestors, although dead, are still believed to be part of the living community and are therefore honoured and respected. This belief in the living-dead is one of the cherished and preserved values in African religion. Even when Africans are converted to other foreign religions like Christianity or Islam, their African cultural values such as respect for parents and ancestors are retained. Parents are given a great deal of respect by their children. This is because African culture is built on respect and parents belong to the custodians of this culture. Children look on their parents as their teachers, doctors and spiritual leaders and therefore regard them as their mentors. They strive to model their lives (even their love lives) after the lives of their parents. This is why children rarely argue with their parents when they receive instructions from them on spiritual and moral (or ethical) issues. This indicates that parents in Africa have a strong influence on the religious lives and upbringing of their children. Historically, the indigenous people of the diocese of Ahiara worshipped God through the use of idols before the advent of Christianity. These idols were only symbols and images of the deity in African Traditional Religion (ATR). This is also likened to the use of images in Christianity in which the Crucifix, for instance, is used to signify the image of the crucified Christ.

Although the use of these idols was condemned by the early missionaries who ascribed them pagan connotations, they were not evil in themselves and did not contain any supernatural powers. Although many of the traditional worshippers were not very fast in accepting the Christian religion, they allowed their children to be baptised (before their own later conversion, in the case of very few). They also sent their children to school (primarily) for the quest of Western education, fame and fortune despite the fact that they were illiterate themselves.[35] This indicates that some parents can strive to give their children those fundamental values which they themselves were not privileged to have. Parents can therefore influence the religious lives of their children either through their individual religious actions or through delegation. In this regard, they can either send their children to school where they would be privileged to attend religious education classes or to the Church for catechetical instructions. This proves that non-believing parents can have believing children. A more concrete way through which parents influence their children religiously is family prayer and regular Church attendance especially on Sundays. They also engage in family pilgrimages to some holy places or designated centres, discussions, songs and the use of sacred images in their homes. In this way, the family can be described as a genuine, independent and idiosyncratic place of faith communication.[36] Such family catechetical activities can indeed help the children to get attuned to their religious practices as well as to become more aware of the Christian (or Catholic) religious beliefs and principles.

In the archdiocese of Munich and Freising, some parents do not exhibit much influence on the religious lives of their children, especially because of the fear that they might infringe on their personal freedom. Due to a lack of knowledge, some parents do not understand their role in the religious upbringing of their children. This is because they are not religious and therefore cannot give what they do not have. As a result of their material affluence, some of them do not recognize the need for religion in their lives and therefore cannot inculcate it into their children. A common practice which is to the detriment of religion is the act of some parents who regularly attend Church services without the company of their children. Such parents allow their children to get more sleep especially on Sundays in order to be fit for other programmes, such as sports, which will occur in the course of the day. Although some of these children may be very good in the religious education classes, they may not be

35 Cf. Isichei E., A History of Christianity in Africa. From Antiquity to the Present, London, 1995, 270.

36 Cf. Bendel H., Biesinger A., Familienkatechese, in: Bitter G., Englert R., Miller G., Nipkow K. E. (Hg.), Neues Handbuch religionspädagogischer Grundbegriffe, 2. Auflage, München, 2009, 310.

religious in their daily lives due to the lack of religious practices and exercises. In this way, the action of some parents influences the children negatively in their practice of religion.

5.2.2 The Influence of the Religious Education Teacher on Religious Education

In many schools, the religious education teacher is often very positively assessed.[37] His or her acceptance by the students is often based on his or her ability to win the attention of the students during the lessons. A religious education teacher who does not appeal to the taste of the students is often despised and the rate of attendance at his or her lessons is often very low. Even the few who attend do not show the desired interest in his or her lessons. A religious education teacher should be able to command influence and respect from his or her students. He or she is above all expected to exhibit a positive influence in the class so that his or her subject can be loved by the students. Some of the basic required expectations of the religious education teacher are: factual competence, personal mastery and good educational skills. These qualities are very significant for religious learning and make the religious education teacher highly recognized and esteemed by the students.

A tactical mastery of the teaching materials boosts the personal ego of the religious education teacher and brings him or her to the admiration of the class. The manner of delivering the lessons defines the teacher's factual competence as well as his or her teaching charisma. The most significant quality of the religious education teacher according to Kunstmann is the ability to translate personal knowledge into the present life.[38] This means that the religious education teacher should be able to demonstrate the value of the (Christian) religion to individual life activities.

The personality of the religious education teacher plays a fundamental role in the transmission and assimilation of his or her lessons. The teacher should be willing and able to be in control of the class.[39] He or she is expected to posses an authentic personality in the sense of being devoted to his or her duty. The need for this is based on the fact that students like harmony and do not like thoughtfully negligent teachers who posses poor personal qualities.[40] Such teachers cannot comport themselves before their students and do not show any mastery of their subject. For a positive influence on his or her subject, the re-

37 Cf. Kunstmann J., Religionspädagogik, Eine Einführung, 2. Auflage, Tübingen, 2010, 207.

38 Cf. Ibid., 209.

39 Cf. Ibid.

40 Cf. Ibid.

ligious education teacher should be convinced of his or her role and be able to show empathy and understanding to the students. Above all, he or she should carefully relate with the students in a manner of commanding authority before them in order to give meaning to the importance of his or her subject.[41] This will help in keeping a balance between controlling the class and winning the attention of the students.

The educational competence of the religious education teacher helps him or her to psychologically understand the experiences, needs and attitudes of his or her students and be able to offer solutions to them.[42] From the perspective of Christianity, the religious education teacher has to understand the essentials of the Christian doctrines, be able to analyse and present them to the students so that old experiences can produce new ones. The ability of the teacher to generate thoughtfulness and enthusiasm for the Christian religion in the students signifies his or her competence as a teacher of the Christian religion. This is often the case when the teacher not only informs, but also moderates religious experiences.

The importance of the above-enumerated qualities of the religious education teacher for a positive influence on religious education is based on the fact that students of the contemporary era are not so much interested in the credibility of the religious belief and practical life of the religious education teacher, but rather in his or her authenticity, life experience, style of appearance and personal charisma.[43] The religious education teacher therefore is not to be seen as a representative of his or her religious denomination in the school. Although he or she may have the theological knowledge of his or her personal religious beliefs and thus can be a witness and herald of the tenets of this religion, he or she is expected in recent times to be only a knowledgeable teacher of religion and not of faith.[44] He or she is only expected to be a competent advocate of the existential religious questions of the students, a facilitator of the discussions on social issues, a therapeutic counsellor and a psychologically trained promoter of religious socialization.[45]

The above situation applies to both the schools within the diocese of Ahiara and those in the archdiocese of Munich and Freising.

41 Cf. Ibid.

42 Cf. Ibid., 210.

43 Cf. Ibid.

44 Cf. Ibid.

45 Cf. Ibid.

5.2.3 The Influence of Peer Group on Religious Education

At the first African Synod, the Bishops of Africa identified young people as the proper evangelizers of their peers. This is because young people know and understand themselves better than any other group of individuals. This was articulated as follows:

The Church in Africa knows well that youth are not only the present but above all the future of humanity. It is thus necessary to help young people to overcome the obstacles thwarting their development: illiteracy, idleness, hunger, drugs. In order to meet these challenges, young people themselves should be called upon to become the evangelizers of their peers. No one can do this better than they.[46]

This role of evangelization by young people makes them co-educators and co-formators of their age mates. They play this role by encouraging themselves to attend religious education classes, to participate in youth pastoral care and to attend regular Church services. The peer group in this sense serves as a means of promoting religious education. However, the peer group can also play a negative role in religious education. This is often the case when some students are mobbed, jeered at, booed or taunted because of their religious inclinations. Such students may be altar servers, choristers or lectors in their various Churches. The members of their peer group sometimes mock them and give them abusive names such as: sancta, pastor, angel, holy man, etc. Victims of such situations are often frustrated and even withdraw themselves from the group or sometimes give up their religious beliefs. Cases of depression and a state of deep melancholy have also been recorded as a result of a miserable experience from the peer group. In some cases, victimized students react violently against the members of their peer group thereby causing suppression and rancour or even a stampede. The peer group in this instance plays a negative role in religious education and clamps down on the spirit of religiosity in some young people. This influence of the peer group is applicable to the two areas of investigation – the diocese of Ahiara and the archdiocese of Munich and Freising. This is because the youth exhibit similar characteristics and express similar problems wherever they are located.

From the overall analysis, it can be seen that religious education favours and promotes the pastoral care of youth. This is especially seen in the areas of study, prayer and reflection which take place in the school, in the family and in the Church.[47] The major concern of this work at this point is to propose some

46 Ecclesia in Africa (EA), 1995, 93, http://www.vatican.va/holy_father/john_paul_ii/apost_exhortations/documents/hf_jp-ii_exh_14091995_ecclesia-in-africa_en.html, 09.11.2012.

47 Cf. Ibid.

measures which will help to improve the teaching of religion in the three principal places of religious education – the school, the family and the Church. The need for such a proposal is to ensure that religious education is relevant to young people in all categories taking into recognition the technological advancements of the contemporary time. This leads to three important topics of this chapter which are the contents of religious education in the family, in the school and in the Church followed by recommendations that can enhance a larger participation in religious education and a greater involvement in the pastoral care of the youth.

5.3 Contents of Religious Education in the Family

In the family, religious education is concerned mainly with God, prayer, songs, Bible reading and the sacraments. As a result of their curiosity for knowledge, children first develop their idea of God based on their questions to their parents. They also learn some of the basic Christian prayers such as Grace before and after meals, the Our Father, the Hail Mary and the Creed. With the help of Biblical stories, they get to know some Biblical personalities and their importance in Christianity. The parents also play a significant role in preparing their children for the reception of the sacraments. The mode of doing this differs in the two dioceses under investigation. In the diocese of Ahiara, the parents help in teaching their children catechism and explaining some basic mysteries of the faith to them. In the archdiocese of Munich and Freising, the parents participate, in addition to the teaching of catechism, in the so-called “parents’ evening” during which they come together with their children in the Church as a means of showing their support for their children’s participation in the reception of First Holy Communion and other sacraments. In this “special evening”, they rehearse the order of the Eucharistic celebration with their children so that they will know their seating positions, be informed of their various roles during the Mass and the specific time at which they are to participate in the celebration of the Eucharist. Some of them will participate in the readings, prayer of the faithful and the presentation of gifts to the altar. The following table will illustrate what role the family has in the religious education of their children.

TABLE 1: FAMILY CATECHESIS

Ahiara Diocese	Archdiocese of Munich and Freising
1. God 2. The Sign of the Cross	1. God 2. The Sign of the Cross

3. Grace before and after meals	3. Grace before and after meals
4. The Our Father	4. The Our Father
5. The Hail Mary	5. The Hail Mary
6. Glory Be	6. Glory Be
7. The Creed	7. Bible reading (stories)
8. Bible reading (stories)	8. Parents' evening
9. Catechism	9. Youth Catechism
10. Songs	10. Songs

5.4 Contents of Religious Education in the School

The religious education curricula of the schools in both the diocese of Ahiara and the archdiocese of Munich and Freising contain laudable themes which can doubtlessly enlighten the religious lives of their recipients. The schools in the diocese of Ahiara present basically a Bible-oriented religious education programme with only one topic dealing with leadership. In the archdiocese of Munich and Freising, the curriculum contains teachings on the Bible, life experience and the didactic of other religions. For a better analysis of the two curricula, the two school systems will be discussed separately in this sub topic.

5.4.1 Religious Education in the Schools in the Diocese of Ahiara

The schools in the diocese of Ahiara use the Bible as the primary source of teaching religion. This is mainly due the religiously pluralistic nature of the environment. Children of various Christian denominations attend the same school. This makes it difficult to use denominational terms in religious education. Denominational and doctrinal teachings are reserved for home training and catechism classes. The aim of using the Bible as the primary source in giving religious instructions is to place emphasis on the oneness and universality of the Gospel of Christ so that all Christians will benefit from the lessons on an equal basis. This is why religious education in the schools is limited to the following themes:

1. "Primary One: God's goodness; Jesus, my brother and friend; God our Father
2. Primary Two: talk to God through Jesus Christ; the life of Jesus Christ; God the Creator and Father of all
3. Primary Three: God fulfils His promises; faith in Jesus Christ my Saviour; knowing God through our relationship with others"[48]

48 Federal Ministry of Education, 9-Year Basic Education Curriculum, Christian Religious Studies for Primary 1 – 3, Abuja, 2007, vi-vii.

4. "Primary Four: God as Father guides His children; Jesus the way to the Father and our guide
5. Primary Five: God wants to save all men; Holy Spirit working in us
6. Primary Six: Paul the Apostle; Nigerian Christian leaders and leadership"[49]
7. "JSS One: God and His creation; relationship with God and man; God's call
8. JSS Two: the early life of Jesus Christ; the ministry of Jesus Christ; the Passion, Death and Resurrection of Jesus
9. JSS Three: the beginning of the Church; the life and teaching of Paul and the Christian Church today"[50]
10. "SSS One: Jesus' teaching about Himself; love; justification; new life in Christ; son-ship; faith and works; fruit of the Spirit; spiritual gifts; forgiveness; the family; humility; effectiveness of prayer; Christian living in the community; the Christians and persecution; impartiality; and the Resurrection and the second coming of Christ
11. SSS Two: the sovereignty of God (as manifested in the creation stories); the leadership of Moses, Joshua, Joseph and Deborah; God's care for His people; parental responsibility; the consequences of obedience and disobedience; forgiveness; friendship; submission to the will of God; making decisions as a Christian; greed and its effects; the supremacy of God; religious and personal reforms; concern for one's nation; faith in God; true religion and social justice (from Amos); and Divine love (from Hosea)
12. SSS Three: Baptism and temptation; call to discipleship; mission of the Apostles; the Trial, Death and Resurrection of Jesus (all from the synoptic Gospels); communion and fellowship; the Holy Spirit and mission to the Gentiles; stories of opposition to the Gospel (all from Acts of the Apostles); civic responsibility; HIV/AIDS; skill acquisition and empowerment; dignity of human labour; and dignity of human life (contemporary issues)"[51]

These themes are further broken down into topics for easier and faster understanding. They will now be illustrated with the help of tables.

49 Federal Ministry of Education, 9-Year Basic Education Curriculum, Christian Religious Studies for Primary 4 – 6, Abuja, 2007, vi-vii.

50 Federal Ministry of Education, 9-Year Basic Education Curriculum, Christian Religious Studies for JSS 1 – 3, Abuja, 2007, vi-vii.

51 Federal Ministry of Education, Senior Secondary School Curriculum, Christian Religious Studies for SS 1 – 3, Abuja, 2010, iii-iv.

TABLE 2: PRIMARY ONE

Theme	Topic
1. God's goodness	1. God the creator 2. The goodness of God 3. God the provider of good things 4. God the giver of family 5. God the helper 6. Using God's gift of sight 7. Using God's gift of hearing 8. The birth of Jesus Christ
2. Jesus my brother and my friend	1. Jesus our brother 2. Jesus our friend 3. Jesus wants us to make friends 4. Jesus wants us to love one another 5. Jesus wants us to enjoy playing and living together 6. Obeying God 7. Using God's gift of strength and ability
3. God our Father	1. God our Father 2. Discovering God through Jesus 3. We are children of one God 4. The joy of having God as a Father 5. Children of God help one another 6. Thanking God our Father 7. Praising God our Father 8. Talking to God our Father in prayer[52]

In primary one, children are introduced to God as a loving and caring Father who created the universe and all that is in it. The act of creation portrays God's goodness to mankind and also to all His creatures. Human beings, who are created in the image and likeness of God, are entrusted with the care of God's work of creation. God also instituted the family as a means of ensuring the propagation of the human species. The children are also brought to the

52 Federal Ministry of Education, 9-Year Basic Education Curriculum, Christian Religious Studies for Primary 1 – 3, Abuja, 2007, 1-20.

knowledge of Jesus Christ, the son of God, who lives in the midst of human beings. He is therefore seen as a brother and friend who leads us back to the Father through His teachings.

TABLE 3: PRIMARY TWO

Theme	Topic
1. Talking to God through Jesus Christ	1. The meaning of prayer 2. Jesus the man of prayer 3. Jesus' teaching on prayer 4. Types of prayer 5. The power of prayer 6. God cares for us 7. God announces the coming of a Saviour 8. God gives the world a Saviour
2. The life of Jesus Christ	1. The early life of Jesus 2. Jesus' preparation for His ministry 3. Jesus' power over natural forces 4. Jesus' power over diseases and death 5. Jesus' teaching on God's love 6. Jesus' teaching on the kingdom of God 7. Jesus teaches us how to behave
3. God the Creator and Father of all	1. God creates everything 2. God creates a nation (Abraham) 3. Jacob 4. Joseph 5. Moses the liberator 6. Judges as leaders 7. Saul and David as kings in Israel[53]

The topics of primary two bring the children to the awareness of communication with God through prayer. Jesus taught his disciples how to pray and thereby introduced them to the image of God as "Our Father" (cf. Mt. 6:9-15).

53 Ibid., 21-41.

This prayer, which is the standard of all Christian prayers, is also the bulwark of our communication with God. By teaching his disciples how to pray, Jesus wants them to imitate His life style which is characterized by prayer to God (cf. Mt. 14:12-25, Lk. 12:12, Jn. 6:1-14). The children are further brought back to the theme of God as our loving Father, through whom all human beings come into existence. This is concretized in God's choice of Abraham through whom He begot for Himself "a nation". To this nation belong some Biblical personalities such as Jacob, Joseph, Moses and Saul the first king of Israel.

TABLE 4: PRIMARY THREE

Theme	Topic
1. God fulfils His promises	1. God fulfils His promises to Abraham 2. Deliverance from Egypt 3. The Passover 4. Moses and the bronze serpent in the wilderness 5. Entry into the promised land 6. The promise of the Saviour 7. Announcement of the coming of the Lord 8. The birth of Jesus
2. Faith in Jesus Christ my Saviour	1. Jesus the way to the father 2. The goodness of Jesus 3. Jesus the Good Shepherd 4. Jesus the Bread of Life 5. Christians as salt of the earth 6. Christians as light of the world 7. Suffering 8. Suffering of Jesus 9. Death and Resurrection
3. Knowing God through our relationship with others	1. Showing hospitality 2. Showing love and unselfishness 3. Showing desire for peaceful co-existence 4. Forbearance and understanding 5. Kindness in action

	6. Helping people in trouble 7. The blessedness of peace makers[54]

In primary three, the pupils are given a further picture of God as the One who fulfils His promises. This is brought to light in His promise to Abraham to make him the father of all nations and how He fulfilled this promise through his son Jacob. From this background, the children are taught to trust God because He keeps to His words and stands by His people in times of need as in the story of the deliverance of Israel from Egypt. The children are also brought to the awareness of helping one another in difficult times following the example of Jesus Christ who suffered the death of the cross for our deliverance from sin and eternal death.

TABLE 5: PRIMARY FOUR

Theme	Topic
1. God as Father guides His children	1. God speaks to us 2. We are children of one father 3. God calls us for a purpose 4. God gives His law to us 5. God reveals Himself to us
2. Jesus the way to the Father and our guide	1. Jesus' power to forgive sins 2. Jesus loves all people 3. Jesus prayed to the Father 4. Jesus gives His life for us on the Cross 5. Jesus guides us by His Spirit 6. Jesus gives us a new life[55]

The above table containing the lessons of primary four illustrates mankind as originating from the same source – God. God cements this unity by handing the Ten Commandments to Moses (cf. Ex. 20:1-11). These commandments are meant to regulate the relationship between God and His people. The children are brought to the awareness of unity among themselves. This unity of man-

54 Ibid., 42-71.

55 Federal Ministry of Education, 9-Year Basic Education Curriculum, Christian Religious Studies for Primary 4 – 6, Abuja, 2007, 1-12.

kind makes it possible for them to accept one another and learn from the same environment. Jesus illustrates this unity by caring for all people; curing many people of their sicknesses and praying to the Father for the unity of all people (cf. Jn. 17). From the idea of the Ten Commandments, the pupils are taught to obey the school rules and regulations which are meant to regulate their behaviour in the school.

TABLE 6: PRIMARY FIVE

Theme	Topic
1. God wants to save all men	1. God creates and wants us to create 2. God saves us from danger 3. God supplies our needs 4. God wants us to work 5. God shows mercy to us 6. God saves His people
2. Holy Spirit working in us	1. The Pentecost 2. The Holy Spirit inspires us 3. The Holy Spirit makes us faithful 4. The Holy Spirit guides us to the truth 5. The Holy Spirit makes us love one another 6. The rewards of working in the Holy Spirit[56]

In primary five, the children are brought back to the theme of God as the Creator of mankind and the entire universe. The earth and all its contents are handed over by God to human beings to be taken care of by them (cf. Gen. 1:28-30). Human beings exercise their control over the universe by taking part in the creative work of God. This idea of sharing in the creative work of God introduces the children to the issue of also working and earning a living. God further works in us through the Holy Spirit, but we work with our hands in order to sustain our lives. The work of the Holy Spirit is to sustain the life of God in us, which is the life of truth and love for one another.

56 Ibid., 13-22.

TABLE 7: PRIMARY SIX

Theme	Topic
1. Paul the Apostle	1. Paul's early life 2. Paul's conversion 3. Paul's mission 4. Paul in Europe 5. The letters of St. Paul (Epistles)
2. Nigerian Christian leaders and leadership	1. Goals setting 2. Decision making 3. The value of hard work 4. Temptation and corruption 5. Moderation in Christian life 6. Love of money 7. God made man and woman 8. Choosing a career 9. The biographies of Christian leaders[827]

The lessons of primary six as seen in the above table are meant to give the children the examples of some people who have used their lives to serve others. The Apostle Paul stands out as a principal Biblical personality, who used his strength and intelligence to lead others to faith in Jesus Christ. The children are also given the examples of some Nigerians, whose lives are worthy of emulation. This is meant to bring them to the awareness of selfless sacrifice for the good of others.

TABLE 8: JSS ONE

Theme	Topic
1. God and His creation	1. Who is God? 2. God's creation 3. Human beings share in God's creative activities 4. Disobedience 5. Reconciliation

57 Ibid., 23-38.

2. Relationship with God and man	1. Relationship in family 2. Relationship in school 3. Relationship in the community and in the Church 4. Relationship with God
3. God's call	1. Call to obedience 2. Call to freedom 3. Call to service 4. Call to repentance[58]

Junior secondary school is the beginning of secondary education. The children are once more introduced to the theme of the nature of God and His creation. They are taught the names of God in different Nigerian languages such as: Ubangiji (Hausa), Olorun (Yoruba), Chineke (Igbo) etc.[59] Such names are meant to denote the closeness of God to all peoples. They also learn some attributes of God so as to understand His nature and appreciate His work of creation. They will also learn how to participate in the creative work of God for the propagation of the human species through marriage which leads to a life of togetherness in the family. This life of togetherness leads to human interaction which can give rise to misunderstanding due to acts of disobedience and recalcitrance. Hence is the need for reconciliation with the aggrieved parties. They will also learn how to avoid misunderstandings among themselves by paying heed to God's call to obedience, freedom, service and repentance.

TABLE 9: JSS TWO

Theme	Topic
1. The early life of Jesus Christ	1. The birth of Jesus 2. Presentation of Jesus in the temple 3. Jesus and His family 4. The Baptism and temptation of Jesus 5. Call of the disciples

58 Federal Ministry of Education, 9-Year Basic Education Curriculum, Christian Religious Studies for JSS 1 – 3, Abuja, 2007, 1-18.

59 Cf. Ibid., 1.

2. The ministry of Jesus Christ	1. Mission of the disciples 2. Jesus' teaching on the mount/the demand of the kingdom 3. Jesus' teaching in parables 4. The miracles of Jesus 5. Jesus subjects Himself to civil and religious law
3. The Passion, Death and Resurrection of Jesus	1. The passion 2. The Death and Burial 3. The Resurrection and appearance 4. The Ascension of Christ[60]

In JS two, the students are brought back to the theme of the life of Jesus Christ, beginning from His birth, to His ministry and finally to His Death and Resurrection. The lessons here are meant to bring them to the awareness of the Christian teachings which have their roots in Jesus Christ. They should therefore appreciate the saving ministry of Jesus and find meaning in their profession of the Christian faith.

TABLE 10: JSS THREE

Theme	Topic
1. The beginning of the Church	1. The promise of the Holy Spirit 2. Fellowship in the early Church 3. Opposition to the Gospel message 4. The ministry of Peter
2. The life and teachings of Paul	1. Paul's early life and his conversion 2. The missionary activities of Paul 3. Some of Paul's teachings 4. Paul and his trials
3. The Christian Church today	1. The growth of the Church 2. Unity among Christians 3. Christians living among non-Christians 4. Peaceful co-existence[61]

60 Ibid., 19-36.

The lessons of JS three are centred on the beginning of the Church and the ministry of the Apostles. The Holy Spirit is introduced to the students as the guiding force that ensures the unity of the Christian faithful. Christians are to see themselves as people of one faith and should live peacefully with people of other religions. This is incorporated in the ecumenical movement which is promoted by the "Christian Association of Nigeria" (CAN).

TABLE 11: SSS ONE

Theme	Topic
1. Jesus' teaching about Himself	1. Jesus as the Lamb, the Door and Good shepherd 2. Jesus the Light of the world 3. Jesus as the True Vine 4. Jesus as the Living Bread and Water
2. Love	1. God's love for man 2. Love one another
3. Justification by faith	1. Justification by faith
4. New life in Christ	1. New life in Christ
5. Son-ship	1. Son-ship
6. Faith that works	1. Faith and works
7. The fruit of the Spirit	1. The fruit of the Spirit
8. Spiritual gifts	1. Spiritual gifts
9. Forgiveness	1. Forgiveness
10. The family	1. Rights and obligations of family members
11. Humility	1. Humility
12. Effectiveness of prayer	1. Effective prayer
13. Christian living in the community	1. Living a life of witnessing to Christ

61 Ibid., 37-52.

14. The Christian and persecution	1. Christian attitude towards persecution
15. Impartiality	1. Impartiality
16. The resurrection and second coming of Christ	1. The resurrection 2. The second coming of Christ[62]

In senior secondary one, the students are brought closer to the person of Jesus Christ through His teachings about Himself. This teaching will help them to understand the mission of Jesus in the world. They will also learn to understand the love of God manifested in human beings. With the help of some Biblical references, they will also be introduced to other Christian virtues which are meant to promote mutual love among human beings.

TABLE 12: SSS TWO

Theme	Topic
1. The sovereignty of God	1. God the Creator 2. God, the Controller of the universe 3. The Apostles Creed
2. Leadership of Joseph, Moses, Joshua and Deborah	1. Joseph as leader 2. Moses as leader 3. Joshua as leader 4. Deborah as leader
3. God's care for His people	1. Guidance 2. Provisions 3. Protection
4. Parental responsibility	1. Examples of Eli and Samuel 2. Example of Asa
5. Consequences of obedience and disobedience	1. Consequences of obedience 2. Consequences of disobedience
6. Forgiveness	1. Forgiveness

62 Federal Ministry of Education, Senior Secondary School Curriculum, Christian Religious Studies for SS 1 – 3, Abuja, 2010, 1-18.

7. Friendship	1. Friendship
8. Submission to the will of God	1. Trust in God
9. Making decisions as a Christian	1. The wisdom of Solomon 2. Unwise decisions of Solomon and Rehoboam
10. Greed and its effects	1. The effects of greed (Ahab and Gehazi)
11. The supremacy of God	1. The supremacy of God 2. Elijah at Mount Carmel
12. Religious reforms	1. Religious reforms
13. Concern for one's nation	1. Concern for one's nation
14. Faith in God	1. Faith in God 2. Faith and power of God
15. True religion and social justice	1. True religion and social justice
16. Divine Love	1. Divine Love[63]

The religious education curriculum provides the students in senior secondary two the opportunity of encountering God once more as the Creator and Controller of the universe. This knowledge demands faith in Him as manifested in the profession of the apostolic creed. God exercises His control over the universe through human agents such as: Joseph, Moses, Joshua and Deborah. Through these agents, God manifests His guidance, provisions and protection for His people. In the contemporary period, God exhibits His love and care for His people through parental care. Children are therefore to obey their parents as a means of submitting to the will of God and learn how to make true friends at school and in their immediate environment.

TABLE 13: SSS THREE

Theme	Topic
1. Baptism and temptation of Jesus	1. The Baptism 2. The temptation of Jesus

63 Ibid., 19-45.

2. Call to discipleship	1. Call to discipleship
3. Mission of the disciples	1. Mission of the twelve disciples
4. The Trial, Death and Resurrection of Jesus	1. The Trial of Jesus 2. The crucifixion, Death and Burial of Jesus 3. The Resurrection of Jesus
5. Fellowship in the early Church	1. Communal living in the early Church
6. The Holy Spirit and the mission to the Gentiles	1. The Holy Spirit at Pentecost 2. Mission to the Gentiles
7. Opposition to the Gospel message	1. Opposition to the Gospel message
8. Civic responsibility	1. The need for order in society 2. Good citizenship
9. HIV/AIDS	1. Care for the sick
10. Skill acquisition and empowerment	1 Independence and self actualization
11. Dignity of labour	1. Dignity of labour
12. Dignity of human life	1. Dignity of human life[64]

The lessons of senior secondary three are centred on the practice of the Christian faith. Following the example of Christ's Baptism, the students are to learn the importance of Christian initiation and the tasks of the Christian life. Jesus underwent temptations and trials which He overcame through the power of the Holy Spirit. The same Holy Sprit guided the Apostles in their mission to the gentiles. The students will learn to recognize the presence of the Holy Spirit in the Church and be able to persevere in their Christian praxis. They will learn how to be good citizens by fulfilling their civic responsibilities as well as being aware of the scourges of some deadly deceases like HIV/AIDS.

64 Ibid., 46-60.

5.4.2 Religious Education in the Schools in the Archdiocese of Munich and Freising

In the schools located within the archdiocese of Munich and Freising, both Biblical and denominational teachings are incorporated into the curriculum. Although the environment is also religiously pluralistic, children receive holistic religious teachings that can help in developing their life orientation and religious background. At the beginning of every school year, the children are offered lessons that can help them in coping with their new environment and class mates. These lessons will first of all offer them a sense of togetherness so that they can appreciate themselves in order to work and learn together in a meaningful manner. Some of the basic topics are: God the Creator, Jesus of Nazareth, sense of togetherness, prayer, the Bible, life experience, Didactic of other religions, the Church, the sacraments and some Christian feasts – Christmas, Easter and Pentecost. A comprehensive and detailed analysis of the religious education curriculum of the schools in the archdiocese of Munich and Freising has already been given in Chapter Three. The aim of this section is to compare the religious education curricula of the schools within the diocese of Ahiara and the archdiocese of Munich and Freising in order to find out their similarities and differences as well as what can be exchanged between them for the improvement of the other.

5.4.3 Comparison of the Religious Education Curricula of the Schools within the Diocese of Ahiara and within the Archdiocese of Munich and Freising

The schools within the diocese of Ahiara and the archdiocese of Munich and Freising have both different systems and curricula. The only little similarity is that both of them have the same primary school for all the children. Because of the three different secondary schools in the German school system, there are also three different curricula for the three secondary schools. This is in contrast to the Nigerian situation. There is only one secondary educational system and the same curriculum for all the secondary schools in Nigeria. In the two instances (Nigeria and Germany), the students are offered religious educational lessons which are meant to shape their lives in recognition of an encounter with God based on an interaction with human beings.

5.5 Contents of Religious Education in the Church

Religious education in the Church takes place as a parish activity. This is carried out in different ways in the diocese of Ahiara and in the archdiocese of Munich and Freising. The only similarity is their structure which is the teaching of catechism, youth associations and their activities. In the diocese of Ahiara, the teaching of catechism is the primary responsibility of the priests and catechists. There are employed and voluntary catechists. The employed catechists are the co-ordinators of catechetical activities in the parishes. Children are taught the catechism as part of their preparation for the reception of the sacraments, especially the Holy Eucharist and Confirmation. They are also encouraged to join any one or two of the six youth associations in the diocese namely: the Catholic Youth Organization of Nigeria (CYON), Mary League Association, The Young Catholic Students of Nigeria (YCS), Man of Order and Discipline (MOD), Boy Scouts/Girl Guides and the Altar Servers (cf. 4.2.3.1). These associations are means of encouraging young people to concretize their membership in the Church with various activities that can help them in the practice of their faith.

In the Archdiocese of Munich and Freising, parish catechesis is carried out through the teaching of catechism and the formation of some youth associations. These associations vary in character and activities from those found in the diocese of Ahiara. Some of these differences will be concretized better with a table.

TABLE 14: PARISH CATECHESIS

Ahiara Diocese	Archdiocese of Munich and Freising
1. Catholic Youth Organization of Nigeria 2. Altar Servers 3. Mary League Girls 4. Young Catholic Students of Nigeria 5. Boy Scouts and Girl Guides 6. Man of Order and Discipline 7. The Block Rosary crusade 8. The Age Grade	1. Federation of German Catholic Youths 2. Christian Youth Workers 3. German Boy Scouts of St. George 4. Catholic Youth Society 5. Altar Servers 6. Catholic Rural Youth Movement 7. Catholic Students and Young Christian Life Societies 8. Kolping Youths 9. Female Scout Union of St. George 10. Youth Action

The above table indicates the reality of pastoral care of the youth in the diocese of Ahiara and the archdiocese of Munich and Freising. However, this table clearly shows that this apostolate is better organized in the archdiocese of Munich and Freising than in the diocese of Ahiara in terms of numbers and activities. The youth of the former demography have a greater variety of associations which offer them more opportunities for self-expression and leisure. To achieve greater goals in the archdiocese of Munich and Freising, some catechetical programmes such as retreats, as seen in the diocese of Ahiara, need to be introduced into the normal activities. Such catechetical activities promote an on-going formation of adults. This will help in dealing with the in-flux of anti-religious ideas of the secular society which may turn the youth away from the Church and its membership. More youth associations with an African background need to be created in the diocese of Ahiara so that the youth can have more time to interact among themselves in the African context. Such associations can also be named after some Nigerians (or Africans) who have contributed to the promotion of the youth movements or the pastoral care of the youth. Some names like that of "Ambrose Ali" who founded the "Nigeria Federation of Catholic Students" (NFCS) can be used to form another youth association which can serve the leisure of many Nigerian youth. This is likened to the naming of a German youth association after "Kolping" because of his vigorous contribution to the growth of the pastoral care of the youth in Germany. The need for more youth associations in the diocese of Ahiara is to give the youth a greater sense of belonging in the Church and to offer them better opportunities to spend time together in order to understand themselves and recognize their status as future leaders, both in the Church and in the larger society. However, the formation of any new youth association in the diocese of Ahiara should take the issue of gender into consideration. This is because gender differentiation affects the ordering of things in the Church and in the society. Many young people of the present age would not like to participate in any activity which encourages gender differentiation. They would like the company of their counterparts of the opposite sex in order to add excitement to their programmes. Such a combination of genders may also result to an eventual founding of families.

5.6 Some Relevant Measures for the Promotion of Religious Education

The religious problems of young people are not intractable. They originated within time and space and therefore are surmountable within the same time and space. In chapter one of this work, religious praxis was identified as one of the goals of religious education (cf. 1.3.1.1). This means that the aim of religious education is not only to educate young people in the area of religion but also to encourage their participation in religious programmes and activities. None of these two objectives is to be taken for granted. In the present section of this chapter, attention is to be focused on making some practical and realizable recommendations that can help in achieving these two vital goals of religious education. Earlier in this work also it had been postulated that religious education will benefit from a reasonable and meaningful use of some modern technologies, especially the media (cf. 0.5).[65] Some of the advantages that can accrue from such use will be articulated in this section.

5.6.1 Training of the Agents of Religious Education

The agents of religious education are the transmitters or teachers of religious knowledge to others (especially to young people) who look on their teachers as models and people of respectable personalities. The teachers not only impart knowledge of the Christian faith to others but also train them in the practice of the Christian life.[66] Such people include priests, deacons, catechists, parents and religious education teachers. By undertaking this ministry, agents of religious education perform a Divine function because God is the Teacher par excellence, the Educator and Formator of His people (cf. Hos. 11:3). They are collaborators with God in the formation and guidance of His people. Some Biblical personalities like Moses and Joshua played this role in the name of God before the people of Israel (cf. Ex. 3:10, Deut. 31:7-8, Josh. 1:1-9). Agents of religious education are mediators between God and His people. They convey God's message to His people and instruct them on the mode of their relationship with God. In order to effectively fulfil this function, agents of religious education need to receive regular training so as to update their knowledge with some social, cultural and environmental developments of the contemporary era. Such developments are the changes in human mentality which result from the rapid advancement in technology and reasoning. Some of these changes are seen in the unprecedented consumption of the media services which has greatly reshaped the human society. Agents of religious education need to be given an on-going formation in order to be acquainted with current developments in the society. This on-going formation, according to Leimgruber can be based on the following four thematic principles:

1. Substantive individual elements of the religious education curriculum in modular design
2. Methodology and didactics in relation to the arrangements of the learning process

65 Cf. Leimgruber S., Woran wird gelernt? Medien in Religionsunterricht, in: Hilger G., Leimgruber S., Ziebertz H. G., Religionsdidaktik, Ein Leitfaden für Studium, Ausbildung und Beruf, München, 2010, 242.

66 Cf. Nwaoru E. O., Youth Upbringing: A Process of Making Adult Christians, in: Nwatu F., Eze A. (Eds.), Bigard Theological Studies, 27, 1, Enugu, 2007, 76.

3. School experiences in the present social and multicultural context
4. The improvement of certain communicative and spiritual powers.[67]

In this on-going formation of the teachers of religious education, exchange of experiences and learning through encounters play a significant role. The formation is generally based on a strong back-up and the widening of the intellectual horizon of the teachers of religion and not necessarily on a short-term teaching. This on-going formation can be achieved through seminars, workshops, symposia and conferences which provide opportunities for substantive discussion and debate on policy issues. The discussion and debate session of their formative programme is better achieved by dividing the participants into working groups and initiating project-based learning and craftwork training. Religious education teachers are encouraged to take part in on-going formation sessions in order to update their knowledge with relevant information that can facilitate their personality competence and educational career. To achieve this, Leimgruber is of the opinion that education authorities should, as a general principle, grant special leave and reimbursement for the programme.[68] This is because the further training of the agents of religious education relates to the acquisition of updated qualification skills after the initial training phase and may include part-time, personal or even university training programmes.[69] In this context, teachers of religious education are required to acquire additional skills as prospective developers and designers of the learning environments. The training is always concerned with the preparation and promotion of a directed individual, social and religious learning. It is meant to help the teachers of religious education undertake more functions as coaches, counsellors, communicators, initiators of the learning processes and project managers. The on-going formation of the agents of religious education can take place during the school session (since it may involve attendance of university lectures) or during a holiday period (in the case of seminars, symposia and workshops). In both instances, it involves an in-depth religious learning, which takes new developments in the society and scientific research into consideration.[70]

67 Cf. Leimgruber S., Religionslehrer/innenaus-, -fort-, und -weiterbildung, in: Mette N., Rikkers F. (Hg.), LexRP. 2. Band, Neukirchen – Vluyn, 2001, 1694.

68 Cf. Ibid., 1695.

69 Cf. Ibid.

70 Cf. Ibid., 1692.

5.6.2 The Media in Religious Education

The media in religious education are technical helping tools through which religion can be learned electronically and also in a printed form. They contribute in the realization of the general educational and religious learning processes. As helping tools, they are meant to revive or promote religious education and not to dominate it.[71] For a reasonable use of the media in the teaching of religion, both the teachers and the students who take part in the formative mission of religious education must have expertise in this area. This is based on the fact that the media have changed the daily lives and habits of many people in post-modern times. Hence, they are not to replace direct communication and the importance of the religious education teacher, who functions as a personal medium in the teaching of religion.[72] They are only meant to support, deepen and help in the visualization of the learning processes of religion. Religious education benefits from the various functions which they play in the overall life of individuals. Such functions are: formation (education), entertainment, communication and interaction. A well-founded use of these functions of the media can enrich religious lessons.

The media can be very educative and instructive. They bring us closer to peoples and countries that we would probably never visit. With the help of the media, we travel through forests, over polar ice caps, onto mountaintops and into the depths of the oceans. We learn about the fascinating worlds of atoms and stars and experience within seconds what is happening in other parts of the earth. The media give information about religion, politics, history, current affairs and culture. They make it possible for people to share in the tragedies of others without their physical presence. These educative functions of the media were expressed by Leimgruber as follows:

> *The media have an educative function insofar as they offer the users some learning opportunities. The media themselves are places and objects of education. They can present a multiple sense of the perspectives and modes of behaviour. In this way, the media expand our horizons, bring the world to us in the room, familiarize us with the problems of our one world and challenge us with personal opinion.*[73]

71 Cf. Nwaoru E. O., Youth Upbringing: A Process of Making Adult Christians, in: Nwatu F., Eze A. (Eds.), Bigard Theological Studies, 27, 1, Enugu, 2007, 76.

72 Cf. Ibid.

73 Leimgruber S., Woran wird gelernt? Medien in Religionsunterricht, (trans. by Nwandu P), in: Hilger G., Leimgruber S., Ziebertz H. G., Religionsdidaktik, Ein Leitfaden für Studium, Ausbildung und Beruf, München, 2010, 243.

The educational function of the media makes them very beneficial in the teaching of religion. This is especially true in connection with the Internet which supplies a tremendous amount of information on religious matters. Researchers of today can also express how cumbersome their work would have been without the fascinating help of the Internet. Hence the Internet stands out as a standard medium that boosts the study of religion and other disciplines of learning. Other forms of communication media apart from the Internet are also very useful in the study of religion. These include television, radio, mobile and landline telephones as well as computers. These bring information nearer to us than we could imagine. Through the television, religious programmes are broadcast to millions of viewers at the same time. This applies to religious plays, drama, films, movies and clips. This is why Leimgruber is of the opinion that television has given an impetus for a change in social behaviour and the institutionalization of ecological thinking.[74] Radio has a similar function as television but only in an audio capacity. Through radio, informative religious programmes are brought to the hearing of many within a wide range of time and space. Such information helps in expanding the religious horizon of many hearers and at the same time deepens their religious awareness and inclination. Of greater benefit to the teaching and learning of religion is the use of mobile telephones. With the current easy Internet access through mobile telephones, young people experience inter-connectivity with their peers. This is especially true through the "short message service" (SMS) with which they communicate directly with their friends, relatives and age mates.[75] Mobile phones are also used for chatting and therefore can serve as a means of exchanging religious views and ideas. Among the enumerated communication media, the computer can be said to be all-embracing. This is because of its ability to render "instant message service" (IMS) and also to serve as both a television and a radio through the use of the Internet. Hence through the use of "chat rooms", young people can use the computer as a means of evangelization of their peers.[76]

The entertaining function of the media will also be of immense benefit to religious education. This is especially true with regard to boredom. Through home videos and religious films as well as religious programmes on the radio and television, the daily lives of many people can be filled with interesting spiritual images that can give rise to meditation and mutual interaction. In this instance, the media can save people from some of the isolating problems of the world and the burdens of their daily lives especially in the lives of elderly

74 Cf. Ibid.

75 Cf. Ibid.

76 Cf. EA, 1995, 93.

people by presenting alternative beautiful realities and representations.[77] Such is also the case with new multimedia digital devices like MP3, with which one can transfer and play back some religious music on digital audio players anywhere and anytime. Such pieces of music can enliven the soul and put one in a lighter mood. Students can also store their lessons in religious education on their MP3 and listen to them as part of their daily activities or also save them on their flash drives or hard drives. These new digital media can in this way serve as means of communication and interaction in religious education in so far as they can be used to extend relevant information to those who did not have the opportunity to receive such information directly and immediately from their primary sources.

The above-described uses of the media are devoid of neither the situation of young people in the diocese of Ahiara nor in the archdiocese of Munich and Freising. In these two demographic areas, the media present new modes of awareness which can be applied to a meaningful access and perception of religious education. The only clear difference is the rate of consumption of media services due to the technological yawning gap existing between the two areas. Access to the Internet is also not at the same level. However, it is an obvious fact that media awareness can be profitably utilized in religious education in both places. Hence, the underlying reason for its recommendation.

5.7 African Elements in Religious Education

In the fourth chapter of this work, the absence of African elements in religious education was lamentably decried (cf. 4.4). This absence was attributed to the failure of both the missionaries and the colonial administrators to integrate African values into their work of evangelization and governance respectively. This is particularly seen in their negligence to include the use of African languages in their system of teaching and ruling. As a result of this situation, the teaching of religion did not permeate the cultural background of African people. This explains the reason for this section. It is aimed at demonstrating the need for the use of African languages such as the Igbo language in the teaching of religion in the schools within the diocese of Ahiara.

Language is identified as the key of integration with a people. It underlies the root of every act of socialization, enculturation and identification. In concrete terms, it characterizes communication among human beings and enhances learning. In many African communities, educational activities are carried

77 Cf. Leimgruber S., Woran wird gelernt? Medien in Religionsunterricht, in: Hilger G., Leimgruber S., Ziebertz H. G., Religionsdidaktik, Ein Leitfaden für Studium, Ausbildung und Beruf, München, 2010, 243.

out in foreign languages. This is likened to the case whereby the "oppressed" can only air his or her "voice" in the "language of the oppressor".[78] Teaching religion in a foreign language for example cannot guarantee a proper assimilation of the lessons by the students. According to Mandela:

> *If you talk to a man in a language he understands, that goes to his head. If you talk to him in his language, that goes to his heart.*[79]

In the schools within the diocese of Ahiara and indeed in the entire school system in Nigeria, religion is taught in the English language and not in the spoken language of the people such as the Igbo language. This is because English is the first and official language in the school curriculum. It is the acclaimed lingua franca in Nigeria. Such a situation cannot be seen in England. Due to colonial influence, the use of Nigerian languages is suppressed in the schools. Although the grammar and rudiments of these languages are learned in the schools, they are not used in the teaching of other subjects. One clear fact is this; there is no better way of teaching and talking to a people than in their own native language or mother tongue. The use of Nigerian languages as a medium of teaching religion in Nigerian schools is therefore strongly recommended. This will give rise to a proper understanding as well as an in-depth Christianization of the people in their mentality, culture and identity.

This view was also expressed by Emenanjo in his Ahiajoku lecture of 2001. Arguing about why he should deliver his lecture in the Igbo language and the need for people to communicate among themselves in their own native tongue he said:

> *Ahịajọkụ bụ mmemme. Ọ bụkwa emume ndị Igbo. Otụtụ ndị bịara mmemme a, n'ebe a, n'afo a, bụ ndị Igbo. Nga a anyi guzọrọ ugbu a bụ ala Owere Nchi Ise, n'ala Igbo. Ebe ihe ndị a niile dizi etu a, ọ bụ gini gbochiri anyi iji asụsụ Igbo gawa n'ihu? Nga olee ka mba ọ bụla si akpata nkụ ha ji esi ihe? Kedụ ebe mba ọ bula si enweta mmiri ha na-anụ? Ọ bụ na mba ndị ọzọ? Olee ebe e si agbata mmiri e ji esi ụgụ? Eche m na ọ bụ mmiri ụgụ gba(pụ)tara ka e ji esi ya? ELo m na ọ bụ ife di n'ubi ka wa ji esili ubi nni?*[80]

78 Voice of the Oppressed in the Language of the Oppressor is the title of a book based on a discussion of selected Postcolonial literature from Ireland, Africa and America by Daniels J. P., New York, 2001.

79 Mandela N., http://www.brainyquote.com/quotes/quotes/n/nelsonmand121685.html#mlMQWyBS8UADf1Um.99, 03.09.2012.

80 Emenanjo E. N., Language in Igbo Civilization, 2001 Ahiajoku Lecture, Owerri, 2001, 3.

Although there is an enshrined principle of free choice of language, between Igbo and English, in the delivery of the Ahiajoku lecture, he found no reason for the use of English language since the majority of his audience (if not all) were Igbo people. He further presented his argument as follows:

> *In the extant and pristine citation crafted by those who thought of and through Ahịajọku, (sic) it was explicitly stated that each lecturer is free to choose his or her 'language of delivery' because the audience understands both 'Igbo and English.' Simple, children like statements are rarely childish. Are choices really ever free? Aren't they hemmed in by the imperatives of context-time, space, dramatis personae? Again, who says the typical Ahịajọku audience 'understands' both Igbo and English? And when we talk of both Igbo and English, are we talking about conjunction, disjunction or co-ordination? Are we talking of a monolingual presentation through and through in either Igbo or English or of the bilingual presentation in both Igbo and English, in one text, or of the same text presented simultaneously in Igbo, and in English all bound together as a book in the Aboyedean sense? We know that bilingualism has as many types as it has varieties. Ladies and Gentlemen, I will stoutly resist the temptation of being drawn from ikpọta ụtaba to iba n 'ime ahịa.*[81]

The use of English language in Igboland is one of the fruits of English colonization of Nigeria. The colonizers, also known as "oppressors" educated their subjects in a culture and language that was foreign to them. This education included the learning of the English language otherwise known as the "language of the oppressor", and the reading of English literature. As a learned language, English cannot favourably compete with the acquired native language of the people in teaching and instructing them in religious education. Hence, there is need to emancipate Africa from linguistic colonialism especially in religious education. This need is also contained in UNESCO's recommendations for the implementation of mother tongue education in the schools:

> *It is important that every effort should be made to provide education in the mother tongue...On educational grounds we recommend that the use of the mother tongue be extended to as late a stage in education as possible. In particular, pupils should begin their schooling through the medium of the mother tongue, because they understand it best and*

81 Ibid., 4.

because to begin their school life in the mother tongue will make the break between home and school as small as possible.[82]

In comparison to their counterparts in the archdiocese of Munich and Freising, children in the diocese of Ahiara are greatly disadvantaged because they use a foreign language (English) as a medium of instruction in religious education in the school. This is identified by Phyak as one of the reasons for a poor educational production by children who are not educated in their native language:

> *If children are not provided education in their own language i.e. in their mother tongue, their achievement in comparison to the children who are getting education in their own mother tongue becomes lower and they face different types of difficulties in learning others' languages in school. This is an injustice for the children who are from different linguistic groups.*[83]

Apart from language, other values of African culture such as symbols, rites, songs, proverbs and folk tales are also important in the teaching of religion at home, in the school and in the Christian communities. This calls for the introduction of intercultural learning in religious education. Intercultural learning, according to Leimgruber, arises from the perception of different cultural systems and is evident in the encounter between people of varying cultures.[84] It involves a comparison of cultures, strives to achieve personal-realization in the face of an individual's cultural origin and guarantees his or her self-orientation in a foreign culture. A person is said to be interculturally competent, when he or she can easily transform from a particular culture to another and be able to understand the rudiments of that culture. Intercultural learning will help an individual to recognize the peculiarities of a particular culture and the similarities between two different cultures and be able to draw conclusions with appropriate attitudes.[85] It gives rise to the practice of enculturation, which is a conscious act of living with two different cultures. In the present context, reference is made to African culture and Christian culture. Intercultural learning will dispose an African to know both his or her African culture and the Christian culture, gain a self-appropriation and a self-empathy of the two cultures, make a critical reflection of his or her dual identity (as an African and as

82 *UNESCO, 1951: 691.*

83 Phyak P. B., Mother Tongue Education: Practices and Problems with Reference to Limbu Language, Nepal, 2007, 2.

84 Cf. Leimgruber S., Interreligiöses Lernen, Neuausgabe, München, 2007, 19.

85 Cf. Ibid., 20.

a Christian) and take appropriate action in the horizon of these two cultures. Intercultural learning will help in creating a balanced interaction between the two cultures, so that an African can realize himself or herself from the background of African identity and at the same time be able to practice his or her Christian faith.

5.8 Evaluation

Religious education in the diocese of Ahiara and the archdiocese of Munich and Freising is encountering some challenges ranging from social, environmental and individual hindrances. Some of these difficulties as described above have contributed in thwarting the teaching of religion in the family, in the school and in the Church as well as its practice among young people. The influence of social norms and nuances like religious pluralism and secularism are very devastating to the teaching of religion and its acceptance by the students. As new phenomena, these have contributed to the reshaping of the society. Many heterogeneous societies have become pluralistic as a result of migration and the social encounter among people of different linguistic, cultural and religious backgrounds. New waves have also been introduced into the human society as a result of secularization which has created the notion of separating the supernatural from human engagements especially in the field of politics. As a result of this development, young people, especially in the archdiocese of Munich and Freising have discovered a freeing situation in which the practice of religion is no longer considered necessary in all spheres of human life.

The media have also contributed to the clamping down on religious and moral values especially through the unrestricted presentation of human sexuality. That is why there is a pertinent call for a more positive use of the media for the promotion of religious education and religious values. This would be realized especially when young people are brought to this awareness. Through a more reasonable use of the media, young people can withstand some of the negative influences of their peer groups and help themselves in the acceptance and practice of their religious beliefs.

Religious education is also encountering challenges from the family. Many modern families have experienced divorce and many conjugal relationships have no marital status. This presents obvious problems for the children who come from such backgrounds. The new trend of many couples living together from the point of view of social interaction and partnership (in some parts of the Western world) is paving the way for the eradication of the institutional character of the family and is creating a situation whereby the raising of children will become a private matter. Such a trend will reduce the status of the family to a mere patchwork. Religion will have no place in such unions especially with regard to the upbringing of children and the future of the family as an institution is no longer guaranteed.

The religious education teacher needs to be acquainted with the social and environmental phenomena affecting religious education negatively so as to present his or her lessons in a way and manner that can adequately ameliorate them. This then calls for a proper formation of the religious education teacher and a regular updating as well as the mastering of his or her teaching materials. This updating is aimed at keeping up with the rapid changes in human development. That is why the teaching of religion has to run on a par with the use of modern technologies in order to meet the taste of the contemporary society. Reference is made here to the advantages of the media in religious education. The media have brought rapid changes into the society and therefore can be used to improve the teaching of religion in the school, in the family and in the Church.

5.9 Summary

Religious education will immensely benefit from the use of some of the modern technologies especially the media. However, care should be taken to curb some of the excesses of the media especially in their presentation of the Church, the family and human sexuality. This is because the media presentation of these values is sometimes only very aesthetic and does not take their fundamental orientation into consideration. Although such an artificial and flowery presentation is sometimes very popular and beloved by the society, it cannot be said to be in favour of religious education because it undermines the authentic teaching of some established religions like Christianity. In such presentations, the atmosphere and the images are more important than contents.[86] They show a growing image of disenchantment between what is presented and what should be viewed. Hence there is a conflict between the ideal and the actual. Children who constantly consume such presentations may no longer differentiate between authentic religious teachings and the conceived religious presentations of the media. Although the media bridge the religious gap between distances, they cannot replace a physical Christian community which encourages personal encounter among its members. The media can also not take the place of teacher-student relationship in which the classroom presents the most conducive atmosphere for learning using a question and answer method. The role of the media in religious education lies in conveying impulses from the world

86 Cf. Kunstmann J., Religionspädagogik, Eine Einführung, 2. Auflage, Tübingen, 2010, 269.

into the classroom and transporting the ideas of the society and the Church to their vicinities, so that both teachers and learners are challenged to work out a synthesis for a balanced spirituality.[87] The media therefore can only help the Christian community to grow when reasonably and positively used in religious education. The goals of religious education can only be realized by the individual participants, using the media as a means.

The use of some African elements such as language and songs in the teaching of religion in the diocese of Ahiara will play a significant role in the grass-root understanding and acceptance of Christianity. This can be achieved through enculturating African values into Christianity as against the act of the early missionaries, who saw these values as tremendous threats to the spread of Christianity. Enculturation will reduce the idea of seeing Christianity as a foreign religion and integrate it into African culture.

87 Cf. Leimgruber S., Woran wird gelernt? Medien in Religionsunterricht, in: Hilger G., Leimgruber S., Ziebertz H. G., Religionsdidaktik, Ein Leitfaden für Studium, Ausbildung und Beruf, München, 2010, 253.

6. General Evaluation and Conclusion

In the course of developing this work, efforts had been made to trace the process of faith formation, maturity and praxis in two demographic areas – the diocese of Ahiara, Nigeria and the archdiocese of Munich and Freising, Germany. This process had been undertaken in order to depict the role of religious education in the practice of the Christian faith in the lives of young people and its contribution in ensuring a sustainable development of the human person. To this effect, the previous chapters of this work had taken an in-depth look at the teaching of religion in the schools, in the families and in the Christian communities within the two areas of investigation. Attention was focused on the religious education of young people throughout their school years as well as the pastoral care of the youth which takes place in the Christian community.

Although this work is not strictly about Nigeria and Germany respectively, care had also been taken to describe the two countries from their historical backgrounds so as to dispose the reader to understand the conventional setting in which religion is taught in the two countries. The two countries are meant to represent the level of religious awareness in a technologically developing and developed environment respectively. This is the reason for the description of the geographical location of the two countries and the origin of their religious backgrounds. Some characteristics peculiar to the youth of the two countries were also described, paying particular attention to the immediate areas of investigation – the diocese of Ahiara and the archdiocese of Munich and Freising.

The two countries have experienced numerous turbulences in their history especially with regard to wars. The present Germany was rebuilt after the Second World War that lasted between 1939 and 1945. Nigeria was greatly shackled by a Civil War that lasted from 1967 to 1970. Each of the two countries has different school systems. Nigeria has a uniform primary and secondary school systems which are open to all Nigerian children irrespective of their academic performances. Germany has the same primary school for all German children but three different types of secondary schools (the grammar school, the intermediate secondary school and the general secondary school), the attendance at which depends on the academic ability of the students in the primary school. This makes a comparative study of the school systems in the two countries rather difficult but not impossible. Nigeria operates a uniform school system in all the states of her Federation while school policies in Germany are left for the respective states to determine. This is why a national curriculum is operative in all the schools in Nigeria including the schools within the diocese of Ahiara. The school curriculum presented in this work for the schools in the archdiocese of Munich and Freising is that of the State of Bavaria in which the archdiocese is located. The learning environment of the schools within the diocese of Ahiara is very poor. The classrooms are not only overcrowded but are also filled with dilapidated and out-moded furniture which may cause discomfort and a lack of concentration for the students. The school authorities do not see to the welfare of the teachers. This is why the teachers most often do not deliver their lessons with commitment and devotion. Sometimes they abandon their school programmes to run their private businesses in order to gain a means of livelihood, since they do not receive their regular salaries. This lackadaisical attitude of the teachers towards teaching also affects the mode of learning of the students. Many students do not do their home works and the teachers do not care about it. This results in a poor academic record at the end of the school year. In the schools within the archdiocese of Munich and Freising, the classrooms are spaced out so that the teacher can assess the learning ability of his or her pupils. The classrooms contain both audio and visual teaching aids in order to ensure that the pupils are able to hear and see the demonstration of the lessons. This promotes a better perception and understanding of the lessons so that the pupils will achieve convincing results at the end of the academic year. In order to improve the situation in the schools within the diocese of Ahiara, there is need to establish better learning environments which will include good recreational facilities, classrooms with comfortable furniture and modern teaching materials.

In contrast to Nigeria, Germany is a country with national unity and purpose. The spirit of nationalism and patriotism ranks high among its citizens. Religion plays a significant role in the upholding of its national unity. This is why religious education or its equivalent is compulsory in all the States. Nigeria on the other hand is a country united in disintegration. There is no serious emphasis on the issue of nationalism both in the mode of life of the people and in their system of studies. Although Nigerians share one central Government, they are not one people. This is because the coming together of the Nigerian people to form one country did not dissuade their strong attachment to ethnicity and religion. This explains why religious education serves as one of the means of searching for the promotion of national unity, patriotism and sustainable development. From this background, religious education plays a fundamental role in inculcating the spirit of oneness into Nigerian children. Hence, care is taken not to mingle religious education with some issues of differentiation such as denominational teachings. Every Nigerian child learns the same thing under religious education so that they can understand religion and its praxis from the same platform without creating much difference among them.

Children at school age approach religious education with zeal and keen interest. They manifest a great deal of religiosity which sometimes is not nurtured and encouraged due to some influences accruing either from the family or from the larger society. School catechesis affords them the opportunity of knowing God and sharing their religious experiences with their schoolmates. The teaching of religion in the schools begins at the primary school which lasts for a period of six years for the schools in the diocese of Ahiara, and four years for the schools in the archdiocese of Munich and Freising. At the secondary level, students spend a total of six years in the learning of religion in the schools within the diocese of Ahiara. Due to the different types of secondary schools in the archdiocese of Munich and Freising, students do not spend an equal number of years in religious education. In the grammar school, this lasts for a period of eight years while five years are required in both intermediate and general secondary schools respectively. The mode and curriculum of religious education in the diocese of Ahiara and the archdiocese of Munich and Freising differ, but the goal is the same – the religious formation and sustainable development of the human person.

In the religious education of the two places under investigation, certain factors come into play and determine the rate of the religious development of the participants: the school environment, the historical background, the family setting and the disposition of the Christian community. In the school, the religious education teacher plays a predominant role. His or her method of teaching and self-mastery characterize the level of the involvement of the students. The religious background of the students also plays a fundamental role. Children of poor religious upbringing may lure their peers to shun religious practices and beliefs. Families with decadent religious foundations may not provide enough "soil" for the growth of the faith of their children and therefore cannot encourage them to live up to its praxis. In many cases, this leads to a total "black out" in the area of religion.

The secular nature of the contemporary society has also affected religious education and the practice of religion. This is greatly seen in the fact that religion is no longer occupying a position of primary importance in human life. It has been classified as a "private matter" and no longer a "sine-qua-non" in many societies, especially in the Western world.[1] Questions of the ultimate reality are now replaced with questions of the self. Belief in God has been ascribed many options thereby making the human society very pluralistic. This idea of pluralism presents a problematic situation for religious education since children of different beliefs are in the same learning environment. Hence the

1 Cf. Taylor C., A Secular Age, Harvard, 2007, 1.

question: "which religion should be taught?" This is as a result of the presence of many religions in the same locality.

In the Christian community, children have the opportunity of acquiring a denominational religious education in which they are prepared for the reception of the Christian sacraments and are given a wider scope of sustainable human development. This is achieved through a guided effort of the priest, catechist or other voluntary agents who team up in the work of parish catechesis. Under the pastoral care of the youth, young people are given the opportunity of belonging to various youth associations for closer formation and development. These associations exist both in the diocese of Ahiara and in the archdiocese of Munich and Freising, though not at an equal proportion. The striking thing is that the youth of both areas are not "left like sheep without a shepherd" (cf. Mt. 9:36). Parish catechesis begins in the two areas of investigation from the time of the preparation for the reception of the sacraments of initiation until the celebration of Confirmation and continues under the "pastoral care of the youth" until the time of marriage. Due to unprecedented attachment to their careers, many young people do not have time for a meaningful participation in the youth apostolate and some even drift from their faith. This is especially the case in the archdiocese of Munich and Freising where some secular trends are seriously militating against religion and its praxis.

In the schools within the diocese of Ahiara, religion is taught from the background of a divided Christendom. The missionaries established Christianity with the spirit of division among the various Christian denominations. During the missionary era and shortly after the Civil War in Nigeria, Catholics and Protestants had little or nothing in common. They did not attend the same school, were forbidden to inter-marry and could not worship or pray together. They also used different recreational facilities and places. Thus, a wrong method of Christianization thwarted the already existing cordial relationship among "brothers and sisters". The document, "What are we Anglicans doing?" describes a typical relationship between Catholics and Protestants during the days of the missionaries.[2] This time was characterized by the "survival of the fittest" and a struggle for supremacy. The people of this time lived with feud, envy and suspicion among themselves as a result of denominational differences. This division was also inculcated into the school children in their religious education in the sense that Catholics taught their children that they are the true Christians and vice versa. This is why the establishment of the "Christian Association of Nigeria" (CAN) under ecumenism is a welcome development. This association is aimed at the unity of all Christians in Nigeria so that Nige-

2 Cf. Enemo E. O., What are we Anglicans Doing?, A Lecture Presented to the Teachers' Week, Awka, 1950, 1.

rians can imbibe the spirit of oneness among themselves. It works hard in the eradication of the spirit of hatred, pride and slander which characterized the behaviour of the various Christian denominations towards one another. This is why religious education in the schools within the diocese of Ahiara and indeed throughout Nigeria is ecumenical and not denominational. No denominational literature such as catechisms and prayer books is used in religious education. Teaching materials are drawn primarily from the Bible for the sake of unity and acceptability.

Christianity was also established in Africa without any recourse to African culture, identity and mentality. These values were regarded as pagan oriented and therefore were not patronized. Serious efforts were made by the missionaries to suppress or even to eradicate them. African culture was replaced with European Christian culture, a new mode of dressing was introduced and Western mentality was popularized through the establishment of Western education. This was the view of Achebe in the saying:

The white man says that our customs are bad. He came quietly and peaceably with his religion. We were amused at his foolishness and allowed him to stay. Now he has won our brothers, and our clan can no longer act like one. He has put a knife on the things that held us together and we have fallen apart.[3]

As a result of this lack of respect and recognition for African tradition, the worship of Africans was devoid of African culture and mentality. This is why there is an ardent call for an enculturization of Christianity in Africa. There is need to teach religion in Africa within the context of an African background and in an African language. The Africans need to understand themselves first of all as Africans and then as Christians. Christianity is meant to shape the culture of a people and not to revamp it. Hence, a deep rooted sense of enculturation needs to be imbibed into African children in their religious education. This involves a Christianization of African culture and values and not an eradication of them so that the Christian teachings can find their roots in African ideologies and mentality.

Religious education in the archdiocese of Munich and Freising has the background of a Christian culture, though greatly influenced by the current waves of post-modernism as realized in the post-modern technologies, pluralism and secularism. The effects of these post-modern trends can be felt in almost every sector of the society, especially in the teaching and practice of religion. Under this dispensation, religious education has been ascribed many options. One of such options is ethics. Parents are now free to choose between religious education and ethics for their children and students are also free to make personal decisions with regard to their participation in religious educa-

3 Achebe C., Things Fall Apart, Essex, 1986, 126-127.

tion at the attainment of 14 years of age. This situation affects their religious lives. Many young people are not motivated to put their religious knowledge into practice because they lack parental encouragement to take an active part in religious programmes. Parents for instance do not regularly take their children to the Church. They thereby fail to hand over their faith to the next generation. This is the reason for the absence of young people in the Church in the archdiocese of Munich and Freising and indeed in the entire Western world. Parents need to realize this omission and make serious efforts to reverse it. They should always attend Church programmes with their children in order to ensure their sustainable and holistic development as well as an on-going transmission of the Christian faith.

7. Bibliography

Literature

Abba J. B. C., The Need for Basic Pastoral Formation for Youths in Africa of the 21. Century, Aachen, 2005.

Achebe C., Things Fall Apart, Essex, 1986.

Adogame A., Weissköppel C. (Eds.), Religion in the Context of African Migration, Bayreuth, 2005.

Africae Munus, 2011.

Ahlbrecht A. (Ed.), Concilium, 21. Jahrgang 1985, Zürich, 1985.

Amaechi M. I., Comprehensive Christian Religious Knowledge for Senior Secondary Schools, Lagos, 2003.

Bayerisches Staatsministerium für Unterricht und Kultus (Hg.),Lehrplan für das Gymnasium in Bayern, München, 2009.

Bischof F. X., Leimgruber S. (Hg.), Vierzig Jahre Vatikanum, zur Wirkungsgeschichte der Konzilstexte, 2. Aufl., Würzburg, 2005.

Bitter G., Englert R., Miller G., Nipkow K. E. (Hg.), Neues Handbuch religionspädagogischer Grundbegriffe, 2. Auflage, München, 2009.

Britannica World Language Dictionary, Vol. I, Part I, A-P, Chicago, 1964.

Brunk J. W., Child and Adolescent Development, New York, 1975.

Buetow H. A., Religion in Personal Development, An Analysis and a Prescription, New York, 1991.

Carr W., A History of Germany, 1815-1945, Second Ed., London, 1979.

Carson T., Cerrito J. (Eds.), New Catholic Encyclopedia, 2nd Ed. Vol.3, Detroit, 2003.

Carson T., Cerrito J. (Eds.), New Catholic Encyclopedia, 2nd Ed. Vol.4, Detroit, 2003.

Carson T., Cerrito J. (Eds.), New Catholic Encyclopedia, 2nd Ed. Vol.6, Detroit, 2003.

Chidester D. (Ed.), Journal for the Study of Religion Vol. 22, Nr. 2, Cape Town, 2009.

Chikwe V., Catholic Diocese of Ahiara Mbaise, Diary and Calendar of Pastoral Events, Nguru, 2009.

Daniels P. J., The Voice of the Oppressed in the Language of the Oppressor. A Discussion of Selected Postcolonial Literature from Ireland, Africa and America, New York, 2001.

Eicher P. (Hg.), Neues Handbuch theologischer Grundbegriffe, Band 4, München, 2005.

Eluwa G. I. C., Ukagwu M. O., Nwachukwu J. U. N., Nwaubani A. C. N., A History of Nigeria, For Schools and Colleges, Onitsha, 2005.

Emeis D., Grundriss der Gemeinde- und Sakramentenkatechese, München, 2001.

Emenanjo E. N., Language in Igbo Civilization, 2001 Ahiajoku Lecture, Owerri, 2001.

Enemo E. O., What are we Anglicans Doing?, A Lecture Presented to the Teachers' Week, Awka, 1950.

Federal Ministry of Education, 9-Year Basic Education Curriculum, Christian Religious Studies for Primary 1 – 3, Abuja, 2007.

Federal Ministry of Education, 9-Year Basic Education Curriculum, Christian Religious Studies for Primary 4 – 6, Abuja, 2007.

Federal Ministry of Education, 9-Year Basic Education Curriculum, Christian Religious Studies for JSS 1 – 3, Abuja, 2007.

Federal Ministry of Education, Senior Secondary School Curriculum, Christian Religious Studies for SS 1 – 3, Abuja, 2010.

Federal Ministry of Education, 9-Year Basic Education Curriculum, Islamic Studies for Primary 1-3, Lagos, 2007.

Federal Ministry of Education and Research, Germany's Vocational Education at a Glance, Bonn, 2003.

Filser H., Leimgruber S. (Hg.), Petrus Canisius, Der Große Katechismus, Regensburg, 2003.

Flannery A. (Gen. Ed.), Vatican Council II, More Post-Conciliar Documents, Mumbai, 2007.

Flannery A., (Gen. Ed.), Vatican Council II, The Conciliar and Post-Conciliar Documents, Mumbai, 2007.

General Directory for Catechesis, Third Reprint, Nairobi, 2003.

Hanisch H., Unterrichtsplanung im Fach Religion, Theorie und Praxis, Göttingen, 2007.

Harris M., Moran G., Reshaping Religious Education, Conversations on Contemporary Practice, Kentucky, 1998.

Heinemann C. (Hg.), Gottes Wort im Kirchenjahr 2006, 3. Band, Würzburg, 2006.
Hilger G., Leimgruber S., Ziebertz H. G., Religionsdidaktik, Ein Leitfaden für Studium, Ausbildung und Beruf, 6. Auflage, München, 2010.
Hofrichter C., Färber E., Vogelmann W., Ich glaube, Handreichung zur Firmvorbereitung, München, 2005.

Idowu E. B., African Traditional Religion, A Definition, London, 1973.
Igbokwe J., Igbos 25 Years after Biafra, Enugu, 1995.
Ikein A. A., The Impact of Oil on a Developing Country, The Case of Nigeria, New York, 1990.
Ikime O. (Ed.), Groundwork of Nigerian History, Ibadan, 2004.
Imoagene O., Know Your Country Series, Handbooks of Nigeria's Major Culture Areas Vol. 1, The Hausa and Fulani of Northern Nigeria, Ibadan, 1993.
Imoagene O., Know Your Country Series, Handbooks of Nigeria's Major Culture Areas Vol. 2, The Yoruba of South Western Nigeria, Ibadan, 1993.
Imoagene O., Know Your Country Series, Handbooks of Nigeria's Major Culture Areas Vol. 3, The Ibo of East Central Nigeria, Ibadan, 1993.
Isichei E., A History of Christianity in Africa. From Antiquity to the Present, London, 1995.

Jakobs M., Neue Wege der Katechese, München, 2010.
Job F. A., The Order of Mass, Nairobi, 2011.

Kalloch C., Leimgruber S., Schwab U., Lehrbuch der Religionsdidaktik. Für Studium und Praxis in ökumenischer Perspektive, Freiburg, 2009.
Katholisches Schulkommissariat in Bayern, Lehrplan für die Berufsschule und Berufsfachschule, München, 1997.
Katholisches Schulkommissariat in Bayern, Lehrplan für Katholische Religionslehre an den bayerischen Grundschulen, München, 2000.
Katholisches Schulkommissariat in Bayern, Lehrplan für Katholische Religionslehre an den bayerischen Hauptschulen, München, 2004.
Katholisches Schulkommissariat in Bayern, Lehrplan für Katholische Religionslehre an den bayerischen Realschulen, München, 2001.
Kaupp A., Leimgruber S., Scheidler M. (Hg.), Handbuch der Katechese für Studium und Praxis, Freiburg, 2011.
Kitchen M., A History of Modern Germany, 1800-2000, Malden, 2006.
Kunstmann J., Religionspädagogik, Eine Einführung, Tübingen, 2004.

Kunstmann J., Religionspädagogik, Eine Einführung, 2. Auflage, Tübingen, 2010.
Kuru T. K., Secularism and State Policies Toward Religion, The United States, France and Turkey, Cambridge, 2009.

Leimgruber S., Ethikunterricht an den katholischen Gymnasien und Lehrseminarien der Schweiz, Analyse der Religionsbücher seit Mitte des 19. Jahrhunderts, Freiburg Schweiz, 1989.
Leimgruber S., Interreligiöses Lernen, Neuausgabe, München, 2007.
Lines T. A., Systemic Religious Education, Birmingham, 1987.

Mbiti J. S., Introduction to African Religion, London, 1986.
McClelland V. A. (Ed.), Christian Education in a Pluralistic Society, London, 1988.
Meijer W. A. J. et al. (Eds.), Religious Education in a World of Religious Diversity, München, 2009.
Mette N., Rickers F. (Hg.), LexRP. 2. Band, Neukirchen – Vluyn, 2001.
Moran G., Religious Education As A Second Language, Birmingham, 1989.
Münk H. J. (Hg.), Wann ist Bildung gerecht? Ethische und theologische Beiträge im interdisziplinären Kontext, Bielefeld, 2008.

National Economic Empowerment and Development Strategy, Meeting Everyone's
Needs, Abuja, 2004.
Nwatu F., Eze A. (Eds.), Bigard Theological Studies, 27, 1, Enugu, 2007.
Nwele C., Fatherhood and Child's Education: Exploring the Effects of a Father's Absence on the Social, Moral and Religious Lives of Children, New York, 2010.

Odiaka M. O., Garba A. M., Fadeyi Y., Udom M., Basic Primary Christian Religious Knowledge, Pupils' Book 2, Onitsha, 2000.
Okonkwo P. I., Minorities and the Problem of Fairness – A Social Ethical Inquiry, Aachen, 2002.
Oonk G. H. (Henk), Internationalisation in Primary and Secondary Education, Alkmaar, 2007.
Osewska E., Stala J. (Eds.), Religious Education/Catechesis in the Family: A European Perspective, Warszawa, 2010.

Pals D. L., Seven Theories of Religion, New York, 1996.
Parrinder G., West African Religion, London, 1961.

Peters R. S. (Ed.), The Philosophy of Education, London, 1975.
Petersen K. H. (Ed.), Religion, Development and African Identity, Uppsala, 1987.
Phyak P. B., Mother Tongue Education: Practices and Problems with Reference to Limbu Language, Nepal, 2007.
Pobee J. S. (Ed.), Religion in a Pluralistic Society, Leiden, 1976.
Pocket Ritual (Rituale Parvum), Bangalore, 2008.
Polkinghorne D. E., "Language and Meaning, Data Collection in Quantitative Research", in: Journal of Counselling Psychology 52, no. 2, 2005.

Quarcoopome T. N. O., Obinna A. J. V., Daudu M., Ilori J., Christian Religious Education and Moral Instruction for Junior Secondary Schools 1, 3rd Ed., Ibadan, 2005.

Rego A.J., How to Develop a Pleasing Personality, Mumbai, 2006.

Schulze H., Siedler Deutsche Geschichte, Weimar Deutschland 1917-1933 Band 2, München, 2005.
Schwachulla, W. (Red.), Der Brockhaus in einem Band, Leipzig, 1998.
Schweitzer F., Biesinger A., Religiöse Erziehung in evangelisch-katholischen Familien, Freiburg, 2009.
Shanley B. J., O.P., The Thomist Tradition, Dordrecht, 2002.
Skeie G. (Ed.), Religious Diversity and Education, München, 2009.

Taylor C., A Secular Age, Harvard, 2007.
The Catechism of the Catholic Church, Revised Edition, 2004.
The Code of Canon Law, Fifth Reprint, London, 1994.
The Holy Bible, The New Standard Version, Catholic Edition, Bangalore, 2005.
The New Encyclopaedia Britannica Vol. VIII, Chicago, 1984.
Thompson H. N. (Ed.), Religious Pluralism and Religious Education, Birmingham, 1988.
Timm H., Das ästhetische Jahrzehnt. Zur Postmodernisierung der Religion, Gütersloh, 1990.

Unegbu M. O., Doctrine for Adults, Second Edition, Owerri, 2000.
Unegbu M. O., Katikizim Nke Abuo, Owerri, 2000.
Uwalaka J. N., The Struggle for an Inclusive Nigeria: Igbos: To Be or not to Be?, A Treatise on Igbo Political Personality and Survival in Nigeria, Enugu, 2003.

Webster's Third International Dictionary, Vol. I, Chicago, 1981.
Webster's Third International Dictionary, Vol. II, Chicago, 1981.
Webster's Third International Dictionary, Vol. III, Chicago, 1981.
World Population Prospects, The 2006 Revision, Highlights, New York, 2007.
Youth Catechism of the Catholic Church, Wien, 2011.

Ziebertz H. G., Kalbheim B., Riegel U., Religiöse Signaturen heute, Ein religionspädagogischer Beitrag zur empirischen Jugendforschung, Gütersloh, 2003.
Ziebertz H. G., Riegel U. (Eds.), How Teachers in Europe Teach Religion, An International Empirical Study in 16 Countries, Berlin, 2009.

Internet Sites

http://www.nysc.gov.ng/history2.php, 09.06.2011.
http:/www.nfcsnigeria.org/, 09.06.2011.
http:/www.nysc.gov.ng/history2.php, 09.06.2011.
http//www.infoplaese.com/ipa/A0107568.html, 25.07.2011.
http://www.state.gov/r/pa/ei/bgn/3997.htm, 24.08.2011.
http//esa.un.org/unpd/wpp/Sorting-Tables/tab-sorting_population.htm, 29.08.2011.
http//esa.un.org/unpd/wpp/Sorting-Tables/tab-sorting_mortality.htm, 29.08.2011.
http//www.asiarooms.com/en/travel-guide/germany/-culture-of-germany/languages-in-germany.html, 30.08.2011.
http://www.state.gov/r/pa/ei/bgn/3997.htm, 24.08.2011.
http://library.thinkquest.org/26576/kindergartenpage.htm, 03.10.2011.
http://library.thinkquest.org/26576/gymnasiumpage.htm, 03.10.2011.
http://www.germanculture.com.ua/libraryfacts/bl_vocational_education.htm, 04.10.2011.
http://histclo.com/act/rel/altar.html, 13.02.2012.
http://cyonanniversary.blogspot.com/p/history.html, 16.02.2012.
http://saintcypriancathchurch.org/cyon.html, 16.02.2012.
http://ourlady.bulletinstudio.com/parish-groups/mary-league-girls-association/, 06.03.2012.
http://www.ycsnigeria.org/?u=page&page_id=2, 05.05.2012.
http://www.ycsnigeria.org/?u=page&page_id=8, 05.05.2012.
http://www.nigeriascouts.org/index.php?option=com_content&view=article&id=25&Itemid=28, 13.02.2012.

http://modwarridmc.com/index.php, 16.02.2012.
http://modwarridmc.com/membership.php, 16.02.2012.
http://modwarridmc.com/aim.php, 16.02.2012.
http://www.eja-muenchen.de/bdkj.html, 12.03.2012.
http://www.eja-muenchen.de/bdkj/die-organe-in-der-erzdiözese/mitgliedsverbaende/caj.html, 12.03.2012.
http://www.eja-muenchen.de/bdkj/die-organe-in-der-erzdiözese/mitgliedsverbaende/dpsg.html, 12.03.2012.
http://www.kjg-muenchen.de/seite/index.php?id=42, 21.03.2012.
http://www.kjg-muenchen.de/seite/index.php?id=183, 21.03.2012.
http://kljb.org/internationale-vorstellung/english/, 06.03.2012.
http://www.eja-muenchen.de/bdkj/die-organe-in-der-erzdiözese/mitgliedsverbaende/kljb.html, 12.03.2012.
http://www.eja-muenchen.de/bdkj/die-organe-in-der-erzdiözese/mitgliedsverbaende/ksj-gcl.html, 12.03.2012.
http://www.eja-muenchen.de/bdkj/die-organe-in-der-erzdiözese/mitgliedsverbaende/kolpingjugend.html, 12.03.2012.
www.kolping-muenchen.de/jugend/kolpingjugend.html, 21.03.2012.
http://www.eja-muenchen.de/bdkj/die-organe-in-der-erzdiözese/mitgliedsverbaende/psg.html, 12.03.2012.
http://www.junge-aktion.de/, 21.03.2012.
http://www.brainyquote.com/quotes/quotes/n/nelsonmand121685.html#mlMQWyBS8UADf1Um.99, 03.09.2012.
http://unesdoc.unesco.org/images/0012/001202/120240e.pdf, 08.10.2012.
http://ubeconline.com/about_ubec.html, 07.11.2012.
http://ubeconline.com/index-2.html, 07.11.2012.
http://nigeria.unfpa.org/youngpeople.html, 08.11.2012.
http://www.vatican.va/holy_father/benedict_xvi/apost_exhortations/documents/hf_ben-xvi_exh_20111119_africae-munus_en.html, 09.11.2012.
http://www.vatican.va/holy_father/john_paul_ii/apost_exhortations/documents/hf_jp-ii_exh_14091995_ecclesia-in-africa_en.html, 09.11.2012.
http://www.papalencyclicals.net/Pius10/p10quam.htm, 09.11.2012.
http://www.vatican.va/holy_father/john_paul_ii/apost_exhortations/documents/hf_jp-ii_exh_16101979_catechesi-tradendae_en.html, 10.11.2012.
http://www.nigeria-law.org/ConstitutionOfTheFederalRepublicOfNigeria.htm#Chapter_4, 12.11.2012.

EOS-VERLAG ▪ THEOLOGISCHE REIHE

BAND 92

Markus Schrom

Die Kirche als Gebetsgemeinschaft

Überlegungen zum Verhältnis von Kirche und Gebet in der Liturgie auf dem Hintergrund der Texte des Zweiten Vatikanischen Konzils

402 Seiten, € 29,80, ISBN 978-3-8306-7452-8

BAND 93

Edith Olk

Die Barmherzigkeit Gottes als zentrale Quelle des christlichen Lebens

Eine theologische Würdigung der Lehre von Papst Johannes Paul II.

468 Seiten, € 34,95, ISBN 978-3-8306-7476-4

BAND 94

Hyacinth Nwankwor

Religious Freedom,

the Bed-rock of National Unity in Nigeria

286 Seiten, € 24,95, ISBN 978-3-8306-7514-3

BAND 95

Michael Joe Okpalanozie

Christianity, Islam and African Traditional Religion in Nigeria

Conflicts and Challenges to Peaceful Co-existence

306 Seiten, € 29,95, ISBN 978-3-8306-7500-6

BAND 96

Xaver X. Kazimoto Komba

Die Selbsterhaltung der afrikanischen Kirche

Eine sozio-theologische Analyse der heutigen „Kleinen christlichen Gemeinschaften", dargestellt am Beispiel der Ortskirche von Tansania

292 Seiten, € 29,95, ISBN 978-3-8306-7540-2

EOS Editions Sankt Ottilien

www.eos-books.com | mail@eos-verlag.de